# How
# I Became
# What
# I Am

ATROPOS

Andrzej Jachimczyk

# How
# I Became
# What
# I Am

YOUNG NIETZSCHE EMBARKS
ON LIFE'S ODYSSEY

ATROPOS PRESS
new york • dresden

ATROPOSS PRESS
New York • Dresden
151 First Avenue # 14, New York, N.Y. 10003
Mockritzer Str. 6, D-01219, Dresden, Germany

Cover designed by Ola Maslik/David Crixel
Interior designed by Milene Ney

ISBN: 978-1-7375591-9-1

*For Zosia*

# CONTENTS

# ACKNOWLEDGEMENTS

I want to thank Alexander Nehamas, Graham Parkes, and Robert Holub for their productive conversations with me when I was working on a film essay project about Friedrich Nietzsche's idea of self-creation. Their inspiring contributions propelled the film's original idea into a book about Nietzsche's formative years.

I owe profound thanks to Friedrich Ulfers and Graham Parkes for reading the manuscript and for their valuable comments and corrections.

I want to thank Arti Grabowski for his commitment while working on the essay film and for inspiring me through his art and conversations to dedicate myself to exploring the emergence of Nietzsche's thought.

My greatest thanks, as always, go to my wife, Ola Maslik, for her unfailing support when *How I Became One What I Am* was conceived and written and for reflecting the crux of this book in her ingenious design of its cover.

*Part I*

# Under the Rule of *Bildung*

# 1

## CHILDHOOD MEMORIES

It is a late summer night at the end of August, 1858. By the flickering light of an oil lamp, in a room on the main floor of a house standing alongside the medieval stonewall that once closely encircled Naumburg, a town in Prussian Saxony near Leipzig, a chubby, dark-haired, myopic teenage boy named Fritz sits behind a large table cluttered with books and notes, leaning over a sheet of paper, writing rapidly with a slightly oblique, beautiful script.

"Let's take a look at the city," he takes his readers on a stroll about the town. "Let us first enter by the pretty Jacob's Gate. If we now walk down the beautiful, broad street with its very old houses, we will arrive at the marketplace. Behold, right in front of you is the town hall. How big it is! How expansive! Its four sides almost form four streets, and with dark turrets, it towers into the sky. Its dark gray color, its ancient oriels, always made me regard it reverently. Now turn your attention to the right, there in the middle, the green house! That's the Pinder residence! Councilor Krug lives here; Frau Grandmother Pinder lives here, the honorable proprietress of the house. Friedrich the Great allegedly stayed here once, likewise Napoleon; and a great eagle from that time is still there…. Left of the town hall you see the high, venerable town church jutting out. Look at what an ugly building stands in front of it! Ah, if only it were torn down, it would not block the view of the house of God?! Past the church is the royal provincial court, which towers over the market with high twin gables. Let's bypass the church; we will look at it on another occasion when we have more time. Let's take a walk along the Priestergasse! Right at the start is the boys' public school. At present, it finds itself in quite a good condition, which is perhaps primarily thanks to its director, the splendid

Doctor Neumüller. Right next to it, we come across the Superintendent's place. …Through a large gateway, we arrive in the courtyard with its many auxiliary buildings until we reach the residence that, with its facade, ends at the corner of the Neugasse. If we walk down this street a little further, then we immediately catch sight of the large, beautiful building of Mayor Rasch. The end of the street contains the stately presidential residence that at present houses Herr Pr. Koch. To the right of this is a pretty house, to which I have gone so often and from which I have always brought home my knowledge a little more enriched. Of course, it's Herr Weber's Institute. The dear man is now employed as pastor of the nearby St. Othmar church but nevertheless maintains his school, which, however, has now moved to a public building. —Well, onward! Beyond these houses, grassy fields and groups of trees extend up to the Salztor gate. The sentry buildings on both sides are decorated with simple Doric columns, making them appear impressive. A little further on, again, a pair of very pretty houses appear. Both were built just recently. They form the beginning of the Salzstrasse. If we leave these aside and continue along our way, we arrive at the Lindenstrasse, planted with a median of linden trees, creating an avenue. Towards the middle, it gradually rises and, at the top, forms the junction of Steinweg and Herrengasse. I still want to mention the latter with its gloomy, ancient buildings, since the residence of Councilor Pinder is there. The Domrich bookstore is also located in the same area. I also want to mention the part of the town hall that is located along this street, because concerts and dances often took place there. —Well, now we have seen enough; more on another occasion,"[1] the boy finishes with the tour of his hometown.

All is silent, only "my pen scratching on the paper, for I love to think by writing."[2] He turns to focus on himself and his upbringing—"by and large, I am in charge of my own upbringing.… I have had to do without the strict and senior guidance of a male intellect"[3]— before launching into his life's story of assembling an image of himself for posterity. Not yet fourteen, he works relentlessly late into the night, completing his first autobiography, titled "From My Life. The Years of My Youth 1844-1858" *(Aus meinem Leben. Die Jugendjahre 1844-1858),* which, though he did not know it yet, would become another turning point in his life.

Just a few months before, he had completed Tertia at the Naumburg Domgymnasium and was at a crossroads of where to go to continue his education. Probably expecting to be admitted to a nearby prestigious Schulpforta, he celebrated this forthcoming momentous event by reminiscing about his entire short life. Although he wrote with an audience in mind, it seemed to be truly for himself, for the process would allow him to look uninhibitedly at his past and evaluate it.

Producing an autobiography, probably more emotionally spontaneous than rationally intended, was an important event in his life, affecting him as a future thinker. From the strongly affectional beginnings as a child poet, his writing, begotten from the need for artistic self-indulgence, became the key to self-knowledge, creative expression, and a way to think. On January 2 of that year, his mother Franziska's thirty-second birthday, Fritz decided to give her a poem, then write a new one each following day. It would be an incessant gift to her, but at the same time, a gift to himself, providing an enlightening probe into his ever-changing soul.

As he writes, he realizes, a method is taking shape: introspection through retrospection. The pleasure of seeing a finished piece of work, "a new production of my spirit laying before me,"[4] fulfills his compelling desire to write about his own significant—he is convinced—life.

He calligraphed evenly, emphasizing details with methodical precision, composing his memories "into a painting." However, his precise style did not take precedence over his attention to content, following his own advice: "while writing, one must especially bear in mind the thoughts, since a negligent style is forgiven more easily than a confused idea." He then enlists the guiding principles, not only in writing poetry but also in reading, listening, and composing music: avoiding clichés, emphasizing creativity, working tirelessly, and taking responsibility for his life by building his character.

Young as he was, this boy named Fritz was exceptionally mature and had a piercing, self-critical perspective regarding his person. As writing developed into his primary tool of self-expression, alongside improvising and composing music, he refined it by reading his written thoughts to himself. "It was always my plan to write a little book and then to read it myself,"[5] repeatedly maintaining that it was only for himself. Or possibly, he only assumed this hedonistic pose to free himself from the ordinary rigors and writing conventions as a method to become a better writer. This technique of vivisecting his soul in an exhibitionistic gesture would become, in later years, the mode of his philosophy.

When he was about ten years old, during the Crimean War (1854–1855), Fritz began to compose his first poems. Nonetheless critical of their formal qualities, in this initial phase, he already mused about "the transience of happiness," which probably refers to bouts of melancholy and the difficulty of expressing himself, "as his soul bestowed [these poems] upon him."[6] He was not alone in those early intellectual endeavors. His two schoolmates, Gustav Krug and Wilhelm Pinder, were the zealous participants in these poetic undertakings, although from the beginning, Fritz was their initiator. He describes their trio as "quite indispensable to each other, never lacking material for our conversations. We exchanged ideas about poets and writers, about works that we had read, about new publications in the field of literature, made joint plans, submitted poems to each other, and did not rest until we had opened our hearts completely."[7]

However, according to one of the leading historians of Nietzschean philosophy, Thomas Brobjer, during Fritz's early years in the Domgymnasium, Fritz was not as intellectually inclined as he was profoundly pious. He demonstrated his intense religious devotion by memorizing passages from the Bible, so he could recite them by heart at one's beck and call. He was so dedicated to it that his schoolmates called him "the little pastor,"[8] mocking his performances. Fritz was utterly smitten by the mystery of faith, as only a child could be; nevertheless, he was also reading other works and authors like *Der Cid* by J. G. von Herder, *Meditations* by Marcus Aurelius,[9] most likely Goethe's *Faust,* and a lot of poetry, which enlighten him with its "profound thoughts, clear as gold."[10] He read Xenophon's *Anabasis* and Homer's *Odyssey*, the works of Julius Caesar, and Ovid's *Metamorphoses* for the Greek and Latin classes. But outside his schoolwork, he was reading poetry by Friedrich Schiller, other works by Johan Wolfgang von Goethe, Friedrich Hölderlin, Johann Gottfried Seume, Klaus Groth, Henrik Hertz, Esaias Tegnér, Carl Theodor Körner, Franz von Gaudy, August von Platen, Adelbert von Chamisso, Nikolaus Lenau, and Friedrich von Matthisson.[11]

Fritz worked very hard at the Domgymnasium, staying up late into the night, then waking up at 5 in the morning to continue with his home-work, but surprisingly, to rather mediocre results.[12] Outside of schoolwork, undaunted by his modest achievements at school, Fritz offers some over-confident advice on writing good poetry. He refers again to the requirement of substantivity over empty formality, criticizing "thoughtless poems that are overwrought with clichés and metaphors."[13] Self-confident, young Fritz sees himself as a creative artist who recognizes that "the frequent use of clichés is evidence of a mind that is incapable of creating something by itself."[14] And, not only did he know that he was not one of these incapable writers, but Fritz was sure, without a doubt, that he could create something utterly original. It was apparent right from the beginning that Fritz was not an obedient follower within an education system, but rather a devotee of expanding one's intellectual curiosity through self-education, self-explora-tion, and free, unfettered creativity. His autobiography from 1858, Brobjer asserts, "is excellent and ought, without doubt, to have received the highest grade had it been handed in at school, which it was not."[15]

At his young age, he recognized in the biographical retrospection or retroactive autobiography a method of inquiry, which could reveal him to himself, within the grand scheme of existence:

> *Life is a mirror.*
> *To recognize ourselves with in it,*
> *This, I would like to call the first thing,*
> *To which we can hope to strive!*[16]

Writing about one's life, one bares the naked truth of one's development before the calculating gaze of one's mind and, in that, acknowledges oneself as the creator of one's life. It is an ingenious tool to continuously realize oneself a new by repainting oneself repeatedly throughout one's life. "If only one could write quite a lot of es-says of this sort!"[17]– Fritz yearns for the future version of "From My Life."

While composing the work, he recalls the past, and expects to be his own reader later on, therefore reaching out simultaneously into the past and the future. By recognizing the future, he anticipated the more mature, wiser version of himself, nevertheless, still only a disciple of the historical person.[18] Recognizing himself in "the mirror of life," this early autobiography created an opportunity for Fritz to have a conversation with himself outside the boundaries of time, where the past and the future overlap, dissolving into a temporality.[19]

Then, if we look at this project even closer, we should consider the subsequent autobiographical experiments. As one would expect, to write about himself for the future and to be honest in that endeavor—up to certain limits, of course—one would need to be cognizant of one's life's contingent events as a potentiality for their future consequences, *a priori* to any decision-making as a collaborator of their outcomes. In that scenario, the subsequent retrospection would be the automatic documentation of a decision-making processes' accuracy and outcomes. As one puts this impossible yoke of responsibility onto oneself, the critical moment is to come later, when one reads the text about himself. What should have been a moment of evaluating our past behavioral trends in contrast with the present situation instead becomes a process of assessing one's predictive abilities concerning one's decision-making choices. But in that regard, one must be aware that any decision-making is an a-rational and mostly automatic process within the necessary contingency of events and the contingent necessity of experiences and is beyond one's ability to realize and address every event in one's life.

So, the only time we can direct ourselves onto a specific path is in the act of composing, and enjoying the ever-changing, timeless "painting" of an impression of ourselves, hoping that it will impact our future "I". Through creating a story of ourselves and experiencing it once again later in life, we continuously carve ourselves into the irrational, spontaneous, and accidental work of art. Considering it, we should not forget that in his vanity, Fritz always envisaged the future readers, the main audience of his writing, so he never missed an opportunity to present himself as an ideal of himself.

# REMEMBRANCE OF RÖCKEN

Fritz opens his life story with introductory remarks about writing an autobiography. "Some things are clear and vivid within my soul, and along with those that are vague and gloomy, I will combine them into a painting. It is beneficial to look at the gradual formation of the mind and heart, and in that, the almighty guidance of God!"[20] – he discovers a method of self-knowing not as a finished picture, but a formative process of the character.

With this new brush in hand, he began to paint his portrait starting October 15, 1844, in a parsonage in Röcken, a tiny village near Lützen, where "I was born as a plant close to the churchyard (graveyard); as a human being I was born in the rectory."[21] He evokes his father, Karl Ludwig, a Lutheran pastor, who succumbed to illness and died at 35 when Fritz was barely five years old. He provided details of his father's ailments—as of some he was already suffering himself—expecting the same end to his own life. He listed painful headaches, blindness, and going in and out of consciousness, which was diagnosed as a softening of the brain—in other words, mental illness.

Despite being barely five years old at the time, Fritz remembers his father, or perhaps imagines him, as a pious man with "a talented mind and spirit, invested with all the virtues of a Christian.... The perfect picture of a clergyman," who loves the "fine scholarship and music and achieved a considerable skill in piano playing, especially in free variations."[22]

From the onset of illness through the months of his father's decline, culminating in his death, Fritz was tormented by nightmares, which persisted beyond this period. Six months after his father's demise, he writes: "I once dream that I heard organ music in the church, like at the funeral. When I looked for what was causing it, a grave suddenly rose, and my father emerged from it in his winding sheet. He hurried into the church and soon returned with a tiny child in his arms. The gravemound opened, he climbed inside, and the slab closed over the opening. All at once, the roaring sound of the organ stopped, and I awoke. On the day after this night, little Joseph suddenly got sick, had convulsions, and died in a few hours. Our grief was enormous. My dream had been completely fulfilled. The tiny corpse was laid in his father's arms. —God in heaven was our sole consolation and refuge from this double misfortune. This happened at the end of January 1850."[23]

When Fritz wrote this passage, almost a decade had passed from these tragic events, which had occurred when he was merely five years old. He had more than enough time to ask himself an accusatory question: Why me? Or, being such a religious devotee: Why does God punish me to such a degree? But he never asked himself these questions. It could be that he was in such trusting devotion to God, that he had accepted His judgment unreservedly like Job, where there would be no place for such questions. Or, he stoically accepted his fate as a blessing—not in the sense of a masochistic punishment, but a nurturing trial to enrich his character's development. Fritz never blames God for his misfortune, but writing about his father and brother's deaths, with the inclusion of the terrible nightmares, he re-experiences them to the letter. One would expect that the healing process had been completed after such a long time. But Fritz repeatedly brought them back as though he enjoyed them or was thankful that he experienced them.[24]

Undoubtedly, his household's pietism had an imperative influence on the young Fritz's zestful submission to Christianity. From birth, he could take solace in the fact that his life path was already chosen for him, a condition which changed, however, upon his father's death. Tradition had required him to become a clergyman in acquiescence with his father, grandfather, great grandfather, and other ancestral family members. There was no other possibility, no way for Fritz to disrupt the pattern. But then, his father, his role model to follow, whose provenance would have been Fritz's fate, was suddenly gone, his death broke the chain of repetitive and identical career choices. Fritz was on his own.

Let's consider the historicity of relevant facts to be included in the retrospection as introspection into oneself, which Fritz took upon himself as his modus operandi of self-development. The task is implausible to realize. Fritz did not remember all the relevant events that occurred when he was a child. In mid-August, when preparing to write his first autobiography, he wrote a letter to his aunt Rosalie from Plauen: "Now, that I want to write my biography, I notice with horror that I am in great uncertainty about the life of Papa, the great-uncle Krause, and the great-grandmamma, and I do not have any memory of them. Oh, would you be so good and write me short life stories and character descriptions of these dear people."[25] The autobiographical exercise is not based on facts but instead an invented picture that mixes reality with illusion. "When we have grown up," Fritz begins his first biography, "we usually remember of our earliest childhood only the moments that stand out the most. Right, I am not yet grown up, hardly have the years of childhood and boyhood behind me, and however, so much has already slipped from my memory, and the little that I know about them I have probably retained only through tradition. The sequence of years rushes past my gaze like a confusing dream. Therefore, I can't establish the facts of the first ten years of my life. Nevertheless, some things are clear and vivid within my soul, and these, along with those that are vague and gloomy, I will combine into a portrait."[26]

Apart from recalling all the facts he could remember of his childhood, he made in some instances connections between his past and present self, pointing, for example, to his migraine headaches. "I was not permitted to attend school in the last semester of the *Quarta* due to headaches," he complains, suspecting that he had inherited other qualities of his father's illness as well.

"His headaches were already bad enough to keep him in bed," Ronald Hayman explains, "and from the age of nine onwards, he missed a good deal of school through illness. Between Easter 1854 and Easter 1855, he was absent for five weeks and six days.… After starting at the Dom Gymnasium in 1855, he missed twenty days of schooling in his first year, and thirteen in his second. Then when he was twelve, he began to have serious trouble with his eyes. He had inherited myopia from his father, and one of his pupils was larger than the other, a feature he had inherited from his mother."[27]

If we consider suffering as a gesture of sacrifice for the greater purpose, as Fritz did, and who, at fourteen, had already anointed himself a sacrificial lamb then, perhaps we could explain Fritz's stoical acceptance of his afflictions.

Since, after Karl Ludwig's death, there was not enough money for medicine; therefore, Franziska's remedies for Fritz's health complaints were compresses and cold-water treatment. "Throughout his life, he was to torment himself by dousing his body with cold water – it was, after all, what his mother had always prescribed."[28] At the time, it was not unusual or uncommon to bring your children through such harsh methods, his sister Elisabeth writes later: "We were never subject to the enervating influence of blind maternal affection."[29] Severity was a virtue that was highly prized at the time. Orders were carried out to the letter. Often a stern look sufficed: Franziska could show both approval and disapproval—more often the latter—with a mere glance. The children showed her total respect, not least because, like God Himself, she reprimanded lesser misdemeanors on the spot. If, on occasion, she displayed tenderness toward them, Fritz was effusive in his gratitude. On the other hand, he was always prepared to accept punishment for a minor transgression. The hardest thing to bear, however, was when she made fun of him. "'What torture it is for a child', he lamented years later, 'always to find that his ideas of right and wrong are the opposite of his mother's and be mocked and despised for what he most values!'"[30]

Throughout his first autobiography, Fritz evokes God so often that it gives the whole piece the impression of a prayer. It appears that his religiosity is so profoundly engraved within his soul that it overshadows his other qualities, namely, his intellectual curiosity and love of music inherited from his father. Being such a pious child, he was never happily accepting of the joys and sorrows that life delivered, but rather, out of mourning after his dead father, developed an almost paternal authority over himself to motivate, control, and advise himself. Thus, following his pastor father, he offered his entire life to service to God: "By now, I have already experienced so many joyful and sorrowful, cheering and depressing things, but in everything, God has safely led me like a father leads his weak little child. He has already inflicted upon me much pain, but in everything, I acknowledge with reverence his power on high, which carries out everything so magnificently. I have firmly resolved within me to devote myself forever to his service. May the dear Lord give me strength and power for my purpose and protect me on my path of life. I trust in his grace like a child: he will watch over us all so that no misfortune saddens us. But his holy will be done! I will joyfully accept all that he gives, happiness and unhappiness, poverty and wealth, and boldly look even death in the face, who will someday unite us all in eternal joy and bliss. Yes, dear Lord, let your face shine upon us forever! Amen!!"[31]

However, it was never as much of a blind devotion as it appeared to be. Young Fritz, already at twelve, raised the topic of good and evil in a now lost essay "On the Origin of Evil."[32] Some historians and biographers, along with Fritz himself, consider it his original excursion towards philosophy.[33] "The problem of the origin of evil pursued me even as a boy of thirteen," he writes in *On the Genealogy of Morals*, "at an age in which you have 'half childish trifles, half God in your heart,' I devoted it to my first literary trifle, my first philosophical effort—and a for the 'solution' of the problem I posted at the time, well, I give the honor to God, as was only fair, and made him the *father* of evil."[34] He writes about his original philosophical effort some twenty-six years later, but it appears that from the depths of his faith arose a question of moral concern. The problem that stayed with Fritz into the end of his productive life "is concerned with *morality*, with all that has hitherto been celebrated on earth as morality— a scruple that entered my life so early, so uninvited, so irresistibly, so much in conflict with my environment, age, precedents, and descent that I might almost have the right to call it my *'a priori'*—my curiosity as well as my suspicions were bound to halt quite soon at the question of where our good and evil really *originated.*"[35]

## MY ENCHANTMENT WITH MUSIC

Fritz's profound devotion to God was inseparably interlaced with music. From his earliest childhood, he was exposed to it either in the Röcken's small, stone church or at the adjacent parsonage, when his father often improvised on piano. When the family moved to Naumburg after his father's death, he attended masses filled with musical liturgy at the Dom Cathedral, went to concerts, or enjoined with his friend Gustav at his house, the evenings filled with music.

Gustav's father, Herr Krug, Councilor of the Court of Appeals in Naumburg, was a music connoisseur and regularly hosted famous musicians like Felix Mendelssohn-Bartholdy and the Müller brothers. Often, when on his way from school, Fritz stopped, mesmerized by sounds coming from the Krugs' house. When invited, he could listen to the best interpretations of "the sublime melodies of Beethoven"[36] played by Mendelssohn. Recognizing his sprouting passion for music, Fritz's mother, Franziska, bought a piano and took piano lessons herself in order to teach him to play. Later, she hired a woman, one of the best teachers in Naumburg,[37] to deepen Fritz's musical skills.

Fritz perceived music as a divine gift from "God, [Who] has given us music so that, first of all, we could be guided upwards by it.... All qualities are combined in music: it can uplift, divert, cheer us up; with its soft melancholy notes, it can even break the toughest disposition. But its chief purpose is to direct our thoughts to the heights, elevate us, even jolt us."[38] He considered music as essential in reaching the realm of transcendence; it cannot merely serve as an entertainment or amusement.

However, not all types of music were equally worthy to Fritz. He was moved when listening to "the sublime chorus from the Handel's Messiah, the Hallelujah." Or considered the classical music of Mozart, Haydn, Schubert, Mendelssohn, Beethoven, and Bach "the pillars upon which German and [his] music rested"[39] but, he developed an "inextinguishable hatred" for anything that was not classical, "the so-called music of the future" by Liszt, Berlioz, and Wagner. And all his earliest experiences with music were always heightened by attempts to compose his own pieces.

At eleven, in April 1855, Fritz began to take piano lessons from the local precentor, G. Fr. M. Steeger.[40] Almost immediately, he started composing and, following his father, improvising on the piano while developing an acute sense of criticism. He was unscrupulously finger-pointing at people without the ability to appreciate music, calling them "unimaginative, animal-like creatures."[41] He considered his musical taste as an ultimate standard in the judgment of music preferences. "This most glorious gift of God, my companion on my life's journey," he writes praising it to the heavens. And God heard Fritz. Love for music would stay with him till the end of his life.

Writing about himself quite in detail, Fritz sketches his persona to lay it bare before himself. "My character already began to reveal itself." He was aware of his unique personality, formed by the exposure to different life experiences, which he outright welcomed. His solitude and seriousness, hard work and perseverance, enjoyment of communing with nature, suffering, and sadness, being compliant and traditional were the intrinsic elements in his developing identity. He considered himself the most joyful when alone, reading, writing, walking, experiencing nature, and thinking. "I sought solitude and found myself happiest when I could be left to myself undisturbed; usually, in the open temple of nature, I found the most genuine joy. A thunderstorm always made the finest impression on me; the distant, booming thunder and the brilliant, flashing lightning only increased my reverence for God,"[42] he confessed, elated.

On vacation, instead of playing with the other children, he rummages among the books and notebooks in his grandfather, David Ernst Oehler's study with the "greatest pleasure."[43] "David Ernst regarded teaching as an important component of his duties and expended a considerable amount of energy on educating the children in the village as well as his own offspring. He greatly enjoyed spending time in his study, which had a comprehensive library where works of theology by no means predominated. 'His study was his own special realm. Books that he had opened and wanted to consult further would lie open, and pieces of paper on which he had made notes also had to be left where they were.' Unsurprisingly, young Fritz especially enjoyed spending time in his grandfather's study when he visited Pobles: 'My favorite occupation was to be in grandpapa's study, and my greatest pleasure was browsing through all the old books and magazines there.' An indication of the breadth of his grandfather's intellectual interests is the fact that young Fritz found numerous works on such relatively occult subjects as magnetism and somnambulism in his library, including Justinus Kerner's well-known *The Seeress of Prevorst,* which appear to have influenced Nietzsche's later ideas about the multiplicity of the psyche."[44]

Fritz swam in the Saale River and went for long walks in the hills above the town. In afternoons, instead of playing outside with his peers, he spent hours in the library where he read the philosopher Novalis, "who had maintained that all experience was magical, using the term *Magische Idealis-*

*mus* for his conception of romantic idealism that would subsume the idealism of Kant."[45] Later, in his notes, Fritz wrote, Novalis's "philosophical thoughts interest me,"[46] but he never followed up with further discussion, mentioning him only three times in his writings. But the seed was sown.

While in Pobles during summers, he learned how to swim and skate in the winter. And again, it is not merely swimming or skating. His acute awareness and sensitivity provide him with different textures of experience in addition to straightforward enjoyment. "To give oneself over to the current, and to glide along effortlessly upon the gentle tide, can one imagine anything more delightful?" – he rejoices. Then, when skating during winter, he depicts his surroundings with acute awareness: "All around, the deep silence, which is broken only by the cracking of the ice and the clinking sound of those moving over it, has something majestic about it that we seek in vain on summer nights."[47] But, in the end, he cannot escape being a bit condescending. One can always sense the undertones of bragging and patronizing. Our novice swimmer, putting himself on a pedestal of significance and superiority, advises that swimming is advantageous for young people's physical development and learning. Being not yet fourteen, it sounds ridiculous, but he takes on the attitude of a preacher, perhaps in anticipation of becoming a future prophet.

In the same spirit, he organizes games with lead soldiers for himself and his two friends. They are not just for fun, but lessons of the history of wars and political strategies of winning them. Passionate about militarism, monarchism, tradition, patriotism, German supremacy, and God, Fritz was an inventor of learning experiences disguised as games, so he could satisfy his cravings to learn something he could not find in the school's curriculum.

He was well-mannered and obedient to rules, to the point of absurdity. "The exuberant prodigy took an awkward and precocious stub at self-discipline,since there was no parental authority to impose discipline on him,"[48] Safranski writes.

Once, as eye-witnessed by his sister Elisabeth, when returning home from school, Fritz was caught in a rainstorm. Instead of running, as the other boys did, Fritz walked calmly in the pouring rain. When his mother Franziska asked him why he did not run to avoid becoming soaking wet, he explained that "according to the rules, boys going back from school must not run or jump but proceed in a quite orderly fashion."[49] The performance must look not just absurdly comical, but also intently theatrical. Undoubtedly, there were various rebellious reasons behind his performance, e.g., defiance of the common rules; cleverness in showing incoherence of rules; signaling his presence and uncommonness; performing radical individualism; emphatic self-awareness and self-discipline. But, in the end, Fritz was noticed. He was not like everyone else who tried to blend in within the background of others.

Being a mediocre student, Fritz was hardly an ideal advocate of the benefits of education. Something of a poseur, a pretender shined through his opinions. However, as Ronald Hayman claims in his biography, Fritz, to withstand the teasing of his schoolmates, appropriated a pose of superiority which "probably give him his earliest practice in what he was later to call self-conquest."[50]

Nonetheless, there is no question that whatever he learned and deemed valuable, he adopted immediately, if he saw it as beneficial to his growth and development—then quite vague and not jet precisely defined—but which, undoubtedly, could be described as aspiring upwards to surpass his contemporaries, colleges, teachers, family members, and so-called friends.

When introduced to Greek and Latin culture at the Weber Institute, he started on a new path, perhaps without realizing, of thinking in terms of the Greek philosophy, which would derail him from becoming a pastor. It was not precisely the way to merely surpass his contemporaries but leave them behind.

The only path of life Fritz identified with at that age was to become a pastor, which, considering his background, should have been relatively straightforward, an almost automatic development. Nonetheless, it is surprising that, having such a precise goal in life supported by his strong faith and possibility of social advancement, he wondered about life's meaning. Already as an early teenager, he was doubting the infallibility of moral and cultural values.

So, the retrospection as a way to find out who he was put Fritz on the path of the history of the future. Probably instinctively, through reminiscing about his past, Fritz projected his future person, already anticipated in the past events. Thinking and analyzing, if not to say writing about past events and their impact on one's personality, is in itself an event anticipating a new person in the future.

With full awareness he accepted all the events and traits of his character. Becoming what he already was, he turned to his advantage his father's death, physical health, grandiose personality, friendships, Christian faith, the necessity of music, readings, need to write autobiographically, writings, communing with nature, walking about, education, German culture, changing schools and friends, becoming a pastor, becoming an artist, becoming a thinker. But there was not much Christian humility in that process of cultivating himself, or belief in the transcendence of the afterlife.

# 2

## SCHULPFORTA - THE PRUSSIAN UPBRINGING

While completing his first autobiography by the end of August and probably not yet aware of upcoming changes, Fritz was getting ready to begin a new semester at the Naumburg's Domgymnasium. He did not expect that his life would radically change soon, yet again. In September, his mother received a surprise letter from the Rector of *Landesschule Pforta* offering Fritz a tuition-free placement. The Pforta school was a prestigious boarding institution, religious and oriented towards classical study, whose noble pupils include Johann Gottlieb Fichte, Friedrich Gottlieb Klopstock, and Ulrich von Wilamowitz-Moellendorff, among others, located around five kilometers west of Naumburg. Fritz received this scholarship for being an orphan of a state-employed Lutheran pastor, not—as many academics claimed—because of his high academic qualifications.[51]

The school, situated in an old Cistercian monastery, was a self-sufficient enterprise with its own farm, livestock, mill and church, which specialized in producing a new clergy for the Lutheran Church. Fritz himself accepted the offer since his mother asked him to decide whether he wanted to continue his education at the Domgymnasium and stay at home or move away to Pforta. "It was completely up to me if I want to accept or reject the offer. Already since earlier times, I had had a partiality for Pforta, partly because I was attracted to the good reputation of the school and the famous names of those who had been there in the past and are there at present, partly because I admire the beautiful location and the surrounding nature. I quickly decided to accept the offer and have never regretted it," he wrote in one of his successive autobiographies.[52]

Therefore, it was his sole decision to move out from his family home. Although not too far, it was still a permanent move. He was about to leave behind the family home's stagnant tranquility to live from now on in impermanent, transitional places for the rest of his life. It was one of the pivotal decision moments that would be repeated throughout his life, and mapped his trajectory towards becoming his own creation. He would return home only as a guest, for holidays and in the interims between changing locations in his travels. He would never create a home of his own but move incessantly, from place to place, in search for a right location to carry out his ventures.

He moved out without hesitation, but the trip, the new residence, and the new life customs would strongly impact him during the next six years. Pforta was more prestigious than Domgymnasium, but their education levels were almost the same.[53] Considering this, Fritz could continue attending the Domgymnasium without exposing himself to the austere regiments of the Prussian system of *Bildung*, applied with the verve of monastic rigor. But he chose otherwise.

On October 5, 1858, Fritz arrives at Pforta, having the impression that it feels more like entering a prison than a boarding school. The compound of different structures was built first in 1127 A.D. as a self-sufficient Benedictine monastery, and then in 1132 A.D. as a Cistercian abbey with "walls twelve feet high and two and a half feet thick."[54] In the middle of the sixteenth century, the abbey was converted into a boarding school as "a self-contained school state in which the life of the individual is wholly absorbed. The parents entrust the young scholars to their alma mater not only for instructions but for their moral development as well. The parents transfer all parental rights to the school, so that the school finds in the totality of their education even more than a second-father house."[55] On his way to Pforta, Fritz was overflowing with conflicting emotions: "It was on a Tuesday morning when I drove out through the gates of Naumburg. The dawn still lay around the meadows, and on the horizon, only a few dimly lit clouds showed the coming day. There remains a sunset in me: not yet had a joy of sunrise risen in my heart. The horror of the anxious night still enveloped me, and the future lay before me in a gray haze. For the first time, I was to move away from the parental home for a long, long time. I approached unknown dangers; the farewell had baffled me, and I was trembling at the thought of my future. It was good that I should leave my dear friends and step out of the comfortable circumstances into a new, unknown, rigid world. It cramped my breast, and every minute became more terrible to me. Even as I saw Pforta shining forth, I perceived her more like a prison than recognize as an alma mater. I drove through the gate. My heart was overflowing with divine sensations; I was lifted up to God in silent prayer, and great peace came over my soul. Yes, Lord, bless my arrival and also protect me physically and spiritually in this sanctuary of the Holy Spirit. Send down your angel so that he may lead me victoriously through the trials I am going to encounter, and let this place become my true blessing for eternity. So, help me, God! Amen."[56] He conveyed his first encounter with the school in the letter to Pinder in the middle of February 1859.

The motive to move out was loftier and more complex than just the simple necessity of education. Fritz intuitively anticipated that he could not tie himself up to the convenience of a certain inertia at home in Naumburg. Even if the consequences of his decision would produce hardship and loss of all entitlements he had at home, they were always the components in fulfilling his pursuit of self-formation.

There is no question that Fritz was trying to leave nothing to chance. His life's conduct had to have a deliberate purpose aimed at the goal of self-invention. Hayman provides an astute analysis of one of Fritz's incongruous performances at Pforta that he initiated to prove an argument, which looked bizarre on the surface, but in fact, screamed to his audience that he existed and was in command of himself.

"The regimen of the school acted like a hot-house on [Fritz's] inclinations to fight for the self-mastery. The sadism in authoritarian oppression always tends to generate masochism in the desire to excel through obedience and, as at the Domgymnasium, one of the ways [Fritz] could feel superior to the boys who teased him was by winning the approval of the teachers and earning high marks for good behavior.

The sadomasochism concealed behind the severity with himself came to the surface when he became involved in an argument about Gaius Mucius

Scaevola, the Roman soldier who, failing to kill Porsena, put his hand into a fire to prove his indifference to pain.

Taking a handful of matches, [Fritz] set them alight and held them unflinchingly in the palm of his outstretched hand until a prefect knock them to the ground."[57]

The strictly controlled residency at Pforta was not easy for Fritz. Homesick, he wrote home and two of his friends, Krug and Pinder almost daily, always requesting something and insisting on prompt replies. In addition to incessant note-making, this compulsive letter writing became his new, controlled way of fashioning his thoughts. "From now on, we want to write to each other back and forth regularly and without interruptions. Tell Gustav this too,"[58] he writes to Pinder. To his mother, regardless of seeing her almost every Sunday in Alm-rich (formerly Attenburg), located halfway between Naumburg and Pforta, he mailed daily lists of requests "which give a very strained impression, bordering on hysteria or tantrums."[59]

"Many thanks for the wonderful grapes," he writes his mother, "they taste great. Anyway, I was pleased to see you. Well, maybe next Sunday again. – I remember many things that still I have not yet received, such as glasses, chocolate powder, *Prussian History* by Hahn, scissors, sewing kit, spoon and knive, and many more. Oh, send these to me as soon as possible. It will be good enough for now! – I wish Lisbeth and uncle good health. Write to me soon. Send me the box for scissors, etc.! Tell Wilhelm, he would receive a long letter from me soon. He should now be prepared for regular correspondence. – If only we could have talked longer. In any case, come on Sunday to Almrich. We all will see each other!"[60]

He was lonely at Pforta, incapable of initiating any new friendships, and overwhelmed with a demanding and rigorous schoolwork schedule. All the pupils (around two hundred of them during Fritz's residency) got up at five o'clock in the morning in summer and at six during the wintertime. After a quick breakfast of bread rolls and warm milk, the boys went for classes, which lasted till midday. Each day there was a different lunch: "On Mondays, soup, beef, vegetables, and fruit; on Tuesdays, soup, beef, vegetables and butter; on Wednesdays, soup, beef, vegetables and fruit; on Thursdays, beef, and vegetables, grilled kidneys and salad; on Fridays, soup, pork and vegetables. In addition, each boy was given a twelfth of a loaf of bread at each meal,"[61] Fritz writes at length about his daily diet. It would seem a trivial topic, but Fritz, from early on, paid a lot of attention to his diet, for he considered it throughout his life as one of the main influences on his wellbeing. There is also the first note about his susceptibility to the weather having a strong impact on his moods. Later in life, when he was choosing any specific place of his many residences, he always considered the type of climate and weather patterns. "It is true: gloomy weather evokes gloomy thoughts; a darkening sky makes the soul darken, and when the heavens weep, my own eyes overflow with tears."[62] Fritz's "extreme sensitivity to meteorological phenomena evinces an important respect in which the membrane between the self and the world remains in [his] case unusually permeable,"[63] Graham Parkes, one of the hylozoistic Nietzschean monists, recognizes experience and the world as one.

The school rules were exhaustively applied to every hour of the day: attending classes, doing homework, going to church, sleeping, eating, praying, or performing grueling physical exercise. Fritz hated the Pfotra' s athletics, but in other circumstances, he enjoyed swimming and taking walks. "It is delightful to surrender oneself to the tepid waters of summer [or] walk around aimlessly and without knowing the roads, wherever chance led me,"[64] Fritz writes, emphasizing joyfulness of body activities, contrary to an imposed militaristic routine of drilling young boys into a dutiful cog to fit into future state services. Although Hayman excuses Fritz's dislike of physical exercises at Pforta due to his myopic eyesight,[65] Fritz, from early on, was approaching everything that seemed to have any systemic lineage with a dose of reserve and skepticism. He intuitively sensed that the body's activity should not be a drill in becoming part of a system, but intrinsically related to the process of thinking, and wherefrom he drew his enjoyment.

With limited time for themselves, the students spent just a couple hours a week outside the school's walls. During these time allowances, Fritz usually walked to Almrich to meet his mother and, on many occasions, his sister Elisabeth. He later described this rigorous time control and austere routine of learning as a fabrication of society's elites, clergy, bureaucrats, and teachers to run the country's political apparatus. "What such exclusive schools actually do is to enforce a brutal regime aimed at producing as quickly as possible a large number of young men trained to be of use – more accurately, misuse – to the state," he wrote.[66]

Conceivably, because of Fritz's mediocre achievements at school, Fritz has to repeat his last semester completed in Naumburg. Regarding the educational schedule, most of the weekly classes consisted of ancient languages: Latin, Greek, and Hebrew, some modern French, physics, and mathematics. However, Pforta was an institution specializing in classical education, a school in the business of producing future clergymen, state officials, and scholars. Its program emphasized Latin, which every student was expected to read, write, and speak fluently.

Fritz submitted willingly to such a regimental process of education for two reasons. He was fatherless, thus desiring a strong, masculine, and disciplinarian father figure in response to all-female Naumburg household, unlike an exclusively male school environment, and in his aims at self-mastery, he needed toughness and discipline to be successful in the process. The austere standards of life imposed by the school were what he wanted. He welcomed the daily routine of strenuous exercise with a masochistic thrill but, inadvertently, he paid for it with his fragile health. Which, it almost seems— gathering from his relishing in detailed descriptions of his numerous ailments in his letters—he welcomed; the "rheumatism, catarrh, rheumatic pains in the head and neck, headache, diarrhea, congestions, all entered time and again in the school records."[67]

Already at this stage of Fritz's maturity, one may notice a pattern in his modus operandi concerning his person. As early as his father's death, when he was five, instead of impulsively following the beaten paths of children of his age, he was relentless in his attempts to decide on the most beneficial possibility for himself. It seems that those decisions were not rationally thought through, but rather rooted in the mindset of egocentric self-involvement to control his own destiny. And, undeniably, underneath all his life choices, there is an unstoppable, obstinate will pushing forward, regardless of circumstance.

At a very early age, he decided to write poetry, compose music, read outside school requirements, discipline himself through long hours of work and allot a limited time for rest. Instead of having fun with his two friends, he invented games to practice his personal development, his individual *Bildung*, just for himself. Was this a visceral drive coming from the inside, or was it brought by his father's death and subsequent loss of the family home in Röcken?

When Fritz was working on his first autobiography, besides vulgarly giving himself over to self-indulgence, he produced a tool of introspection, which in its most refined form enabled the possibility of self-mastery. Perhaps, there should be no surprise that he wished to write many more of these autobiographies, suggesting that his entire oeuvre was one continuous autobiographical piece in a variety of forms.

According to Fritz, the physicality of writing demands other somatic activities, like walking, hiking, mountain climbing, swimming, choosing dietary restrictions, and seeking specific places to live and work. He was whimsical about the natural environment and climate, as well as of social milieus producing useful members of the society. He chose to live in solitude, but among people, as an outsider looking inwards, a hermit carefully selecting friends and acquaintances. He practiced the same approach toward his reading and music. He only had the pleasure of self-picked texts and specific music, inspiring spontaneous improvisations which mirrored and perhaps influenced his continuous adjustments of his formative life pathways. While thinking and writing, he preferred not to sit behind a desk, but to experience nature directly, trekking for hours and making extensive notes.

Most likely, because of his fragile health, he dedicated a lot of attention to his body, intending to overcome its frailty. He aimed to realize himself as he felt he already was, an egocentric superior human being, better than any of his so-called friends and acquaintances. He was looking forward to putting a bridle on his afflictions, faith, family and friend relationships, education, philosophical thought, and body, to tame them into one true expression of himself. But, in the end, it was a mystery; for the whole project of Fritz's life was an experiment. It was heroic to aim at the unknown, for it could cost him his life, and it did as he anticipated it.

# PROMETHEUS

During his first Easter vacation in Naumburg, Fritz, trying to use the time to maximum, was so absorbed with work outside the Pforta's program that he forgot to write his two friends. When, by the end of April, he was back in school, he wrote Pinder about his literary efforts back at home: "First of all an unsuccessful play entitled *Prometheus*, cluttered up with countless false perceptions on this topic, secondly three poems on the same subject which I do to death in a third work. This third work, incidentally, is a curious thing but not yet ready: it is six closely typed pages long and is entitled 'Question marks and comments along with a general exclamation mark concerning three poems entitled Prometheus.' It tells the story of a poet's opposition to the public, and the whole thing is a mixture of rubbish and nonsense.... I don't know how I could have such ridiculous ideas,"[68] – Fritz writes self-critically. But then, almost immediately annotated his work: "Why Prometheus? One would like to recreate the era of Aeschylus or, are there no humans left and we have to make the Titans appear once again!"[69] – he asks.

Because of Pforta's classical Greco-Roman literature profile, Fritz, without a doubt, read *Prometheus Bound* by Aeschylus. He followed the German attitude, popular at the time, towards connecting ancient Greek culture with modern Germany as its cultural successor and "the potential for a shared identity that might link them."[70] The character of Prometheus appealed to Fritz as a rebel against the gods and a benefactor of humanity. The Titan stole fire from the gods of Olympus, depriving them of their divine qualities, which discern the gods from us, humans. But sharing the fire with humanity meant that we could become gods also: we could evolve, developing godlike powers, ultimately overshadowing the gods of Olympus and leading to their demise.

The challenge to the gods was not new to Fritz. Regardless of being deeply pious, Fritz asked defiant questions concerning God's absolute power. Through the metaphor of Promethean tragedy, he was not afraid to test His power and need for sacrifice in advancing humanity. Fritz championed the lone revolutionary, mocking the power of authority and, at the same time, fostering the good of humanity. Being quite attractive to Fritz, the Promethean figure would reappear later in his works. He would promote an ideal of continually challenging institutional authority, not only through his writings but his lifestyle. Young Fritz probably saw himself as a lone rebel-philosopher, courageous enough to romantically sacrifice his life for the cause. Later in his life, anticipating perhaps what to expect from the masses, Fritz returned to the Aeschylus' tragedy asking if the public was ready for the Titan's gift. He answered unfavorably, in "opposition to the public," assuming that "there are no humans left."

And so, already at age fourteen, by challenging God's authority and recognizing the lack of humanness within the masses of people, Fritz anticipates his future assaults on faith and the hordes of mindlessly numb humans.

As evidenced by his lifestyle choices, type of education, taste in music, literature and art, career plans, interest in politics, etc., from an early age, Fritz was always intensely conservative. So, wherefrom did the rebellious attitude come? It is a constructive question, but one attitude does not preclude the other. They can exist in chiasmic unity.[71] Both conservatism and rebelliousness create a divergence of ideals, providing a space of tension in between, like any other pair of contradictory values, the most exciting and productive enterprise.


The first half of his summer vacation, Fritz spent with his uncle, Dr. Emil Schenk, the *Oberbürgermeister* of Jena. Uncle Emil took him to the meetings of his old student fraternity Tautonia, regarding Fritz not as an average teenage boy, but a thoughtful young man. Later on, the uncle fraternity's Germanic designation probably inspired Fritz to create his own fraternity, Germania, fulfilling Fritz's patriotic sentiments. Or, as Robert C. Holub claims, "The name Germania was likely drawn from the celebrated history text by Tacitus, *De Origine et situ Germanorum* (98 AD), an ethnographic account that praises Germans (in contrast to Romans of Tacitus times), which became perhaps the central work from antiquity for German nationalism.[72]

The second half of his vacation Fritz spent in Pobles, at his grandfather Oehler's house, where the whole family gathered to celebrate his grandfather's seventieth birthday. Fritz wrote a poem for the occasion, being merely fifteen years old, already nostalgic about his lost childhood and a family home he once had.

*O place that hath always vouchsafed me*
*A fresh glimmer of the homestead*
*That I had lost,*
*Thou art special to me,*
*Helping me to preserve*
*The faithful memories of childhood*
*That would otherwise have faded away,*
*And to satisfy my craving*
*For the home I once called my own.*[73]

The night before the celebration, he had a dream picturing the Pobles' parsonage laying in ruins with his grandmother sitting in despair among the rubble. Franziska being superstitious, asked Fritz not to repeat the vision to anyone; nevertheless, within six months, his grandfather Oehler, although in excellent health, died.[74] Fritz, "who suffered from nightmares throughout his life and exploited them in his works, saw in them the forces that perpetually threatened his life. Masked and otherwise disguised, these forces constantly assumed new forms that always continued to menace and frighten him. His suffering remained hidden, as did, therefore, his attempts to overcome it."[75] Later, in 1878, he seriously considered reviewing the role of dreams in culture and include it in his published work, not just as an anecdotal curiosity, but as his supposed ability to predict future.[76]

Following Fritz's return to Pforta after summer vacation, he joined the school choir, but regardless of being among boys of his age, he could not initiate any friendships. "He gave the impression of thinking himself superior to his classmates,"[77] Hayman describes Fritz's attitude towards his peers. The only friend he considered, in some sense, his equal was his Naumburg friend Pinder, but with whom he could hardly meet in person as both boys were in in different schools. With Krug, the other Naumburg friend, Fritz lost contact, possibly due to his more than frequent and annoying requests for daily correspondence. "From now on, we want to write each other back and forth regularly and without interruptions. Tell Gustav this too,"[78] he commanded Pinder. Then, upon his arrival in Pforta he wrote in his diary: "I longed for

Naumburg and for the hours of pleasant conversations with my friends. Here, I had no one. The whole school building seemed so bleak, so comfortless, and the duskiness everywhere left me with nothing before my eyes except happy memories from the holidays. Oh Christmas, oh, Christmas how long, how long,"[79] he complains.

At the beginning of January 1860, Fritz again suffered from illness. This time, he developed catarrh and was constantly coughing. The school's doctor kept him in the infirmary for almost two weeks, from January 5 to 16. "My cough is almost completely cured, but I am still wearing the shawl," he wrote his mother after his discharge. But he was not tormented only by the physical ailments. Already in February, he lamented to Pinder about his "thoughts of cold, boring existence,"[80] looking forward to Easter holiday at Aunt Rosalie's in Plauen, reminiscing about "lovely meadows, surrounded by green hills with many springs, once revealed to me the awakening of nature. Ponds with goldfish, butterflies, larks, violets and forget-me-nots, cowherds with charming bells."[81] However, besides the melancholy of these colorful recollections, what is more significant is that Fritz showed an acute sensibility to nature. He saw not only its beauty but experienced it corporeally as a formative imprint on human character.

*Spring is coming*
*Very soon, very soon*
*And sprinkles its bliss*
*On the meadows and forests.*

*And love and life*
*And joy and happiness*
*That returns with*
*The approaching springtime.*

*The clouds so fluffy*
*And the lake so pure –*
*Oh, I could die*
*From desire and pain!*[82]

Fritz composed an ad-hoc poem (mailed later to Pinder) eulogizing the future ingrained in the memories of the past.

In his future works, these experiences of nature would augment themselves, forming the connotations of their self-contained immediacy into domains capable of producing ideas.

Although an idea seems independent from its surrounding, nonetheless it raises the questions: to what degree is its appearance about the independency or dependency? To what degree is an experience— as it moves from subconsciousness to conscious realization— entangled with a subsequent or simultaneous thought?

## MY FIRST DISCIPLES

At the beginning of his second year at Pforta, Fritz, a mediocre student lacking any inspiring relationships with the school's teachers or tutors, has had an uplifting revelation.

He realized that his life passes with few scattered moments of happiness but without any lasting changes. "Time goes like the roses of spring and pleasure like the foam of the brook," he reflects nostalgically in his notebooks.

This revelation was probably raised by a lecture of biography of an explorer, scientist, and philosopher Alexander von Humboldt by Herman Klencke, *Alexander von Humboldt: ein biographisches Denkmal* (1851), which began his lasting love affair with learning. "A general drive to knowledge, to universal learning had seized me. Humboldt has awakened this feeling in me. May it be as enduring as my dedication to poetry.... Great is the feeling of knowledge, endless the search for truth! And over everything religion, the fundament of all knowledge!"[83] – he wrote, immediately introducing it into practice.

Within a few months, at the end of the second or beginning of the third year at Pforta, Fritz was nominated as a class Primus, the best student in his class. With it came the responsibility for keeping an eye on his classmates when teachers were not in the room. On one occasion, eager to fulfill his new role, he unexpectedly approached one of his fellow students, who later remembered that event:

"I was sitting quietly in my place, peacefully chewing at my breakfast, a delicious roll. I can still see Nietzsche roaming through the aisles with the uncertain look of a very myopic person, trying in vain to find some occasion to take action. Just then, he passed where I was sitting, bent down to me, and said, 'Don't talk so loud to your roll!' Those were the first words he spoke to me. I no longer remember what first brought us closer together,"[84] Paul Deussen recalls their first encounter.

Later, during their walk, "by coming together in a solemn hour," they made a friendship pact replacing customary *Sie* with the familiar *du* (reserved only for close friends) then, in the dorm quarters, celebrated their brotherhood with snuff instead of wine.

So finally, after two years at Pforta, Fritz solicited a new friend to join the Naumburg's pair, Pinder and Krug. But we cannot forget that at the same time, he had always had a given friend, two years his junior, his sister Elisabeth. Albeit, with the proviso that she was his kin and a woman, she could not satisfy a male friendship's requirements. Still, Fritz corresponded with her by letter almost as often as with his mother, and asked about her frequently in the letters to Franziska.

"Elisabeth was inordinately close to her brother from her earliest youth. Their dealings with each other were characterized by a desire to be helpful to the other. [They] were so closed that [they] had an inhibiting effect on the other's chances of finding a marriage partner,"[85] writes Carol Diethe. It appears then that it was a "friendship" of reciprocal dependency, driven by the desire to possess and use one another, where Fritz felt entitled to demand care from his sister because he was the only male of their household. Whereas Elisabeth was so jealous and emotionally attached to him that "there are alleged indications of sibling incest in the early years. Did little Fritz perhaps even pull Elisabeth into his bed and wind up plagued by a bad conscience?"[86]– Safranski suggests, stirring controversy.

Fritz was on the lookout throughout his entire productive life—until struck by mental illness which prohibited him from any independent endeavor—not so much for a new ideal comrade as for a follower. Repeatedly disappointed, he wrote a versed letter on March 6, 1860, addressed "To a Friend," an imaginary companion, who—inferring from the content—was his *doppelgänger*. Thus, in having a conversation with himself, he initiated a practice which he would continue throughout his life to generate new ideas.

It seems that the spur to search for someone new with whom he could have a constructive argument was a shortage of valid challenges from his childhood friends, Pinder and Krug. Complaining about his learning difficulties and rigid discipline at Pforta, he could not wait for spring vacation. But at home, no one could meet his needs for faithful companionship. Ironically, surrounded by hundreds of schoolmates at Pforta, childhood friends at home in Naumburg, and a large extended family in its vicinity, Fritz, instead of genuinely reaching out to any one of them with a gesture of friendship, chose to turn away preferring his own introverted company. He complained about loneliness, nevertheless running away from any intimacy of friendship. He was a lone wanderer, merely in need of intellectual acquaintances to accomplish his goals, not in want of a companion to whom he could give himself unconditionally. His life choices were calculated moves, targeting, first of all, his *Aufgaben*, the tasks aiming at himself as a constantly renewed person.

From June 12 to 26, Fritz was sick again, this time with rheumatism, but the summer vacations were just a few days away so that he could leave Pforta and his ailments behind at the beginning of July. This time, he visited his uncle Edmund Oehler, the pastor in Gorenzen, a village in the Harz Mountains. He invited Pinder to go with him to discuss "regularizing the literary collaboration they had planned for 'Prometheus,'"[87] an unfinished, but still interesting subject to Fritz. On their hikes in the woods, Fritz proposes establishing a fraternity called Germania. The idea was probably influenced by the call on the Teutonia—during the previous year's summer vacation with Uncle Emil Schenk—uncle's old fraternity. Later in July, after their return to Naumburg, they recruited Gustav and, on July 26, 1860, in the ruins of Schönburg castle, they established a fraternity, celebrating it with a bottle of cheap wine. "We resolved to found a kind of small club [Germania]"—Fritz recalled the event in a lecture, delivered at Basel University a few years later—"which would consist of ourselves and a few friends, and the object of which would be to provide us with a stable and binding organization directing and adding interest to our creative impulses in art and literature; or, to put it more plainly: each of us would be pledged to present an original piece of work to the club once a month—either a poem, a treatise, an architectural design, or a musical composition, upon which each of the others, in a friendly spirit, would have to pass free and unrestrained criticism."[88]

By establishing this club of three members, Fritz found a venue to present his works, which he could not introduce at Pforta. The members were obligated to contribute a small amount of money to purchase books and sheet music. Among the musical periodicals bought for Germania by Gustav, who was in charge of music matters, was the *Zeitschrift für Musik* and the piano score of *Tristan und Isolde*. Very likely, it was Fritz's initial introduction to Wagner's music.[89]

As his first submission, Fritz composed a musical score for a Christmas oratorio, followed by seven poems, which he presented to the members of Germania in January 1861. He argued that the oratorio is of higher value than the opera, preferring the oratorio over any other type of music. "I believe," Fritz writes to Pinder and Krug, justifying the choice of his submission, "that oratorio is higher in its musical genre than the opera." But his choice also signified that his Christian faith was still an essential component of his life and that he minimized opera, dethroning it as worldly music: "In and of itself, the oratorio is already of an imposing simplicity, and indeed it must be so, as uplifting and, moreover, as strictly religious uplifting music. Hence the oratorio spurns all these other means that opera uses for effect; no one can take it for a kind of accomplishment, as opera music is still for the masses. It excites no other sense than our hearing. Its content, too, is infinitely simpler and more sublime and, for the most part, is familiar and easily comprehensible to even an uneducated audience. This is why I believe that, in its musical genus, the oratorio stands at a higher level than opera."[90]

During that time, Fritz was working intensely on school assignments and the Germania submissions despite getting sick again and again, but not reporting it to the school's physician, eager to achieve as much as possible despite his illness. "I have constant headaches; they have taken over my whole head, and my neck hurts each time I move, and my larynx when I breathe. For two nights, I have not slept at all. I was freezing and sweating alternately. I cannot come to my senses; everything around me is like a dream,"[91] he wrote his mother in mid-January. Although, being incessantly sick for the rest of January, he finally reported it and was immediately referred to the infirmary.

In the middle of February, he recovered, but headaches returned. Dr. Zimmermann, Pforta's medical officer, applied leeches behind the boy's ears. After an improvement, he was still unable to attend classes, so the doctor sent him to Naumburg to recover, where he took long, daily walks—in Fritz's opinion, the only effective remedy for his afflictions. However, after his return to Pforta, headaches began again. Facing such long, reoccurring attacks of illness, Fritz realized that the prophecy of his father's inheritance was coming true. There was no way out of it, but to "have to get gradually used to it,"[92] he wrote his mother by the end of February.

In mid-March, on Laetare Sunday, on March 10, 1861,[93] Deussen and Fritz, both kneeling next to each other, were confirmed at the Pforta's minster. Fritz regarded his Confirmation with exultation. "May this holy and solemn day constantly remain before my soul throughout the whole of my future life and remind me of the awe-inspiring oath I have taken and the professions of faith I have made." He thanked his uncle Edmund Oehler from Gorenzen for attending the rite and for a gift of "beautiful books." However, only three weeks later, during Easter vacation, probably under the influence of Professor Steinhardt's lectures,[94] he had a faith-related quarrel with his mother, an inconvincible religious devotee[95]

In any case, the Confirmation is the last ostentatious—maybe even theatrical—manifestation of Fritz's Christian devotion. From then on, he gradually separated himself from it, until reaching a phase of radical atheism, with explicit attacks on religion during the last period of his creative life.[96]

Shortly before the Confirmation, on March 5, Fritz wrote an essay, "Hunters and Fishers" *(Jäger und Fischer)*[97] as a school assignment concerning the possibility of cultural development of prehistoric, primitive communities, without interference from God. He posed the question of how the "early, brutal humans could find the inspiration and means to develop the arts and moral sophistication enjoyed by later generations when they were themselves so primitive. How could this be done through natural means alone and without divine intervention?"[98]

Then, after the Confirmation, a week before Easter break, on March 24, he followed up with yet another essay, "The Childhood of Peoples" *(Die Kindheit der Völker)*,[99] where "the seventeen year-old immerses himself in the genealogy of world religions and concludes that they were in debt to 'profound men who, carried away by the soaring of their unbridled fantasy, claimed to be envoys of the highest gods.'"[100] What is pertinent in this work is that Fritz elaborated his speculations concerning religion's nascency from the primeval idea of spirit *(Geist)* being present in all things as God. At a certain point in man's evolution, it becomes necessary for our "childlike ancestors" to have an explicable relationship with the natural world in terms of good and evil. This idea evolved into religious worship, which, in consequence, led to an ascent of culture. But we do not owe this continuous progress to everyone. For Fritz discerned people as polarized, the evolution of thought only possible through the very few gifted *(begabten)* and most significant *(bedeutungsvollsten)* group members. Thus, the seed of the idea of greatness—realized by the very few great individuals as the movers and shakers of history—was already present, which later developed into profound philosophical claims. There was also a sign that Fritz's religiosity gave way to the realization that religion, based on faith, is not an attempt to explain the world's phenomena but an imposition by an undisputed source, God. Therefore, some philosophers of the Enlightenment (or the enlightened philosophers *(oerleuchtete Philosophen)*, as Fritz sardonically wrote) rejected God as a source of all being *(Gott als den Urquell alles Seins)*.[101] In the end, he proposed two resolves to the problem of the likelihood of developing culture by primitive humans. At first, he rejected the natural way of cultural development, in favor of the idea that culture originally was given by God but was lost to social decline and could be recovered from the memory of the original divinely instituted culture. Alternately, Fritz considered the birth of culture through solely natural means, although, because it was threatening to religion, he rejected it, opting for the first explanation. "It is neither part of my intention to decide this issue, nor does it seem possible to simplify so problematic an issue. Enough. I opt for the first opinion that human beings were at first provided with culture, that under the impress of world events and revolution they turned to barbarism, and partly then began to develop the first paths to civilization."[102]

What is significant in those two essays, besides knocking religion off from the pedestal of absolute authority by merely asking questions about its role in the order of things, is the process of cultural development. Culture (*Kultur*) is an indicator of human advancement, as they go hand in hand, becoming the most meaningful and fertile creation of humanity. Civilization and its devaluation in contemporary, modern times became Fritz's focus in his later years, since, according to him, the vulgarization of culture was the origin of the death drive leading to the annihilation of all life.

## MEIN LEBENSLAUF

In May 1861, Fritz produced an autobiographical piece as a school assignment, in three installments or, as some of the facts overlap, three attempts at the same autobiography. All three of them are entitled "My Curriculum Vitae" *(Mein Lebenslauf).*[103]

The initial piece is most remarkable for, as Graham Parkes points out, it is "one of Nietzsche's first overtly philosophical pronouncements concerning the conception of life."[104] In it, Fritz preaches "a radical hylozoism," stating that "everything that is, is alive," and continues in an essayistic format —surely without realizing, for he had not yet read Montaigne—to indicate salient elements of human development, exemplifying that all matter is alive with the personal events of his own life. Furthermore, Safranski sees in the essay an "intricate analysis of the guiding hand of God"[105] as the rationale for wondering about the absolute of God. A prelude to future criticism.

Whether to be "philosophical pronouncements" or an analysis of Christian faith, the critical idea that emerges from Fritz's line of thought is the development of oneself and its dependence on the circumstances we live in. As there is a potential of self (a germ or seed, *die Keime*) innate to us, which could be activated by the accidental and indifferent circumstances of our milieu or natural environment, he continues with a dependency analysis between himself and his habitat.

As in his piece from 1858, he begins with a postulate concerning history's relevance in one's development. Historical account has a meaning; there is meaning in all things. Therefore, we can deduce how the event-experiences we are exposed to are connected in the process of forming "who we are." He makes a retrospection of one's life indispensable if one would like to have an impact on one's own development. He binds events of one's life, deemed individually significant, but only personally to him, with mental growth. Recognizing the role of heredity as the given, unchangeable traits of personality, he nevertheless acknowledges that if they cannot be changed in themselves, the behavior spawned by them certainly can. One could achieve it by absorbing the experiences that might change one's life's trajectory, even if these events are horrific. And not blaming fate for his misfortune but using the bad experiences to his advantage. Obviously, not everyone can do that. Fritz divided mankind into majority of fate blamers and complainers and minority of the rich, famous, lucky ones, the great individuals. Implicitly, hierarchies arose based on the distribution of mental faculties, in the same way as life; thus, the spirit is spread throughout all creation, with the primordial spirit, on the top of the ladder. "Everything that is, is alive *(Deen alles, was ist, lebt)*. There are hierarchies throughout creation," he writes, "which must extend even as far as invisible beings unless the world itself is to be the Primordial Soul *(der Urseele)*. Thus, we see a progression in life, beginning with stone ... progression to plant, animals, and human beings, and issuing in the earth, air, heavenly bodies, world or space, matter, and time."[106]

On the one hand, we have an accidental, indifferent, and naturalistic intervention influencing human development through environmentally generated events. Fritz categorically rejects this solution, claiming that it is "unthinkable to place the highest interests of the human race in the hands of a thoughtless and indifferent being – it is almost like to entrust it to an original evil being *(urböses Wesen)*. For an abstract, non-creative creature, the same way as an original evil being, cannot guide our destinies, since the spiritless cannot exist – for all that is, lives."[107]

However, humanity's highest purposes are influenced by or coming from "the primeval spirit, which directs our gaze to a higher, more sublime spiritual power."[108]

In both instances— would it be an indifferent chance or divine intervention— the overall mode of influence is deterministic. Surprisingly, Fritz is not lamenting his conclusion, but, on the contrary, he warns to, "not dare to raise the veil, which is spread over the guidance of our circumstances."[109] While he acknowledges a modus operandi shaping our destiny, at the same time, he implicitly suggests that there is a possibility of "raising the veil" without outright stating it. Although, he stops short, putting his fate in the hands of the original spirit.[110]

However, regardless of an intrinsic determinism hidden in these statements concerning meaningful experiences, Fritz believes that only a few of them are significant (*bedeutsam*) to destiny in his life, for most are irrelevant, not even worth mentioning. But does the decision to incorporate any one of them within his writings—sometimes down to minute details—provide him with an opportunity to influence his own life beyond the determinism of interweaving dependencies of meaning qualifying "all creation, guided knowingly and meaningfully by a higher being"?[111]

The process of influencing one's life is a futile fight against the destructive and irreversible process of entropy as the ubiquitous property of the cosmos, including the lifespans of each and every human being. Our attempts to bring order and purpose into our existence through fighting or trying to reverse the flow of the events—which is our natural way of reacting to destruction— provides merely an illusion of doing something constructive. In the end, our lives and the world will, regardless of our attempts, end up as a chaotic and unpredictable pile of rubble. From the moment of conception, we fall into disarray in the same way as the world we are part of is speeding into oblivion.

So, suppose we want to go against the common grain. In that case, it seems that the only solution would be not only to accept defeat but to embrace these chaotic and unpredictable processes with the intention of utilizing them for our purposes. The only solution would be to open yourself up to the entropic mind of the universe.

"[E]very human being contemplates his past life because he must, because he cannot interrupt for one moment the connection with his past – and the more he himself acts, standing above mere contemplation of his changing self, and the further he looks back on this being, so much *the more will he develop his life toward a higher norm*,"[112] Fritz sets up the bar high to which he will adhere for the rest of his productive life.

Writing in this richly picturesque way is an essential aspect of this method, which Fritz exercises throughout his entire output. The details of forms, sounds, colors, light, smells, and feelings are so vivid that we could undoubtedly think of cinema, not of dry philosophical treaties. Perhaps, he could have been an experimental filmmaker, should he have lived a little bit longer or later into the 20th century.

In the third part of his "Curriculum Vitae," Fritz abandons metaphysics entirely in favor of reality-driven examples of significant, according to him, events. Again, as in his first autobiography from two years prior, he begins with his father's death when he was five years old. "The growing sufferings of my father, [in its symptoms similar to the suffering of the most blessed king],[113] his blindness, his thinness, the tears of my mother, the worried glances of the doctors, and the indelicate comments by peasants, had to make me a suspect of [a] threatening tragedy. And tragedy struck—my father died. I overcame my pain, tears, my mother's suffering, and the village people's deep sorrow. How the funeral moved me! How did the leaden deathly bells pierce me through! I felt that I was orphaned and fatherless [,] that I had lost a loving father for the first time. His image is still alive in my soul: a tall, slender figure with delicate features and warm friendliness."[114] Fritz again is despairing at the loss of his father but, at the same time, trying to become a father to himself, unless, enjoying the event by writing about it again and again. From then on though, he is on the continuous search for a father figure to provide him with advice and reprimand him. So, instead of being provided with directions, he was defining his life path by himself, alone.

Then he reminisced again—lifting verbatim the description from his first autobiography—about the day of the departure from the idyllic life. When the family had to move out from the parsonage to make room for a new pastor.

"The evening bells echoed through the corridors of the house with a melancholy sound; heavy darkness spread all over our village, the pale moon rose and looked upon us. I could not sleep. Restless and excited, I threw myself around in my bed, then finally stood up. Below were several loaded cars; the dim light of a lantern illuminated the courtyard. Never did my future seem so dark and uncertain as it was then. As soon as the morning dawned, the horses were harnessed. We drove away through the morning mist and bade a farewell to our dear home,"[115] Fritz said it again.

He remembered the last and only permanent family home, which had to be abandoned. When family moved from house to house in the nearby Naumburg, eventually settling down at 18 Weingarten, he had to move out within a few days to the dormitory at the nearby Schulpforta, yet again. He never returned to Naumburg to live permanently there, except when brought back by his mother, incapacitated by illness. With that sorrowful move out from Röcken, he was stripped out of comfort, safety, and certainty in life. The relocation though, probably provided him with an awareness of new opportunities, but still, in his writing tone, one can detect an immense sadness breaking through.

He recalled making acquaintance with Pinder and Krug and the feeling of being welcome at their homes, having a fantastic time listening to music or discussing literature and art, while becoming a member of Naumburg's elite. He was happy having the same aspirations and desires as the rich and influential families he was visiting.

Fritz was eager to learn, but strangely for his commitment to traditional values, he did not like the institutional way of training. He seldom mentioned any educational experiences that made an impression on him but in general appraised the education he received in Pforta. "I do not fail to recognize how beneficially Pforta acts on me, and I can only hope that I will always prove myself here and even more so in later times as a worthy son of the Pforta."[116] The only question remains; did Fritz valued the quality of learning, or merely appreciate being a pupil in a very prestigious school? Looking through the prism of Fritz's choices in life, I am inclined to observe that the latter was probably more important to Fritz than the former.

Nonetheless, it is astonishing that at barely seventeen, without any formal philosophical training, relying only on his own inquisitiveness, he put on paper some of his most pertinent ideas, including self-creation, heredity, panpsychism, unequal distribution of mental capacities, and hierarchies of social structures: the ideas which, later in life, would develop into subsystems of "the 'essence' of [his] intellectual concerns."[117]

## ERNST ORTLEPP

Two months later, in June 1861, he wrote an essay as a school assignment. He would consider it "the only work of my schooldays with which I was almost satisfied," he wrote in yet another autobiography, at the end of his education at Pforta. It was a work concerning an old Germanic saga of king Ermanaric, titled "Ermanaric, King of the Ostrogoths. A Historical Sketch" *(Ermanarich, Ostgothenkönig. Eine historische Skizze),* dated July 3, 1861. In it, Fritz compares two versions of the same tale, one Nordic and one Germanic, concluding that the latter was the more advanced, where "everything lies more in the realm of historical clarity and humanity,"[118] rather than in the realm of paganism and fairytale, as in the Nordic version. But primarily, he appreciated the power of natural forces, which the great ancient heroes struggle to subdue, or fail and magnificently die:

> *Well have we fought; we sit upon corpses*
> *Felled by us, like eagles on branches*[119]

But on the other hand, Fritz is not as interested in the story itself as he is fascinated with its expressive impact "that stand like rocks towering into the sky in their innate titanic power, gigantic in their form" and with the sheer power of language, where "every word in its story is like lightning, powerful and laden with meaning."[120] Through this, as he called it, "a dry treaty," he reconstructed a great, historically factual hero's personality: "A man who is so deeply rooted in the consciousness of the people that he outlived the saga for 12 centuries and carries his name and fame as far as Iceland, indeed must always be considered as one of the most important personalities in the history of the world."[121]

Fritz was not interested in the plot of the "tragedy" per se but in the way that the idea of this great hero was engraved in people's minds so that it stayed there forever. He analyzed the form and language of the story to provide himself with a method to follow. And he was interested in what makes a man into the great hero people sing songs about.

Obsessed about this project, Fritz spent the next four years creating subsequent versions of treaties, writing poetry, composing a symphony, and even an opera on the theme of Ermanaric. Lecturing his Germania friends, Pinder and Krug, on the subject, he experimented with their response. He searched for a method of presenting a subject matter so it could survive the author's passing, and, through his work, keep him alive.

Fritz presented the essay to his classmates and their teacher, one of the leading literary historians August Koberstein, in his place. As it was common practice at Pforta with upper-class students, in Koberstein's lodgings, among very few others, lived Carl von Gersdorff. Gersdorff recalled that during mealtime, the Professor talked about Fritz's presentation: "Koberstein was highly delighted with it, and was full of prizes for the scholarship, the gift of construction, the penetration and the excellent style of his pupil. As a rule, Koberstein did not talk much at meals; as, however, on this occasion, he expressed himself in such a lively manner to me, I seized the opportunity of communicating what I have heard to Nietzsche. This incident about Koberstein did not, however, lead at once to any intimacy between us; we only began to see and talk to each other frequently when we both in the Sixth grade, and music played no small part in bringing us together."[122] This testimonial provides a glimpse of a time frame of Fritz's relationship with Gersdorff, of whom he left almost no remarks while at Pforta, however, with whom he exchanged correspondence regularly till practically the end of his active life.

Upon Fritz's return to Pforta after the summer break, according to Brobjer, he experiences, on August 19, 1861, the next contributing moment of turning away from Christianity. The departure from his faith was induced by the unexpected death of Fritz's tutor, Professor Buddensieg, an extremely pious, "almost a childlike in his faith in God" teacher of theology, with whom Fritz had a warm relationship.[123] "Oh, you cannot believe how sad my heart is. We all love him so much. Everybody is deeply disturbed. There is deathly silence everywhere…. Oh, it is too painful! Yet what God does is well done," he cries to his mother.[124] Uncannily, right before the incident, Fritz composed the oratorio for the Germania audience of two, titled "Pain is the Keynote of Nature" *(Schmerz ist der Grundton der Natur)*,[125] rationalizing his life's misfortunes and equating God with nature.

The death of Buddensieg marks the end of Fritz's devout childhood, of which Deussen writes later: "I still remember very well the holy, ecstatic mood that filled us during the week before and after the confirmation. We would have been quite ready to die immediately to be with Christ. All our thoughts, feeling, and actions were irradiated with a super-terrestrial joy, which, however, as an artificially grown little plant could not last and, under the pressure of studying and living, very soon vanished just as quickly as it had come."[126] From then on, Fritz's religious poems' production decreased considerably, eventually ceasing, except for birthday gifts for his mother and aunt Rosalie. He began to read books concerning skepticism towards religion. It was reflected in his birthday wishlist, which included the famously irreligious book *Das Wesen des Christenthum* by Ludwig Feuerbach. "It was likely that it was first after the death of Buddensieg, that he became emotionally and psychologically free to question his Christian faith,"[127] Deussen suggests. But that was not the only field of scrutiny. He began to read *Anregung für Kunst, Leben und Wissenschaft*—a journal predominantly focused on Wagner's music and materialistic philosophy.[128]

At Pforta, apart from professors' suggestions and reading newspapers, Fritz could access yet other source of information concerning extracurricular literature. It was Ernst Ortlepp, infamous around Naumburg, a scruffy although brilliant vagrant, writer, and poet who, as an alumnus of Pforta, was allowed on and around the school grounds. Ortlepp was a shabbily dressed genius who, drunk, often disturbed church services with loud recitations of blasphemous verses from his poem "The Lord's Prayer of the Nineteen Century:"

*Old time religion*
*Despised by the new era's son*
*And comes the call throughout the earth:*
*Your name will have no holly worth.*[129]

Apart from being quite famous during his prime as a political poet, writer, translator of Shakespeare, Byron and Adam Mickiewicz, and a prolific editor, Ortlepp was banished from Saxony and Württemberg, under suspicions of pederasty, accused of "cutting himself loose from all religious and moral ties adhering only to the demonic instincts of evil."[130]  During Fritz's tenure at Pforta, Ortlepp, idolized by students, tutored some of them and, during their free time, was getting drunk with them in nearby cafes of Almrich.

According to Helmut Walther, Fritz was close with Ortlepp to such an extent that he wrote a poem in Fritz's student album (*Gedichtsalbum*) from the years at Pforta:

*We have met*
*And learned to love each other,*
*Yet, I would never understand,*
*What separated us so soon, again:*
*And the fine, soft hand*
*Played with my enflamed cheeks,*
*And yet, in my innermost heart arose*
*the image of one who was not unknown, yet. –*
*And you? You would laugh at the song,*
*Even tear my garlands apart.*
*And I would continue to sing*
*And love you ever more. –*[131]

Walther suggests that, whether there was a platonic, or perhaps even a homosexual relationship between them, Ortlepp had definitely an intellectual influence on Fritz's worldview. Whereas Safranski insinuates, relying on other sources, that Fritz—who later described Ortlepp in the poem "Before the Crucifix" *(Vor dem Crucifix)* as "an intoxicated blasphemer who calls out to the man on the cross: "Come down! Are you just deaf? You can have my bottle!"[132]—had a homosexual relationship with Ortlepp. "According to a biographical reconstruction by H. J. Schmidt, Ortlepp may have been the first Dionysian seducer in Nietzsche's life, engaging not only his imagination but also his sexuality. Nietzsche, who was both traumatized and exhilarated by this experience, as some surmise, never, in their estimation, got over this first molestation by Dionysus incarnate. They claim that this incident set the stage for his Dionysian experience, which he later alluded to, covertly and guilt-ridden, in *Ecce Homo*: 'the absolute certainty as to what I am was projected onto some coincidental reality or other—the truth about me spoke out of a dreadful depth.'"[133]

Putting aside Fritz's sexual inclinations, even though vital, we are left with Ortlepp's formative intellectual influence on young Fritz. As he was turning away from Christianity, the rebelliousness reinforced, already in the works Fritz's attitude. Then there were authors that Fritz was reading, discovered on his own or recommended by others, further strengthening his convictions that he was on the right track. Fritz unearthed a scarcely known (at that time) Friedrich Hölderlin; reconnected with Goethe, to whom he was introduced a few years back at the home of his Germania friend Pinder, by his father who read the works of Goethe to the boys. He also discovered, probably through Ortlepp, a true rebel, Lord Byron.

We usually have a tendency to think of a new author or an artist we encounter as a discovery, but, in most instances, we were often introduced to a "discovery" by someone else through reading a book, listening to a lecture, having a conversation or merely leafing through a newspaper. In the instance of Hölderlin, Fritz definitely knew of him through Pinder, who in a letter from November 21, 1858, listed five biographies of German writers, with Hölderlin among them, as a gift for Christmas. Later, in the spring of 1861, Pinder initiated purchasing Hölderlin's poetry, and it was Pinder who gave a lecture about the poet to Germania in the early summer of 1861.[134] There is also a possibility that Ortlepp, who was living in Naumburg at the time, and was known to Pinder and Fritz, had introduced them to this forgotten poet.

Back in Pforta, after the summer vacations, Fritz began to work on his assignments in German literature class. He was given a task by Professor Koberstein, one of the leading literary historians, to write about a favorite German poet in the form of a letter to a friend recommending this poet to him. The essay-letter was titled, "Letter to my friend, in which I recommend that he read my favorite poet" *(Brief an meinen Freund, in dem ich ihm meinen Lieblings-dichter zum Lessen empfehle)*.[135] Having only two weeks for it, Fritz requested that his sister promptly send him the Hölderlin's biography *Moderne Klassiker. Deutsche Literaturgeschichte der neueren Zeit in Biographien, Kritiken und Proben: Friedrich Hölderlin* by William Neumann, which he left at home.[136]

In this essay-letter, Fritz concentrated on two works by Hölderlin: an unfinished drama, *The Death of Empedocles*, and "the magnificent hybrid prose-poem,"[137] *Hyperion*. Reading the texts, he was paying attention to descriptions of human qualities, which seems were his interests from the early years of extracurricular practice of self-inquiry. Presenting Hölderlin, he focused specifically on the poet's personality traits and the themes of his concerns, as if he would have intended to become a poet himself. But it was not anything new. From the beginning of his search for a career-path, Fritz was trying to imitate great personalities—real or fictional—by identifying with them, while seeing in them his deceased father. What he saw in Hölderlin was a "half-mad" genius with "contradictory religious views" and a "disrupted broken mind" producing the "ideas of a lunatic" and "violent outbreaks against Germany and German barbarism," proposing in his "longing for Greece, [the] deification of the pagan world."[138]

But why was Fritz so interested in such a little-known poet like Hölderlin? Here Brobjer confirms our assumptions, claiming that "the reason why Hölderlin became Nietzsche's favorite poet may well not only depend on his poetry but also be due to his biography as described by Neumann. The account of Hölderlin's life probably strongly attracted the young Nietzsche, for there are several obvious similarities in their development and views. In the first few pages it is pointed out that Hölderlin had lost his father at the age of two, had been much influenced by his mother, had had an aversion to everything vulgar, a tendency to melancholy and had showed manly independence. It is emphasized that he loved nature and had an especial love of the classics of antiquity. Like

Nietzsche, Hölderlin studied at a famous *lateinische Schule* and, while there, intended to pursue a theological career. He had little contact with his school friends but had a close friend who was not at the school. Already at school, he showed a love of poetry and wrote a number of shorter poetic works. He also developed a remarkable musical talent at this time. This could almost, even in detail, have been a description of the young Nietzsche instead of Hölderlin."[139]

So, young Fritz was not just looking for an archetype to build up his self-image by associating himself with artists and writers' elites. He was also looking to rationalize his misfortunes experienced through recurrent deaths in his family. To find solace in embracing and identifying with the outcasts who, in his opinion, were the most desired exemplars of the high culture. Regrettably, Fritz was not directly exposed to these ideas at their source because, at that time, he never read Hölderlin firsthand but only consulted secondary sources, and, in the end, plagiarized them. The essay "Letter to a Friend," as Brobjer demonstrated, is plagiarism,[140] a practice Fritz would continue—in different forms and to varied extents—till the end of his writing life. Fritz was appropriating the work of others as his own original ideas without giving the authors credit or, at least, mentioning them as his inspirations.[141]

One could ask then, why such an ambitious, smart, and self-aware adolescent would have risked the embarrassment, or even expulsion from school, should the plagiarism have been discovered by teachers? The answer, I think, lies in our hero's attitude towards the rest of the world. In his self-important opinion, there was no one, in the past or present, who could be better than him. A year later, when he was eventually caught, Fritz regretted not that he was a plagiarist, but that he was caught. For, as he wrote nonchalantly to his mother on November 19, 1862: "there can be no question of influence, for that I would first have to meet people whom I considered my superior."[142] Fritz considered the use of others' ideas within his own narrative as their better application. In other words, these ideas were not utilized as they should have been. According to Fritz, the original authors did not understand them enough to use them correctly. This intellectual arrogance, at that moment, still somehow remained implicit in Fritz's statements, until the last period of his life, when it reached the level of explicitness verging on outright narcissism.

But this is the end of 1861, and the seventeen-year-old Fritz's personality is still an enigma to his teachers. He had not yet been discovered for appropriating the others' work. The essay, evaluated by Professor Koberstein received a high mark, though with a comment: "I should like to give the author one piece of friendly advice: to concern himself with a poet who is healthier, more lucid and more German."[143] And probably at that time, he lost his Primus position, which he could not regain until the next year, in October of 1862.[144] He learned therefore that he must keep his school life separate from his private intellectual endeavors.

By the end of November, in the spirit of that new antichristian leaning, he wrote to Elisabeth, deliberately not mentioning Franziska, suggesting what Elisabeth should ask for the approaching Christmas. According to Elisabeth, Fritz recommended *Church History* and *The Life of Jesus* by Karl Hase, a theologian and an advocate of idealist rationalism[145], which supposedly caused the outbursts of indignation by his mother and Aunt Rosalie. It would make sense if it was accurate, for "Franziska was not even home at that time and that Rosalie would not have found Hase's book intrinsically objectionable, since it was recommended by Friedrich August Wenkel, preacher at St. Wencelas," a historian, Daniel Blue speculates.[146] However, it should be considered that perhaps Elisabeth was not remembering the Hase's book but David Strauss' *The Life of Jesus*, where the author argues for a historical Jesus stripped out of divinity?[147] That book could certainly elicit a storm of outrage. To confuse it even more, Fritz then also asked Krug for an unnamed book that could have been Max Stirner's *The Ego and Its Own* or Bruno Bauer's *Criticism of the Gospels and History of Their Origin.* The request stunned his friend. "I am really alarmed by it since I have heard of problems and other terrible things about it,"[148] he replied, horrified. Or Fritz may as well inquire about the Strauss book, which was more subversive than Hase's. Anyhow, putting speculations aside which book it was, what is relevant is that Fritz was calling into question the status quo of Christianity. It consequently changed his educational trajectory aiming at theology and subsequent priesthood, towards a new, yet unknown, purpose in his life. In the same letter, Fritz suggests another radical choice, but by a non-German writer with whom he was becoming familiar and whose name was Lord Byron.

Although, on December 3, 1860, in the letter to his mother, he requested an edition of Shakespeare as a Christmas gift: "I must have a Shakespeare, for a knowledge of his works belongs to the general program of education, and very often, in the higher classes we receive themes for essays about individual plays."[149] Possibly for financial reasons, he did not receive it that year. However, for the next year of 1861 Christmas, Aunt Rosalie presented him with the standard, Schlegel-Tieck German edition of the complete works of William Shakespeare.[150]

## LORD BYRON

There are unceasing speculations about Fritz's "discovery" of any new writer, but, as it is with anyone who is intellectually inquisitive, Fritz was introduced to any new source of information, by the people with whom he was acquainted, or just by chance. Considering the importance that Byron represented for his old friend Ortlepp, a translator of English writers, especially Shakespeare and Byron, Fritz probably heard about the poet from the vagabond himself. To support this, it should also be mentioned that Fritz owned, as Blue claims, three volumes edition of Byron's works, in Ortlepp's translation, which he extensively annotated.[151]

The other source of information concerning Byron may have been Diederich Volkmann, a new Pforta English teacher, a twenty-three-year-old professor who was offering private English lessons and introduced students to English literature. During the fall semester of 1861, Fritz immersed himself in Shakespeare, Byron, and probably started reading Ralph Waldo Emerson.[152]

Or, it is also possible, he may have known Byron for a while. Before going to Pforta, Pinder's father introduced to him Goethe, who knew and acknowledged Byron. When reading Goethe, Fritz certainly could have been trying to internalize, among the other ideas, *Werther's* concern of "how to employ all one's powers to optimal effect."[153] Nevertheless, his focal point was the interest in Goethe himself. To fulfill his concerns, he read Johann Peter Eckermann's *Conversations with Goethe* (1835), in which the author frequently turns to Byron. "While [Goethe] is clearly aware of Byron's limitations and short-comings, his prize for the work and appreciation of the poet's personality is impressively evident. Such enthusiasm is contagious, and the young Nietzsche was sized by a devotion to the Lord that was anything but short-lived,"[154] Parkes aptly summarizes Fitz's veneration for Byron.

The new interest bore fruit quickly. In December of 1861, during Christmas break in Naumburg, he lectured, probably at his mother home, at Weingarten 18, to the other Germania members, Pinder and Krug, on the theme of Byron's *Manfred*, titling his talk, "On the Dramatic Works of Byron" *(Ueber die dramatischen Dichtungen Byrons).*

As with the other authors, Fritz was keenly interested in the character of a writer he could inquire about. In a result, he discovered in *Manfred*—Byron's "egocentric drama"[155]—a conception of a writer that he could identify with. He described the poet as he would have described himself. "One of those ambivalent men of the moment, sensuous and inspired, yet childlike, their soul concealing a wound, often seeking through their works to avenge the memory of an earlier indignity, often at pains to ward off a spirit of loathing, the ever-recurring specter of a lost faith."[156] He saw in Manfred Byron himself. "A monster in a dramatic relationship, one might say, the monologue of a dying man, burrowing into the deepest questions and problems, deeply moving due to the tremendous sublimity of this spirit-mastering overman (*Übermenschen*),"[157] he wrote. Fascinated with the idea of assuming one's personality, Fitz introduced the infamous term "overman":

"Byron could only portray his own character. In *Manfred's* four characters, we are always confronted, despite apparent significant differences, with the same thing, namely Byron himself in the multifacetedness of his comprehensive spirit. While Manfred emphasizes his gloomy features, his scornful resignation, his superhuman (*übermenschliches*) despair, whereas Sardanapalus sheds light on his sensual nature with the most lurid colors, in *Marino Faliero,* his glowing river of freedom blazes toward us, but also at the same time the southern heat of his emotions; as Jacopo Foscari, he paints for us his enthusiasm for Venice, his noble patriotism.... But for all that, a few features are still missing from this portrait, his almost feminine delicacy of sensibility and subtlety in capturing noble female characters, gifts that manifest themselves especially in the wonderful female figures of Myrrha, Angiolina and Marina,"[158] for the first time in his writings he used the term *Übermensch*.

I wrote above that he introduced it, but he instead reused or applied it within his own thought, borrowing probably from Goethe, as it was the great bard who initially influenced the young Fritz's poetry. Eva Cybulska elaborates where the term originally came from. "Nietzsche did not invent the term *Übermensch*," she claims. "As elaborated by Kaufmann,[159] the concept of *hyperanthropos* can be found in the ancient writings of Lucian; in German, the word had been used before Nietzsche's time by H. Müller, J. G. Herder, Novalis, Heine, and, most importantly, by Goethe in relation to Faust (in *Faust*, Part I, scene 1, line 490). R. W. Emerson[160] spoke of the Over-Soul and, perhaps with the exception of Goethe's Faust, his aristocratic, self-reliant 'beyond-man' was the greatest contributor to Nietzsche's idea of the *Übermensch*."[161] But for our reading, who coined the term and when is less critical than the use of it within a specific context, its subsequent connotations combined with the delivery of immeasurable amounts of highly charged value brought into the culture. Therefore Fritz, undoubtedly, is the one who seems to be singularly responsible for its introduction anew, for he contextualized it within the conceptual milieu which was, and still is, ripe for ideological interpretation.

Fritz, who most likely read all the works by Byron available in German,[162] was infatuated with the poet and *Manfred's* protagonist as an indistinguishably singular character, an indissoluble model of a hero whom he aspired to become. He could have seen in himself a desperate, independent, proud, and lonely soul in the process of emergence. Nevertheless, he longed for indestructibility, indifference, and the superiority of his will. The accruing changes were dramatic and visible. "In the past, he had tended to affect a pose of saintliness, modeling himself on his father and other ministers. Now 'the imitation of Christ' was replaced with 'the imitation of Manfred,' Nietzsche began to evidence kinds of behavior which startled former friends and began to alarm the authorities."[163] He is becoming acutely aware of nature, not as a backdrop or an environment but as an intertwined part of himself. *Manfred* is set in the Alps, which became Fritz's workplace during the warmer seasons in the last, tragic years of his productive life. But, already in his school years he realized, through Byron's poetry, an interdependent relationship between himself and the natural phenomena:

> *From my youth upwards,*
> *My Spirit walked not with the souls of men,*
> *Nor looked upon the earth with human eyes.*
> *The thirst of their Ambition was not mine –*
> *The aim of their existence was not mine –*
> *My joys – my griefs – my passions and my powers*
> *Made me a stranger, though I wore the form*
> *I had no sympathy with breathing flesh,*
>
> *...*
>
> *I said with men and with the thoughts of men*
> *I held but slight communion; but instead,*
> *My joy was in the Wilderness – to breathe*
> *The difficult air of the iced Mountain's top*
> *Where the birds dare not build, nor insect's wing*
> *Flit o'er the herbless Granite; or to plunge*
> *Into the torrent – or to roll along*
> *In the swift whirl of the new breaking wave*
> *Of River–Stream or Ocean in their flow –*
> *In these my early Strength exulted*[164]

Through Byron, he uttered his desire to wander alone, entirely on his own, soaking the power of nature which bestowed him with its might. It is highly romantic, in concord with Fritz's times, and rationalized our protagonist's attitude towards his fellow men, his schoolmates, teachers, and family. Through Byron, he affirmed that his social inadequacies, which further deepened his isolation and one-against-the-world attitude, were correct, and in accordance with his thought. This state of mind exhibited itself in his complete lack of friends, except for perhaps three or four acquaintances (if we count Ortlepp) that he carried on with through swapping communications via letters and notes, which were sporadic but beneficial to him. While introverted Fritz projected himself into Byron, into his works and persona— like in a mirror, he saw himself a *Doppelgänger*.[165]

In the letter with the list of Christmas presents, Fritz requested matter-of-factly Byron's works in English: "As is well known, I will start practicing English in the New Year, and my favorite English poet will be my greatest incentive for this,"[166] he wrote to his mother and sister in December 1862.

## A REBEL

In the fall of 1861, Fritz initiated a relationship with Guido Meyer, a boy he knew formerly from attending preparatory classes in summer 1857. In *Conversation with Nietzsche,* Deussen described the relationship as a rise of "a sort of triumvirate [that] emerged between Nietzsche, me, and [a] certain Meyer, who was handsome, likable and witty, also an excellent cartoonist, but forever at odds with teachers and the school system."[167] Reading Deussen's testimony, one may get the impression that they were a trio of equals, but the reality was entirely different. Fritz and Guido were an inseparable couple, whereas Deussen was a banished outsider. For six weeks, Fritz and his new friend refused to talk to Deussen for being a *Spießer*, a "nerd" in today's terminology, and being too diligent and obedient. And so Fritz began the period of romantic rebellion against the societal status quo.

Carl Pletsch sees it as a "puberty crisis, an ineffectual rebellion against authority. It seems to have been a short-lived protest against the serious person he himself was. [He] seems neither to have been interested in girls nor involved in an affectioned relationship with any of his classmates, 'as was common in boarding schools of the time.' Friedrich's puberty crisis was worked out wholly on the spiritual level."[168]

For Christmas of 1861, Fritz received from Aunt Rosalie the complete works of Shakespeare, yet another source for his examples of great men. Years later, he recommended to Elisabeth that she should read Shakespeare as well, for the author "presents you with so many strong men – rough, hard, powerful, iron-willed. It is in men like these that our age is so poor,"[169] Fritz recounts the ideals of *Übermensch*. He wanted to read Byron and Shakespeare in English to directly experience depictions of these great heroes in whom he could find and recognize himself.

His preference in music changed as well. He was beginning to develop a taste for modern music. But he was still restrained in his praise of the most popular music at that time, Richard Wagner's compositions, even though he listened to Gustav's four lectures which enthusiastically praised Wagner's work. Nevertheless, Fritz was very sensitive to music.

During his tenure at Pforta, he was routinely exposed to it; he participated in the school choir, toured the countryside with their performances, and sang on Sundays at Pforta's church. He studied and composed music in school and at home while on breaks. He improvised on the piano as often as he could to express what he could not through other means.

According to Blue, he read *Gründliche Anweisung zur Composition,* a text on counterpoint by Johann Georg Albrechtsberger, an 18-century instruction book on how to write a fugue. He began producing so many of them that Gustav scolded him in a letter, demanding him to show restraint.[170] Fritz's obsession with Albrechtsbergers and fugue production could be impressive on its own, but what is more intriguing here is that Fritz worked so diligently to improve his skills at composing fugues. Fugues were, according to Albrechtsbergers, one of the essential types of church music. The ability to write this type of music could be advantageous for any pastor or church *kapellmeister.* So, was Fritz still thinking about a church career?

I doubt it. As Elisabeth recalled, he "practiced music zealously already in Pforta and, since I cannot play any instruments, he played for me, many at a time. A lot of Chopin, if I remember rightly."[171] It is conceivable, then, that he was still serious about becoming a composer. Moreover, Fritz "was smitten with the compositions of Robert Schumann, a composer who was romantic in spirit and willing to experiment with form but more associated with the traditionalists."[172] He recommended *Paradise and the Peri (Das Paradies und die Peri),* a secular oratorio for soloists, choir, and orchestra by Schumann, to Elizabeth, "as something adorable for everyone, including you."[173] But beyond his music, Schumann himself was also a fascination for Fritz. As Blue noticed, the composer went insane like Fritz's father, like the king of Prussia, Friedrich William IV, and like Hölderlin, adding yet another madman to the gallery of mirror-images of himself.

During Christmas break in January 1862, Fritz delivered a new essay to Germania fellows. He decided to write about the first president of France, titled *"Napoleon III as President."* [174] As no evident reasons justified his decision, it is difficult to say why he chose to write about Napoleon Bonaparte's nephew, instead of Bonaparte himself, outside some speculations that he confused them.[175] As Hayman interprets political milieu in France at that period, Napoleon III "had become president in December 1848, after setting himself up as both a champion of his uncle's ideas and a defender of orderly stability. A ruthless opportunist, a mediocre man with a huge, waxed mustache, erratically capable, like Hitler, of brilliant statesmanship, he swore an oath of fidelity to the Second Republic overturned in 1851. After twenty-five thousand arrests and ten thousand deportations, a plebiscite gave him presidential power for ten years. Still, by the end of 1952, he successfully proclaimed himself emperor."[176]

Fritz delivered the essay to the synod that was what the Germania's members called, rather pretentiously, their get-togethers during the holiday breaks, which most likely took place at Fritz's house at Weingarten 18. They usually met there if the subject of the meeting was in any way controversial or disturbing to Pinder or Krug's parents, as most of them probably were.

Under the spell of Shakespeare, Byron, Goethe, and Machiavelli's lectures, while experiencing spiritual transformation, Fritz decided he was finally ready to express his fascination with all these antagonistic concepts he was toying with. His boosterism of political genius, ruthlessness, immoral political tactics, militarism, antidemocracy, antisocialism, antiliberalism, dictatorship, monarchism, the superiority of strongmen, Caesarism[177] arose not as a fleeting fancy of adolescence but were to endure as lifelong principles.

Fritz wrote his short essay in two parts; the first part, solely theoretical and shorter, served as an introduction to the whole piece. The second part, although plagiarized Wolfgang Menzel's *Geschichte der letzten vierzig Jahre 1816–1856*,[178] was nevertheless invaluable as a validation of his claims delineated in the first, theoretical section.

The premise of Fritz's argument is that Napoleon III had the right to destroy the republic and proclaim himself the emperor because he was a political genius, an attribute he won through his deeds on the way to the emperorship. "And, as a genius, is subject to higher laws than and different from those intellectually regressive moral laws governing the average person,"[179] Dombowsky reads Fritz's essay.

Right in the opening sentence, Fritz drove his argument explicitly to the point: "The genius is subjected to different and higher laws than the ordinary man; the laws, which often seem to contradict the general principles of morality and justice. *(Das Genie von anderen und höheren Gesetzen abhängig ist, als der gewöhnliche Mensch, von Gesetzen, die oft den allgemeinen Grundsätzen von Moral und Recht zu widersprechen scheinen)* "[180] According to Fritz, it justified "the seizing of the state power which was in unworthy hands *(Das Ansichreißen einer Staatsregierung, die bisher in unwürdigen Händen war)*,"[181] in the eyes of a genius. Next, Fritz lists all the deeds that were the necessary consequence of the power grab to increase it even further: elimination of the new legislation preventing him from being reelected, suppression of the republican press, increasing the loyalty of the army, seizure of power by coup d'état, revision of the constitution and restoration of the emperorship, arrest of all the heads of the opposition parties, and declaring himself an absolute ruler, the Emperor of France.

When criticized by Pinder for glorifying the rogue coup, Fritz evaded the argument by elevating his standing to the abstract level of theoretical thought. He renounced his own convictions: "One can learn much in such times … Above all, one observes how negligible is the power of thought"[182] – he dodged the bullet hiding in emotional, personal and historical circumstances.

The essay was a "declaration of war" in Fritz's incessant search through historical and fictional narratives for the characters of strong and ruthless *Übermenschen* to whom ordinary men's rules do not apply. By bringing the piece to the attention of Germania's members, he declared his alliance not with the common men, but with the men who entirely give themselves to the tasks of achieving the absolute power over the masses and, in doing so, destroy everything that would stand in the way of it. In the quest to establish his superiority, Fritz was looking for a model, an act to improvise upon.

It seems that even the act of plagiarism was deliberate and has its significance in the whole enterprise. Fritz did not ask for permission or give any credit to the original author but took what he wanted, as if the rules of scholarship did not apply to him. He was no longer theoretically speculating about becoming a great man but was already beginning to act out his own principles in transit beyond common morality.

# MY FIRST PHILOSOPHICAL ENDEAVORS

In mid-February of 1862, Fritz fell sick again. He wrote home about his bouts with illness while in the infirmary: "I cannot write anymore; I am still exhausted, and my head is splitting,"[183] but he was still able to read.

During the winter of 1861-1862, probably under the influence of English teacher Diederich Volkmann or Ortlepp, Fritz began to read Ralph Waldo Emerson, and would continue reading him throughout his productive life. There is no evidence of how he got his hands on Emerson for the first time, but we know that the first Emerson essay he read was "The Conduct of Life" (1860). Even though one of his earliest copies of Emerson's *Versuche* is lost, probably stolen from him in 1874 when traveling from Bergün to Basel, he later purchased a new copy, which is still the most annotated volume in his library.[184]

Emerson's works were Fritz's first and foremost introduction to philosophical writing. "This was Nietzsche's first contact with philosophy—it wasn't until the following year that he expressed interest in Plato and another two years until he discovered Schopenhauer. It was Emerson who first introduced Nietzsche about 'philosophy in life.'"[185]

During the Easter break of 1862, at home in Naumburg, under Emerson's spell, Fritz composed two short essays, again for the Germania audience, which are considered his first genuinely philosophical attempts. The first, "Fate and History: Thoughts" *(Fatum und Geschichte. Gedanken),* was written in March, and the second, "Freedom of Will and Fate" *(Willensfreiheit und Fatum),* a month later, in April. Fritz delivered them as usual to Wilhelm and Gustav's intended audience with an occasionally unintended entrant, his sister Elisabeth.

Interpreters of Nietzsche's usually, if not in entirety, read those pieces in forms of comparative studies, pinpointing discrepancies and resemblances between Nietzsche and Emerson. But my approach is entirely different. I will continue—as indicated when talking about the piece, "Napoleon III"—taking Fritz's texts at their face value. What is essential here is what Fritz presumably thought at the time of writing and delivering his essays. The beliefs and considerations expressed by him were of pivotal importance, for they were in a reciprocal relationship with Emerson and his writing. Even if Fritz came to a "wrong" conclusion misreading him, his erroneous thoughts were more significant in erecting his soul and character than the "correct" interpretations brought to our attention by the subsequent readers.

When writing those pieces, Fritz was in a phase of unwinding doubt about his Christian faith. What he sought was a comprehensive argument that would validate and rationalize his scattered feelings about Christianity. With "Fate and History," he provided himself one, which would implicitly reveal that he had changed.

The first essay's central idea was a hypothetical speculation refusing Christianity on the grounds that all its foundations are presuppositions. By doubting "the existence of God, immortality, Biblical authority, divine inspiration, the impressions of our childhood, the influence of our parents, our education,"[186] we unveil the true, godless reality. But "it is folly and doom for undeveloped heads to venture out into the sea of doubt without compass and guide: most will be driven off course by storms; only very few will discover new lands,"[187] Fritz argues. If the experiment had been successful, Fritz would have found himself in the realm of "autonomous gods." Then, "the curtain falls, and man finds himself like a child playing with worlds, like a child who awakens at the glow of dawn and, laughing, wipes the terrible dreams from his brow,"[188] he speculates, trembling. He considered those ideas so bold and courageous that he was in the state of highest excitement and trepidation while conceiving and delivering them.

In the absence of God as the absolute power, he thought-experimented how and by what means "the development of our spirit [and] formation of our temperament" is determined. In other words, Fritz speculated about the development of a human in general, and himself in particular, considering "Christian doctrine and church history" a significant influence on our being. He claimed that our customs, prejudices, and inhibitions prevent us from an impartial, free and appropriate standpoint to make a mere judgment concerning Christianity. Fritz invoked the impossibility of scrutinizing Christianity, which, if attempted, would have been viewed as a transgression and impertinence. Nonetheless, he tried to list his concerns, attempting "to contest views ... that the faith elevated man to a true human being (*wahren Menschen*); to unify natural science with philosophy; to construct (*aufzustellen*) a system of reality out of natural science and history."[189] Predominantly he saw sciences and history as "the harbingers of our future," and a springboard for further philosophical speculations. Albeit, not in a traditional understanding of philosophy, which he dismissed as "a tower of Babel," but through consolidating the natural sciences with philosophy, a combination in which he saw the inevitable potential to destroy (*vernichten*) "the authority of two millennia."[190]

Then he turned towards humankind fooled by Christianity for ages, to face and annihilate the Christian lie. He understood that it is much easier to destroy something than to rebuild it. Nonetheless, there is no other way—all these prejudices cannot be "removed by reasoning or mere will"—but only by "great revolutions" *(große Umwälzungen)*, by inciting violence we can get results.

As a sum of all truths borne of Christian traditions, the system of morality is merely an illusion; therefore, it must be destroyed for mankind to develop. We cannot assume that the contemporary human is the pinnacle of evolution, for we do not know whether the modern human is not just a stage in ongoing human development.

When Fritz wrote his essays, the ideas of Darwin were quite popular and spreading around the world. His use of the concept of evolution was not a surprise, even if he detested Darwin, possibly because "he knew how much he has taken over from him"[191] to develop his ideas without naming his sources, Richardson claims.

Since everything is becoming (*Werdenden*), Fritz lectured to an audience of three listeners, then man is the development (*Entwicklung*) from stone, through plant, then animal.

Subscribing to the idea of spontaneous emergence of life from a dead substance, Fritz unreservedly suggested that life's origins were in nonorganic matter. He could, therefore, ask himself the questions ensuing from it. Should the emergence of organic life, with which philosophers and scientists still struggle, be the uppermost and ultimate event in the existence of matter? Should organic life be the supreme form of becoming? Or is there potential in the next metamorphosis, of life into a new, non-matter-based but nonorganic form of existence?

And he probably did because, by appropriating his bold assumption that life's potentiality is ingrained in all matter, he rejected the teleological idea of humanity as the final stage in evolution. Although he had shed off his God, he still could not imagine the world without a center that made the whole thing tick. "The great clockwork," he called it. An "eternal productive drive, which, in monstrous, ever expending circles,"[192] that through "struggle and undulating of the most diverse currents, produces new events." The center, which is the infinitely small circle, is the common center of all oscillations. To prove its existence is humanity's task, Fritz postulated, to be realized through natural science and history.[193]

The center of that whirlpool, the eternal productive drive is "the will to life as immanent transcendence,"[194] the relationship of "the general will" to "the individual will."[195] The relationship of fate and history. The relationship between the events of the world's history and the impressions of these events' experiences. Fritz provided biological, social, and environmental influences: "a fatalistic structure of skull and spine; the condition and nature of their parents; the triviality of their relationships; the commonness of their environment; even the monotony of their homeland," unconsciously impacting our temperament and mind, which absorbs all experiences without realizing it.

Any of the same biological, hereditary, sociological, or environmental events, when affecting a multitude of people, are experienced differently by each individual. Any person receives the same event most diversely, each time differently, never repeatedly. Therefore, Fritz claims, "It is narrow-minded to want to force the whole of mankind into some specific form of state or society, into stereotypes, as it were. All socialist and communist conceptions lead to this error. Mankind is never the same twice."[196]

However, as most of us let fate dictate our life's events, reducing us to automatons, we still have, perhaps even without realizing it, some amount of choice in our lives. For "fate is the boundless force of opposition against free will. [But] free will without fate is just as unthinkable as a spirit without reality, good without evil. Only antithesis creates the quality."[197] So, there is a free will necessary in the determination of fate and *vice versa*. And they are not standing in the opposite corners, fighting each other, but coalescing in a chiasmic unity[198] of striving opposites, consolidated into one.

The next essay that Fritz delivered to Germania's synod, titled *Freedom of Will and Fate*[199] was a continuation of the first one. Given both essays' subject, it is tempting to ask a few questions: How Fritz felt knowing that these essays of such pivotal importance in his life as a thinker were heard only by two semi-interested boyhood playmates? Was it just a desire to be heard or to see himself climbing a steppingstone in self-development? Was he practicing buffoonery, playing a self-important thinker, or oratory of a budding prophet looking for disciples? In a sense, those lectures were analogous to Fritz walking stoically in the rain on the way from school, while everyone else was running home for cover. Which, regardless of its comicality, marked a significant feature in his development.

An individual's freedom of will is freedom of thought, Fritz claimed. It is restricted only by the biological limits of one's brain. Freedom of will is a part of fate, which is, as a limit-determination, a fatalistic principle. Fate forces man to act in a specific, determined way. However, when a man is stimulated by his own thought to act, he becomes a free agent of self-development. Therefore, the interwovenness of the processes of general evolution determined by fate, with individual self-development affected by free will (still a part of fate's determinism), constitutes human development. "In freedom of will lies, for the individual, the principle of emancipation, the separation from the whole, absolute limitlessness. But fate places man once more in an organic relation to the total development and requires him, insofar as it seeks to dominate him, to a free counteractive development. Absolute freedom of will, absent fate, would make man into a god; the fatalistic principle would make him an automaton."[200] The extremes of fate or free will are the nonexistent ideals, so we can only talk of degrees of determinism and free will, as they are intertwined in one productive force. Regardless of being under a continuous bombardment of deterministic influences of fate, man is entirely responsible for himself. "When we first realize that only we are responsible to ourselves, that accusation that we have missed our life's calling can be directed only at us, not at some higher power, only then will the basic ideas of Christianity shed their outer garment and pass into marrow and blood,"[201] back in Pforta, Fritz wrote to Pinder and Krug. Only then could we become human, not some gods or puppets, when we take responsibility for ourselves. Fritz equated fate with God's will.

The original letter did not survive in its entirety, but we have its outline in *Frühe Schriften,* where Fritz's ideas concerning Christianity, as Blue indicates, are strongly influenced by Feuerbach. From the essays delivered to Germania and a draft of the letter to Wilhelm and Gustav, we can infer that Fritz was losing his Christian faith in favor of scientific materialism.

Those concerns were awakened "by two principal sources: his interest in Ludwig Feuerbach's writings, especially *The Essence of Christianity (Das Wesen der Christenthum, 1841),* (which, along with another work by Feuerbach, *Thoughts on Death and Immortality (Gedanken über Tod und Unsterblichkeit, 1830),* Nietzsche had requested for his birthday in October 1861), and the journal *Anregungen für Kunst, Leben und Wissenschaft,* edited by Franz Brendel and Richard Pohl, which appeared in monthly issues between 1856 and 1861,"[202] and to which members of the Germania subscribed.

Brobjer shows that Fritz encountered his most instrumental philosophical readings by Ralph Waldo Emerson and Ludwig Feuerbach probably right before, or during, the concocting of his essays for Germania.[203] Feuerbach's reputation and fame blossomed from his influence on Marx, Engels, and Wagner, but in 1862 was already fading away. Fritz nonetheless appropriated the philosopher's main ideas concerning Christianity. Blue provides its brief but apt reference: "Feuerbach suggested that human beings created images of God as projections of their own human qualities. When they celebrated the generosity, compassion, or wrath of the Almighty, they were imputing to God their own capacity for generosity, compassion, and rage. In short, Christians worshiped what they had put there themselves, and in the process, they alienated themselves from their own powers, worshiping God and personally disowning the essence of their own humanity. Feuerbach advised that, instead of prostrating themselves to an idol that they had themselves conceived, Christians should look to themselves as human beings first and reconsider their values accordingly."[204]

The experiment of shedding off Christianity allowed Fritz to engage in unrestricted speculation of endless, although dangerous, explorations concerning himself and humanity. But this process of reincarnation demanded more drastic cuts yet to be dealt with. From then on, he hardly wrote to his childhood friends. The Germania contributions declined as well, if not ceased altogether. Pinder and Krug stopped contributing entirely. Fritz delivered mostly poems, concluding a year later, with two criticisms of his friends' work. Finally, he also stopped contributing, and the "society" fell apart.

Continuing further with his makeover, Fritz lets his hair grow Byronically long, posing in June of 1862 for a photograph of himself at Gustav Schultze's studio in Naumburg as if to capture the moment in the process of his transformation. He distributed copies of the picture to his family and three copies to colleagues in Pforta but none to his Naumburg friends. Their relationship, which seems to be sustained exclusively through Germania, cooled down: "There is a fourteen-month gap in which not a single letter from Wilhelm survives. Gustav continued to write, but his letters grew increasingly fawning and self-abnegating, as though he had come to recognize in Nietzsche a dangerous superior, to be placated, flattered, and feared."[205] Fritz was apparently changing. Was it under the influence of his formal education, or inspirations from confidentially acquired books, or through producing writings introducing his own radical ideas? Whatever the cause, Fritz was boldly experimenting with his own selfhood. In contrast, his Naumburg friends were afraid to wander into those forbidden territories, entirely over-whelmed by molds of social norms and mores. They scrupulously followed the beaten tracks provided a priori by society towards readymade goals. Fritz, seeing the widening intellectual gap between himself and his Naumburg com-panions, decided not to continue their so-called friendship because, plainly, there was nothing to gain from it for him. It is difficult to say who besides Deussen, was Fritz's acquaintance, for Fritz destroyed most of the letters and notes from that period of his life. Later, his sister Elisabeth completed the deed when she acquired utter incapacitation care over her sick brother and was trying to retouch his image.

In July 1862, Fritz wrote a poem with a rather lengthy title or, perhaps, an epigram introducing the verse: "The past is dearer to me than the present; but I believe in a better future *(Die Vergangenheit ist mir lieber als die Gegenwart; aber ich glaube an eine bessere Zukunft)*."[206] Further in the poem, he unfolds the concept of the present, clearly in an existential crisis:

> *I do not know what I love,*
> *I do not have peace, nor rest*
> *I do not know what faith is,*
> *What life am I living, and why?*[207]

Fritz spent his summer vacation of 1862 again at his uncle Edmund Oehler's place in Gorenzen. After almost a year in the works, he attempted there a new go at a piece of narrative fiction. He worked on the text, titled *"Euphorion",* but abandoned it again after only an introductory first chapter. Later on, if we are to believe his sister Elisabeth, he destroyed all the copies of this new work, along with many others. "When some time afterwards we were putting some documents in order," she writes in *The Life of Nietzsche,* "my brother, with cheerful indignation, thrust all this youth's productions into the fire."[208] But there is a fragment which survived. It was preserved by one of his Pforta friends, Raimund Granier to whom Fritz mailed it from Gorenzen with a let-ter of July 28, 1962. "You remember my plan for a repulsive novelette–O my God! Don't tell me! You've forgotten that, too! Never mind! –well, after I'd written the first chapter I threw up and then threw it away. I shell send you the monster manuscript for use on the… well, use it as you like. When I wrote it, a burst of diabolical laughter exploded from me–it isn't likely you'll have any appetite for its continuation,"[209] Fritz writes Granier signing it, *FwvNietzky* (alias Muck). The first part of his signature stood in for Friedrich Wilhelm von Nietzky. Fritz, for the first time, explicitly claimed his aristocratic ancestry, while also contradicting it with the second part, his nickname as a sign of degrading affiliation with Byronic, decadent morality of an elite of aristocratic artists and writers.

To a certain degree, it was a joke, but at the same time, it was a serious claim, and Fritz's audience was taking it "half-jokingly, half-seriously,"[210] wrote Granier. Why seriously? As Granier claimed, it was well known that Fritz, from an early age, believed that he came from Polish nobility. The story of Fritz's aristocratic ancestry is collaborated by his sister in her biography of her brother, *The Life of Nietzsche.*

*My brother often refers to his Polish descent and in later years he instituted research with a view to establishing it, which met with some success. I know nothing definite concerning these investigations, as a large number of my brother's documents were lost after his breakdown in health in Turin. The family tradition was that a certain minor Polish nobleman named Nicki (pronounced Nietzky) had obtained the special favor of August the Strong, King of Poland, and had received the title of Count from him. When, however, Stanislaus Leszczynski, the Pole, was made King, our supposed ancestor become involved in a conspiracy in favor of Saxony and the Protestants. He was sentenced to death; but taking flight with his wife, who had just given birth to a son, he wandered about with her for two or three years as a fugitive through the small States of Germany, during which time our great-grandmother nursed and suckled her little boy herself. So, the legend runs, and our great-grandfather Nietzsche, who at the age of ninety could still ride a horse at a gallop, is said to have ascribed his hardiness to those circumstances. Unfortunately, the dates do not seem to tally quite accurately; in any case, nothing definite can be said, as the first certain date which is known about our great-great-grandfather Nietzsche and his family belongs to the year 1709.*

*From his childhood onwards my brother always attached a certain importance to this somewhat mythical Polish descent. He writes in the year 1883: — "I have been taught to trace my descent and name to a noble Polish family called Niëtzky, who, yielding to insufferable religious oppression, give up their homes and their title over a hundred years ago; for they were Protestants. I will not deny that, as a boy, I was rather proud of my Polish descent. Whatever German blood I have in my veins comes solely from my mother's family, the Oehlers, and from my paternal grandmother's family, the Krauses, but it seemed to me that in all essentials I have remained a Pole, notwithstanding. The fact that my appearance has always been characteristic of the Polish type, has often enough been brought home to me. Outside my own country, in Switzerland and in Italy, I have often been accosted as a Pole. In Sorrento, where I spent winters, the people used to call me il Polacco, whilst during a summer holiday, in Marienbad especially, I was often reminded of my Polish nature in a striking manner. Poles would come up to me and, mistaking me for one of their acquaintances, would greet me in Polish and one to whom I said I was no Pole, and to whom I introduced myself as a Swiss, looked me sadly for some time, and then said, It is still the old race, but the heart has vanished, God knows whither. A small booklet of mazurkas, which I composed as a boy, bore the inscription, In memory of our ancient forbearers! and I reflected them in many a judgment and in memory of a prejudice.[211]*

As Fritz, throughout his writings, often reminded his readers that he was a Polish nobleman, his many interpreters omitted or just ridiculed the idea. Throughout the twentieth century, there were numerous speculations, with most of them trying to disregard it as entirely ludicrous, citing, directly or indirectly, as evidence, a short article, *"Nietzsche's Alleged Polish Origin"(Nietzsches angebliche polnische Herkunft)*[212] by Max Oehler, Fritz's cousin, and a devoted Nazi and an archivist at *Nietzsche–Archiv* in Weimar until the end of the WWII. Oehler conducted genealogical research published in the three-page article, dismissing any whatsoever connections between Nietzsche and Polishness.

However, on the other hand, I am not interested if Fritz was correct or if his claims were merely a phantasy. Instead, what I am concerned with here is his life-lasting conviction about his descent and its significance in his grand project of becoming what he was.

The second part of Fritz's signature unveils his, at that time, covert obsession with eroticism, a romantic glorification of decadent morality, and Byron,[213] whose persona was dramatized by Goethe in *Faust*, Part Two as a homage to the poet. "Byron is not classical and not romantic, said Goethe, but he is the present age itself ... He was exactly my man because of his unsatisfied nature and his warlike attitude, which led to his fate at Missolonghi,"[214] writes Hayman. The Faustian figure of Euphorion, the son of Faust and Helen, rendered by Goethe in the context of Greek tragedy is presented by Fritz in "Euphorion Chapter 1" (*Euphorion Cap. I*)[215] as a modern hero. Euphorion is a "played out" author who is writing, as in a full-fledged depressive mood, about his utter disappointment with life. He feels that he "fully emerged from himself" and his only desire at this stage "is only to find now the head of my *Doppelgänger* to vivisect his brain, or perhaps my own little boy's head all goldilocks, oh... twenty years ago," writes Fritz-Euphorion. Fritz goes back again to the memories of the dreams of his father's death of brain disease, fearing that the same fate is, given heredity, inescapably awaiting him as well. And the flies swarming around the rotten cadaver will "guarantee me a token of immortality," *Doppelgänger* comments on the visions of his own death. But "it is more pleasant to decompose in the moist earth than to vegetate under the blue sky [as] these comic humans, these white sepulchers,"[216] he comforts himself.

As Euphorion, Fritz apparently planned to write his new autobiography, this time in a mode of a poetic novel of *épater les bourgeois*. He begins with an absurd, transgressive, erotic, and violent vision: "Across from me dwells a nun, whom I visit now and then, to take joy in her chastity (*Sittsamkeit*). I know her with exactitude, from head to toe, more intimately than I know myself. Earlier, she was all nun, thin and fragile – I was her doctor, and I saw that she soon put on some weight. With her dwells her brother in a common-law marriage, to me he seems too fat and healthy, I thinned him down—to a corpse. He will die in the next day or so—which I enjoy—for I wish to dissect him. But first I want to write my autobiography. Apart from the fact that it is scintillating, it is also full of excellent instructions: it will turn youth into old men... For in this, I am the master. Who is to read it? My *Doppelgänger* and there are many of them in this Vale of Tears (*Jammerthal*).

"Here [Fritz]-Euphorion leaned back a little and moaned, for he suffered from a condition that affected the marrow of his spine (*Rückenmarksdarre*)..."[217] – in the end, again referring to his inherited fate of inevitable decay.

Apart from the intentionally shocking themes of the piece, which provided an entertainment value or a way towards notoriety for the author on the one hand, on the other hand, it was a genuine self-exposure—within limits, of course. Reading probably *Siebenkäs* by Jean Paul Richter, Fritz reformulated his interest in the subject of *Doppelgänger*, which he had initially discovered three years ago. Although this time, he appropriated authorship of the idea. According to Fritz, an apparition or a double is a reflection of the self, realized through writing autobiography, which provides one with the opportunity to perform an act of examination, in effect, determining one's destiny.

Fritz's fragment, Hayman writes, preceded Comte de Lautréamont's *The Songs of Maldoror (Les Chants de Maldoror, 1868)*, unsurprisingly based on Byron's *Manfred*. Although shunned during its initial publishing, it later acquired quite a popularity with the members of the Surrealist movement, especially Salvador Dalí. *The Songs of Maldoror* "describes the violent and perverse character of a despicable protagonist who has renounced God, humanity, and conventional morality," wrote David S. Rubin in the museum catalog for *Salvador Dali's Stairway to Heaven* exhibition.[218]

"The distant lover," Raimund Granier was trusted with the fragment of Fritz's ostentatious declaration of supposedly deep-seated depravity. Luckily, he saved the piece from incineration like many more writings of that type which went in smoke. Granier, a fleeting acquaintance, was forgotten by Fritz, like many other of his predecessors and successors. Years later, he wrote to Fritz, "you will recall a man, who had believed he was loved but now realized that he was being laughed at,"[219] invariably remembering our protagonist with affection.

After a work-filled summer vacation, Fritz went back to Pforta, but he fell ill again. He suffered from such intense headaches that the school physician, Dr. Zimmermann, placed him once more in the infirmary. After nine days, he was sent home to recuperate further. While in Naumburg, he went to see Professor Ludwig Schillbach in Jena, seeking a second opinion concerning his health problems. Prof. Schillbach, in the letter to Dr. Zimmermann, pointed out that more attention should be paid to Fritz's eyes,[220] confirming the eye disease.

Going through the school year without any distinctions, finally in September of 1862, his fifth year at Pforta, Fritz was made Primus again. Naturally, he expected congratulatory notes from everybody, but mostly from his mother. Apparently, Fritz never received one. But he was not discouraged. Instead, he demanded it from her as if it were her duty: "I had kept waiting for a letter in which I had hoped to find at least a few congratulations—especially on Saturday when you knew that promotion would take place.... Do me a favor and arrange that tea party, of which we talked so much.... You know who to invite. See that nothing is omitted," he instructed her, then, as usual, listed things he needed. Lastly, to make a point, he signed it as if it was official business, "—Goodbye, yours, Nietzsche."[221] At that time, Franziska was most likely used to her son's commanding tone, but after all, their relationship from when Fritz was a little boy lacked loving, motherly warmth. It was instead a formal arrangement marked with proper vocabulary, as expected between mother and son. Regardless of declarations of love between each other, it was doubtful that he was loved by her. Instead, she was proud of him and vice versa. He never loved her back. He compelled her to do her duty as a mother, which looked more like ordering a servant.

During the period between September and October of 1862, Fritz dedicates a lot of time to musical compositions and theoretical writings about music,
expanding the horizons of music appreciation by reaching back to Christianity's
origins. He was toying with the idea of composing a musical piece titled *"Satan
rises out of Hell" (Satan steigt aus der Hölle auf)*. Still, he eventually abandoned it because of the difficulties of "striking the exact satanic note."[222] In
the same fragment, he comes up with a profound idea, that "pain is the basic
tone of Nature *(Schmerz ist der Grundton der Natur),"*[223] which later in his
works expanded into the ontological concept of becoming as a chiasmic unity of
two opposites. The idea of pain—implying precedence of violence, avoidance,
overcoming, struggle, tension, pleasure, passion, heroism, release, and erup-
tion, which are in an entangled unity—represents the primary metaphor of the
primordial process of the world's becoming.

Fritz's ontological interests oscillated around, or rather, came from
speculating about language and music's origins. The fragments, written between September and October of 1862 and then, in January of 1863 titled, *"On
the Essence of Music" (Ueber das Wesen der Music)*,[224] dealt with the topic of
interdependence between language and music. They were to be delivered to the
Germania audience as a two-part essay, *"Über das Dämonische in der Musik
I, II"*. Unfortunately, the work itself is lost.[225] However, from the notes to it,
we can construe a core argument that presumably could have scrolled through
Fritz's presentation. Here, he postulates in-depth historical inquiry as an essential framework for grasping the ideas of contemporary trends defining the
world. He analyzes human communication through linguistics, beginning with
an archaic, primordial language as a mode of interaction between the earliest
humans that combined the spoken word and song, not yet separated. "Through
linguistics, we find that the older a language, the richer in tone it is, indeed then
we don't often distinguish speech from a song. The oldest languages were also
poorer in words, lacking general terms. It was passions, needs, feelings which
found their expression in sound. One can almost contend that they were less
a spoken language than a language of feelings, at any rate, forming feelings,
sounds and words in every people according to their individuality."[226] There
were feelings and emotions, interwoven with intellect and rationality—com-

munication as a conglomeration of language and music. And, at the base of it, there was "the original impression [of] demonic nature, neither emotion nor intellect."[227] Thus, in the demonic (*dämonischer Natur, dämonische Kraft, das dämonische*), Fritz recognizes an essential, necessary attribute of artists and composers. The demonic is a characteristic of artistic people—their creative drive—which was, of course, a quality which our young philosopher recognized in himself.

Etymologically, the term demonic came from ancient Greek *diamond*.   It means deity, divine power, a lesser god, guiding spirit, tutelary deity, or one's genius,[228] which later, Fritz replaced with the concept of genius and, one of his main ideas, the Dionysian.[229] It is then the power of divine, spirit, or genius which allows those who are fortunate enough to possess it inquire through feelings—not thinking, but feelings—into the heavens (*Himmelsfunke*). Not the language, but the music, provides the gate through which one must step out to look into the world (*Kosmos*), the gate of *sensations* and experience, not the rationality of knowing, becomes the mode of cognizance. Through his infatuation with music, Fritz posited a way of experiencing the world that could not be described in the cold rationality of language, but in the tragic beauty of emotions.

During this period, Fritz, as usual, acted on what he thought of himself. Abandoning eventuality of a church career, he was toying with the idea of becoming a musician. In that spirit, almost every day while at Pforta, he improvised on the piano available in the music room, between seven-thirty and eight at night. Fritz's schoolmate, Carl von Gersdorff, heir to a noble family from the region of Oberlausitz, the area close to Fritz's heart—as an extensive correspondence suggests had quite an intimate relationship with Fritz—listened to his performances.

"Never in my life shall I forget this impromptu playing. I should have no difficulty in believing that even Beethoven did not play extempore in a more moving manner than Nietzsche, more particularly when a storm was threatening,"[230] he wrote.

In the same period Fritz was "also becoming, gradually, more of a Wagnerian,"[231] Elisabeth, reminiscing about Pforta years, recalled participating in the boys' get-togethers. "I remember that the autumn holidays of 1862 were employed by my brother and his friend Gustav from morning till night in playing the arrangements from *Tristan und Isolde* for the piano. But, as Gustav's father was entirely in favor for classical music, these Wagnerian orgies were celebrated at our house. When Fritz asked me whether it was not 'wonderfully beautiful,' I had to acknowledge that much to my regret the music did not appeal to me." [232]

Regardless of whether played, composed, or listened to, music always offered the possibility of introspection into his soul. According to Fritz, music was not only for mere enjoyment but had a divine function. It was a mirror-image of one's soul, or a way to reflect the indescribable and unknowable world of without and within—the means to become consciously one with it. Music for Fritz replaced the church and God, providing an artistic genius[233] to unveil nature. It is "the paradigmatic vehicle for the expression of the Dionysian mode of self-understanding: – [where] Dionysus stands as a symbol for the mode of self-understanding,"[234] argues Kathleen Higgins.

In October of 1862, Fritz compiled notes for the symphony on the theme of *Ermanaric*, "On the Musical Composition – Ermanaric," of what he made notes on September 29, 1861.[235] "Expressing the mood that the *Ermanaric* saga utterly incarnated in me," he wrote, "the aged Ermanaric, a stern, fierce, heroic personality, far from being mild and tender, who coldly looks down on the worn course of his life,"[236] identifying with the ancient hero. He continuously tries to penetrate and adjust his own psyche through music or a written, historically expansive self-introspection. "It is not only interesting but even necessary to be as faithful as possible to the past, the years of childhood since we can never come to a clear judgment of ourselves unless we have the conditions in which we are trained to look closely and measure their influences on us. How much the life of my first years in a silent vicarage, the change of great happiness with great misfortune, the abandonment of the native village, and the manifold events of city life had an effect on me, I still daily look into in myself. – Serious, tending to extremes, I would say passionately serious, in a variety of circumstances, in joy and in sorrow, even in play,"[237] he makes a personal note again. In the end, describing himself as a joyless fellow, who does not know how to satisfy himself, he revealed his sensitive, deeply depressive, or manic-depressive nature, which is sternly focused on one and only goal of his life—the improvement of himself "as a mark of distinction."[238]

With that guiding thought on his mind, on October 23, Fritz wrote an essay titled, "An Attempt to Characterize Kriemhild after Nibelungen" for the Germania meeting in November. Again, he goes back to an old German saga, *Song of the Nibelungen* (c.1200), the story of Siegfried's deeds, his treacherous murder by Hagen, and the brutal revenge by the widowed wife, Kriemhild. The epic poem serves Fritz as a material for analyzing the relationship between the great and superior and the small and feeble natures. He juxtaposed the demonic or divine nature of great individuals, whose power comes from their hearts, their depths of affection, with a picture of the weak masses, thus spotlighting the great men's character. The weak are the small, frail natures who are not capable of any significant development of power. They can only reflect on their own limitations or tend to mock or moralize over the passionate characters' glory. They are eternally miserable and envious, entangled in guilt and bounded by remorse. However, as Hayman poetically translates the essay, "the weak, who either laugh at the vital fervour of passionate characters or moralize, are easily intimidated (*erschrecken*) when confronted with the demonic."[239]

Evidently, Fritz considered himself one of the great men. He had long seen himself a superior human being, one of the few. But he wanted to test this self-validation in the eyes of the others. How was he perceived by the inferior majority?

Without a doubt, he enjoyed prestige given by his position as a Primus, but at the same time, he had to perform some dull tasks, dictated by the school's Prussian *Ordung*.

He was required to write the reports concerning any repairs or shortages in the dormitories, classrooms, or lockers. To insert some fun into this mindless and boring responsibility, he brightened his report: "In classroom number X, the lights are burning so dimly that [they] are tempted to have their own lamps lit... The benches in the upper second, which were painted recently, become excessively attached to those who sit on them."[240] Apparently, the teachers were not amused and not "easily intimidated" and, furthermore, as it turned out, they were watching Fritz for quite sometimes now, so he was summoned to receive punishment for the insult, which they considered his report. "My strict Master Teachers, astonished to find frivolity introduced to such a serious matter, summoned me to the Synod on Saturday evening and decreed the punishment of no less than three hours detention in dungeon (*Karzer*) and the forfeiture of a few walks,"[241] he wrote his mother, withholding a few vital accusations and addressing his mother and sister arrogantly "Dear Folks" (*Liebe Leute*). Nevertheless, his tutor, Max Heinze wrote with concern to her as well, that "fellow students, had begun to find Fritz vain and that he concurred with this judgment,"[242] and, that the teachers noted in the Synod's minutes that "in January he [Fritz] forgot himself so completely as to try to deceive us by writing someone else's report."[243]

Franziska responded to Fritz's arrogance, probably with a reprimand in her voice, accusing Fritz of being corrupted by his companions, Blue speculates, for the letter is lost.[244] Fritz answered, so sure of himself, almost as though he was playing the system. He was attending gymnasium for four years already, so he knew that Pforta was not in the business of cultivating avant-gardist intellectuals but producing obedient cogs for the Prussian machinery of a militaristic empire. Our angry young man was rebellious, but only to the point of not being expelled from the school, whose education—Fritz also was clearly aware—was *ipso facto*, a path to the elite of society's upper class. Was he cynical? Of course. In the same letter, where he was supposedly confessing to his trespasses, he complained matter-of-factly, needing his linens and undergarments cleaned. It seems from his letter that the whole incident was just a typical day at school. He argued with his mother with a new self-assurance in his voice, with a sense of destiny: "I have astoundingly plenty to do but find myself both physically and mentally better than ever. I am always in a cheerful mood and work with great relish. I can't understand why you can worry even a moment over the consequences of that story, since you have understood it correctly and have reproached me in the letter. I will certainly beware of further indiscretions. But that I should linger in a bad mood, that is out of the question. Let Heinze and others look there for what they want – I know what happened there and I am fully at ease in consequence. As said, I have rarely been in a better mood than now, my projects move forward well, my dealings are various and pleasant – and there can be no question of influence; for that I would first have to meet people whom I considered my superior (*über mir*). I find even the cold temperature pleasant – in short, I feel quite good and have bad feelings toward no one, not even the teachers. Perhaps as teachers they could not understand the situation differently."[245]

Throughout that period, between October of 1862 and January 1863, always dreaming of music in the background, adamant to the admonishment by school authorities, Fritz, convinced that he was right, continued to analyze the idea of the weak versus strong, attempting to delineate the notion of superiority as a trait of character. Almost as though on its own, the concept gradually protruded from Fritz's poetic writings and gained significance. In turn, it affected his psyche, thus strengthening his convictions about it in reciprocal formulation.

Continuing his affair with the airs of superiority, on January 18, 1863, Fritz wrote an essay—inspired by Friedrich Schiller's play *Wallenstein's Camp* (*Wallensteins Lager, 1798*) —concerned with an influence of common men on great individuals. Importing the notion from "An Attempt to Characterize Kriemhild after Nibelungen" that the ordinary men are terrified of the superior individuals, he approached the problem in the same way. He initially formed a proposition, proving and exemplifying it as he continued with Albrecht von Wallenstein's story, the main character in Schiller's play.

Fritz argues that an effect (*Folge*) of the spiritual superiority (*Ueberlegenheit*) of the great men—the greatness of their views and acts—is reflected in the minds of those surrounding them. But it is not shown itself in its entirety. The reflection is only a fleeting glimmer of externalities. So, the mysterious aura which radiates from the leaders (*bedeutende*) irritates (*reizt*) the commoners because it fills them with an indefinite feeling of dependency (*unbestimmten Gefühl der Abhängigkeit*) on them.

However, when the great individuals show themselves in their full glory, the common folk turn away from them. As a result of this entanglement with the common and the ordinary, the great spirits (*geistige Großen*) suddenly appear abandoned and lonely. When they struggle with plebs, they usually lose, for the ordinary's weight will almost always quash even the most significant power of an individual (*bedeutendste Einzelmacht*).

As a result of these ruminations, Fritz came to the conclusion that there is a very delicate balance between the ordinary and the profound. On the one hand, the common and the ordinary folk worship the superior ones, but, at the same time, they are frightened and intimidated by them, which fills them with the feeling of subjugation and helplessness, which in turn saturates them with hatred. Although, quite often, the hatred of the masses is mistaken by their leaders for love. When it happens, a naïve leader falls into the trap of comradeship and brotherhood, which is the beginning of their demise.

To rationalize their feeling of submission, the plebeian masses would not allow anyone to discern their mediocrity. But, if such eventuality would occur, there are two ways to resolve the problem – pulling all who protrude down into the vastness of mediocracy or simply eliminating them. Is there anything more pleasurable than to see the powerful fall into rubble? And that was what happened to the great military leader Wallenstein. Too powerful for his superiors, he died assassinated in exile.

Unexpectedly, in March of 1863, Guido Meyer was forced to leave the school a year before graduation.[246] Deussen, who incessantly sought Fritz's attention, was clearly content with Meyer's departure in contrast to Fritz's devastation. He wrote to his mother about his friend, who "had always been held in high esteem by those who had come to know him more intimately; and that his expulsion was a source of great sorrow to him; that it was the saddest day he had known at the school."[247] However, right after the expulsion, Fritz began to act like Meyer never existed. He stopped mentioning him in his writings and ceased answering his letters. Only years later, he asked Deussen about the boy's whereabouts unconcernedly, if not out of curiosity.

Although, after losing a friend with whom he was revolting against the school establishment and whose companionship, supposedly, was a bad influence by Franziska's Naumburgian morality standards, Fritz unabatedly still continued his rebellious ways. His "conspicuous delinquency culminated in his getting caught drunk in the railroad station."[248] "On Sunday, April 12, 1863, he joined classmates at a railroad station tavern in Kösen and drank four mugs of beer."[249] Upon his return to the school grounds, teachers realized that he was completely drunk. This time, he was stripped out of his Primus privileges for the rest of his stay at school. Probably realizing that he went a bit too far and, seeing that some of his drinking buddies were expelled, he repented, this time sincerely (presumably) as seen by the teachers and his mother, still continuing with the theatricalities but this time with a genuine regret for his past behavior. He wrote his mother: "I write to you today; it is about one of the most unpleasant and saddest incidents I have ever been responsible for. In fact, I have misbehaved very badly, and I do not know whether you can or will forgive me … Last Sunday I got drunk, and I have no excuse, except that I did not know how much I could take … Through this affair, I have spoilt the fairly good position I succeeded in winning for myself the last term … I do not need to give you any further assurances how seriously I will pull myself together, for now, a lot depends on it."[250]

As regularly happened, the crisis brought such incapacitating attacks of illness that Fritz, a little over a week after the drunken escapades followed by interrogation in front of the synod of teachers, wound up in the infirmary. He was suffering from severe colds, throat infection, discharges from and abscesses around the ears, and difficulties with hearing and seeing. He stayed there for over a month, treated with leeches, herbal teas, and warm milk with water. He complained about the missed school events and work; nevertheless, he did not forget to speculate about his future career in almost all letters he sent to his mother. He was interested in so many subjects, he wrote, that it was virtually impossible to choose one. By confessing his indecisiveness to Franziska, he was preparing the ground for the inevitable change in his life to follow, which, he already knew, was in the making.[251] Almost nineteen years old, Fritz was just as confused as when he was fourteen about his future profession. Nevertheless, he maturely and soberly recognized that he was not yet prepared to choose the right life-path for himself: "Certainly, my endeavor is to thoroughly study what I am studying, but the more difficult the choice becomes since one must seek out the subject in which one can hope to accomplish something complete (*etwas Ganzes*). And how deceptive these hopes often are! How easy is it to get carried away by a momentary preference, an old family tradition, or some odd wish, so that the choice of the profession becomes a lottery. Now I am still in the particularly unpleasant position of really having many interests scattered in the most varied subjects, whose universal satisfaction would make me a learned man but hardly a professional.… It is clear to me that I have to get rid of some interests. That I must acquire some new ones, too. But which will be the unlucky ones that get thrown overboard? Perhaps my favorite children!"[252]

As a result of the same uncertainty and hesitancy, he also started to experiment with changes in his appearance, acquiring more of a bohemian look, with long hair and flamboyant dresses, limited though, by his skimpy financial means. On and off, he grew his walrus mustache— a trendy facial hairstyle with the *Szlachta*, a Polish noble class— which, with years, was overdone to almost a comical size, covering an ironic smirk on his face.

All those incidents, changes in taste, appearance, seemed to be outwardly directed, as a rebellion against the *Bildung* aimed at producing the obedient Prussian class of bureaucrats, clergy, and army officers, but in practice, specifically and with the most intensity, were inwardly directed at his own person. He was trying to shed off his compulsory fate of becoming a Lutheran minister. Still, he could not truly free himself from the bounds of perceiving himself as not merely different but superior within his social milieu. So, perhaps he realized that his desire to establish his superiority depended on following the ready-provided, socially established paths, not as an outcast, like his friend Ortlepp, but as a member of an elite bourgeois class. Or perhaps—and this is more probable, for he was a person striving for complete control over himself—he experimented with merely simulating rivalry on the beaten track. Once on the top, rebel against it, playing a dangerous game of manipulating the system. But—there always must be a "but"—deep inside, Fritz was through and through a traditional fellow. In his tastes, likings, intentions, and experiences, he was a conformist, allowing himself some transgressions, which, he knew, would be tolerated, even approved to the certain limits by the school authorities, to add an extra zest to the process of *Bildung*. After all, the subversive Ortlepp was not just tolerated by the Pforta faculty but allowed to tutor some of the students, spending the free time with them. After his deadly accident in the spring of 1864, he was buried at *Kloster Pforte* by the school staff. But Fritz was a keen observer of how the system works. He knew that if certain boundaries of "rebelliousness" were crossed, he could have been expelled, losing the prestigious standing the Pforta's alumni enjoyed, and therefore dismissed into obscurity and insignificance, forever as his drinking buddies were thrown out for "a drunken orgy, which had been accompanied by certain 'aggravating circumstances.'"[253]

In May of 1863, Fritz was given a school assignment of writing a character profile of Cassius from Shakespeare's *Julius Caesar.* The project, titled "Character of Cassius from Julius Caesar" *(Charakterschilderung des Cassius aus Julius Caesar)[254]* appeared to be a new excursion into English literature, but it was presumably a familiar territory for Fritz, a welcome high point of his fascination with the English authors, particularly Shakespeare. Following Christmas of 1861, when he had received the complete works of Shakespeare as a present, Fritz continued to accumulate works about, or by the bard. "Despite his 'small English,' he acquired a thirteen-volume English edition of the plays and Thompson's *Illustrations of Shakespeare*, as well as a verity of works of Shakespeare criticism. He also took every opportunity to attend Shakespeare's performances, which had become staple fare in the theaters throughout Europe by the second half of the nineteenth century.... While still at school, he mentions having attended partial or complete performances of *The Merchant of Venice, Julius Caesar* and *Midsummer Night's Dream, Henry IV, Part I,* and *Julius Caesar* again."[255]

Fritz approached the job well prepared, concerning himself with an incessantly nagging problem of great men, personal relationships, and psychological dynamics of power struggle and violence. As the essay's theme allowed him, he could not write about Caesar, his idol, but about Cassius's character, so he chooses to ponder Cassius and Brutus's friendship. In his analysis, Fritz did not consider Caesar, Brutus, or Cassius's historical personae but focused on the play's characters. "We must not assume without question that he is thinking of Caesar as a historical figure,"[256] reminds Alexander Nehamas. Instead, Fritz searched in the play's characters' representations for glimpses of the author's personality. He "plays the psychological sleuth in reading Shakespeare and is quick to extrapolate from the fictional characters to the character of the poet himself," whose character becomes an exemplar for Fritz himself, continues Large.

Fritz approaches the three characters of the play with the same interest by confronting Cassius with Brutus, who by complementing each other's personalities, form a force sufficient to overthrow Caesar by a vicious and brutal murder.

They both are ambiguous in their lust for power: Brutus, with his old Roman love of freedom and hatred of any autocratic rule, decides that his friendship with Caesar is overruled by his responsibility towards the Roman republic, preventing Caesar from crowning himself a king. On the opposite side, Cassius is more direct and does not hide behind the rationality of choosing his own personal feelings over people's good. He straightforwardly hates tyranny but hesitates whether he hates a tyrant more. But in both cases, the goal is to eliminate Caesar, who is a gigantic personality in Cassius's eyes, and in front of whom Cassius feels like he is hanging around the giant's legs, which fills him with an irreconcilable resentment (*unversöhnlichen Groll*). So, with Cassius, Fritz goes further than merely delineating the ambiguity of his motives. He provides a portrait of a person who is motivated enough to become a great man. Through rendering Cassius' character, Fritz reaches into an idealized image of the poet, a goal for himself. He suggests that Cassius' external appearance unveils his tireless, never-resting soul: a hollow, hungry gaze, a gaunt figure, with the strength and muscularity of his limbs hardened in the war, keen ear and keen eye, a bitter and rare smile that seems to despise the spirit that can still smile. He sleeps little at night, reads and observes a lot, despises the pleasures of life, does not play, is not a friend of music, does not do small talks or drinks, and does not fraternize with anyone.[257] Besides his dislike of music, is it not Fritz's idealized portrait? His alter ego, a *Doppelgänger* in a mirror of Shakespearean poetry? Fritz again killed two birds with one stone: fulfilled his academic requirement and rendered a portrait of himself without explicitly employing autobiography as an instrument of self-modification, as he had previously done. In doing so, he anticipates his future claim that philosophers are writing only of themselves.[258]

The play, being a study of power struggle, which Fritz stresses, is also about the betrayal of friendship as a necessary byproduct of one's craving for an ascent and its price. But in the end, there are no winners. After Caesar's murder, the masses riot, and the republic is lost forever.

After finishing "Cassius' Character" essay, Fritz severed most of his relationships one by one. One could speculate endlessly about the motivations behind it, though he could have assessed some of them useless to him, or plainly, he got tired of his old friends. In the past, Fritz was writing to his two Naumburg friends almost ad nauseam every day. Now, he stopped writing to the point that he forgot Pinder's birthday.

Then in May, he failed to answer any of the letters sent by Guido Meyer, who, just a couple of months ago, was the closest friend of his, and whose departure from Pforta Fritz described as "the saddest day he had known at the school."[259] But now, it was quite the opposite. "A letter! A letter!"– Meyer imploringly pleaded with him, ending with an appeal for Fritz's recent photograph, if available, all without avail.[260]

Finally, in June, back at home in Naumburg, Fritz wrote "Two Pages of Criticism" (*Zwei Bogen Kritik*),[261] an essay in two parts for the upcoming Germania meeting.

The first part, concerning Krug's musical achievements, was written quickly with mistakes and misspellings, without paying much attention to the subject matter. However, one could unmistakably gather from the expressions like "too soft…, too witty…, too artificial…" or, sarcastically, "a nice expression of the demonic song,"[262] an overall insulting critique of Krug's work. Nevertheless, regardless of Fritz's dismissal of his friend's musical attempts, Krug never gave up his musical passion. He worked as a lawyer; however, he composed his own, mostly chamber music, throughout his life and tirelessly promoted Richard Wagner.

The critique of Pinder's work was given more attention and thus was even more ravaging.

Wilhelm's poetry was "awkward, clumsy, muddled, lacking poetic moments, a cliché, a strange but unfortunate idea, trivial to the highest degree, the imitation of unfelt emotions, a very careless work,"[263] he wrote, and within a year or so, he gave up his own poetic productions also. "No more desire to compose terrible poems. End,"[264] he swore, although he still wrote a poem here and there.

The *Kritik* essay was Fritz's last contribution to Germania. When they met in July 1863, probably because of a lack of interest from Pinder and Krug, they decided to resolve the Society. Fritz's friends and the audience were six months ahead of him in school and did not have time for extracurricular activities while they studied for the entry exams to Heidelberg University. After that meeting in July, the group dissolved, and they never met together again.

Then, during the same month, without receiving any answer, Guido sends yet another letter: "Dear God, why haven't I received a letter from you yet, from you, whose letters I would most like to read. Have you already forgotten?"[265] – Meyer begged like a forsaken lover. But invariably, he never got any response from Fritz.

As that was a time of reckoning, Fritz broke his relationship with Erns Ortlepp as well. The end of it is pronounced by the entry in Fritz's diary, a poem by Ortlepp, where the poet prophetically laments of love and anguish: "Now that I no longer have you / I will soon be in my grave."[266] Fritz, for his part, immortalized their adventure by a verse that was probably inspired by witnessing drunken Ortlepp's antics in front of a church crucifix. The piece, titled "Before the Crucifix" (*Vor dem Crucifix*), [267] shows Ortlepp (or his alter ego, the author) shouting at a carving of the Crucified:

*"Block of stone up there, bloody fool,*
*"Down!*
*"What else do you want? What do you see?*
*"On these new wonders?*
*"You have come out now –*
*"Your arm is stiff, your head is muddy –*
*"Have I saw how everyone kneels in front of me,*
*"Was even so muddy,*
*"I jumped down long ago.*
*"I am stumbling here in front of you in dust*
*"And ashes –*
*"Down! Are you just deaf?*

*"Here you have my bottle!"*
*He throws it to shards,*
*The glass rattles, the stone statue stands*
*Still unmoved, raised on the cross,*
*His eye implores*
*To die, to die soon.*[268]

By writing these verses, he acquired the resilience and power to reinforce his separation from and dependence on God. The words of his poem were the words of Ortlepp but coming from Fritz's mouth. The poem, radically blasphemous and full of reproaches, formulated Fritz's loneliness, and in that, his humanity.

Fritz probably realized that all his friends and acquaintances were, in a sense, already slacking behind him. They were establishing their careers' positions, submitting to the society's rules and regulations, where he, on the other hand, was self-evolving with lightning speed. As they could not abide by his autopoietic leadership to keep up with him; hence, they were literally left behind.

And Fritz was alone again. Only Deussen, often rejected, was always ready to be graciously received back. He was not consciously planning these estrangements in advance, although, just a couple of months before, in April of 1863, Fritz predicted in the poem "Now and Formerly" (*Jetzt und ehedem*), what he methodically fulfilled a few months later, even though, it filled him with sorrow:

*My heart is so heavy, the present so gloomy,*
*And never contentment.*
*Melancholy, pain and amusement*
*Overwhelm me.*
*I can scarcely see the*
*May-blue sky anymore:*
*Deep misery deluges me now*
*With happiness and horror.*

*I have broken with the legacy of old*
*With the happiness of childhood bliss*
*Admonishingly called into my memory,*
*I have broken with whatever held me*
*In my childhood faith.*
*I have toyed with my heart*
*And almost let it be taken from me.*
*And what did I find? The past is gone!*
*Only tears!..* [269]

After that house cleaning— it is hard to say, if it was a summertime rapture or a revival after the deed was done—Fritz, as if cleansed anew was full of intense energy. During vacation between July 23 and August 23, he threw himself into work of reading and making extensive notes to "The Gospel of St. Matthew" *(Matthaeus),* [270] and "Beauty" [271] by Emerson.

Then, on August 11, 1863, he wrote yet another poem. Perhaps, in an attempt to go back for a moment to the path of life expected of him, the piece's subject was of the prodigal son, titled "Homecoming" *(Heimkehr).* [272]

*That was a day of tears*
*When once I said goodbye*
*More frightened is my heart*
*When I now return*
*My wandering hopes*
*Shattered in one blow*
*Oh, unhappy hour!*
*Oh, uneventful day!*
*I wept many times at my father's grave*
*And bitter tears fell upon the tomb*
*I became so lonely and sad*
*In my father's treasured house*
*I often wandered into*
*The dark forest, and, in its*

*Roomy shadows, I forgot*
*My pains and sorrows*
*In silent dreams, my heart*
*Fills with peace and*
*Sweet dreams of youth*
*And roses lull me to sleep*
*As I lay in the shadow of the oak tree.*[273]

The poem's confessional form became an instrument of realization, similar to autobiography, that there was no place he could call home, nowhere he could return to in either a metaphorical or literal sense. His true and only family home vanished with his father's death. His mother's house in Naumburg, at Weingarten 18, became a new home for the family, barely a couple of months before Fritz left for Pforta, and from then on, he continued living in the boarding rooms, hotels, and, sporadically friends' houses, never to establish his own home. Considering it, as he never regarded the Naumburg residence his home, he was, in fact, homeless. The only consolation substituting for a home were the fragments of smells, colors, sounds, and dreams dispersed in in his surroundings. Forests and meadows, rocky mountains and gentle slopes, the rain and the snow, the sun and the moon, all these were gloating him with "peace of sweet dreams."

He was again utterly on his own, without the support of friendship, nonetheless always ready to face the pervading problems of his destiny or a choice for the most advantageous career, which would provide means to achieve his—yet unnamed—but nevertheless tormenting purpose of life.

By the end of August of 1963, Fritz, almost nineteen, was invited by his protege pupil (*Unteren*) August Redtel to meet his grandparents in nearby Kösen. At their home, he was introduced to Redtel's sister Anna, with whom he immediately became infatuated, for the first time in his life with a female acquaintance. They met again and—since Anna was a good piano player—soon began to play duets together.[274] He composed rhapsodic poetry (*Rhapsodischen Dichtungen*) and dedicated to her as a present. A few days later, on September 6, forgetting about Elisabeth's possessiveness or just trying to tease her, wrote Franziska and Elisabeth, asking his sister for music scores, including Schumann's *Phantasien* and *Kinderscenen,* which he wanted to present to Anna.[275] Infuriated, Elisabeth never sent them.[276] So, on September 11, he mocked Elizabeth's jealousy, although having his father's inability to directly confront women, he could not stand up to her. "So, you are thoroughly horrified because I did not write, as usual, about dirty socks and my various requirements for food and cash and such like, which always make my letters so endearing to you." Then, by the end, he jokingly asked for a new pair of shoes, for the old ones have an "opening which is called usually a hole."[277] Fritz's brief crush on Anna, whether it was a real thing or just an act, was a turning point in his relationship with Elisabeth. It was the beginning of their drifting apart, mostly initiated and propelled by Fritz.

In that letter, signaling the widening divide between the siblings, Fritz confessed how confused he still was. Unable to find the right path for himself, he did not succumb to it but accepted his fate. He turned around and accepted his indecisiveness as his destiny:

"The autumn and its chilly air drove away the nightingales.... But the air is so crystalline and you can get such a clear view of the heavens that the world lies naked before your eyes. If I think for a moment about what I want, I look for words to a melody I have and a melody to words I have, and the two simply do not match up, although they both came from my soul.
But that is my destiny."[278]

But still, he did not surrender but accepted, even embraced his confusion. In an attempt to resolve this predicament, he turned towards the tool he knew best—writing. He wrote an essay titled "Can the Envious Ever Really Be Happy?" *(Kann der Neidische je wahrhaft glücklich sein?)*[279] Inspired by his sister's possessiveness, or perhaps an attitude rebuking envy in general. Then, he continued with a short life story, "My Life." He needed those exercises to introspect, delving into himself in hopes to generate a new, untraveled path in his life.

Contrary to Fritz's continuous struggle to find a meaningful profession for himself, most, if not all of his schoolmates knew precisely what to do with their lives. They had precise routes marked in front of them, which they simply had to follow. Already at school, they were laying the foundations for their future careers, and all of them had pragmatic and realistic expectations from life. Except for Fritz.

On its surface, the first essay was probably provoked by the outburst of Elisabeth's jealousy in reaction to Fritz's momentary infatuation with Anna Redtel. However, if we look closer, as Fritz suggested, from the perspective of seeking an inner core, we could come to notice an entirely different picture. The alternative, the in-depth view, is indispensable, for Fritz used the same beginning as in his other piece, a brand-new autobiography, which was written immediately after it. "The Envious" attempts to enucleate an internal evil using form of autobiography, which in essence it is.

Again, putting aside the issue of the veracity of his fantastic, self-indulgent ancestral claims, and instead focusing on the reason for these claims, we should be able to assume that Fritz was perfectly aware that he did not belong to the elite class. Nonetheless, instead of submitting to his common origin's unfortunate fate, he persistently sought to become a member of German society's highest echelons recognizing two viable pathways for himself: becoming an artist or academic; or a philosopher or prophet, he stubbornly pursued the not-yet-specific goals of his life. But he surely knew that the prevailing system of values did not suit him.

First, he had to shed all the Judeo-Christian values off of himself. He considered the ideals of equality, piety, chastity, the glorification of poverty, disregard for life in an expectation of reward after death, etc., the antithesis to the Dionysian values professed by the great heroes of past civilizations, especially, in their apogee, by classical Greece. Through reflecting on antiquity, he reconstructed the moral order he could submit to, in consequence, becoming a noble, at least in his eyes. He postulated therefore, a subjective approach towards change, tailored to his own desires and imagination.

The events of 1863 were of critical importance in Fritz's life. It would be a third turning point after his father's death and admittance to Pforta, so it required yet another reassessment through a self-retrospection, which could provide a range of unfolding possibilities.

## MY LIFE. ONCE AGAIN

On September 18, 1863, Fritz sketched a new autobiography, "My Life (1863),"[280] reusing the same introductory paragraph as "Can the Envious Ever Really Be Happy," metaphorically comparing the examination of man's life with the observable organic and non-organic nature. In that approach, he rejected the first impression, a habitual way of looking at a landscape or a person as an external, superficial examination of physiognomic circumstances, which misses the character of a landscape, as well as of man. In nature, he argues, the ambiance of a mountain range is not provided by its physiognomic characteristics (shape, cliffs, and rocks), but by the vegetation that reveals itself to us in time, though they initially seem to be irrelevant details. And it is the same with people. The physiognomic characteristics of a person do not show his inner quality, which lies within.

"We ought not to be guided by chance events, the gifts of fortune, the changing external eventualities which arise from conflicting external circumstances, when, like mountain peaks, they leap first to the eye. It is precisely those little events and inner occurrences we believe we have to neglect which in their totality reveal the individual character most clearly, they grow organically out of the nature of the man, while the former appears only in inorganic connection with him,"[281] Fritz recognizes the small events in human life as the most salient in our nature.

Then, he proceeds to autobiography. He sees himself growing out of the Lutheran tradition, which shaped his character indicated by external conditions, which are misleading. He goes further, designating language as his teacher. Although, he concludes that his autobiography's phrases and words, like polished to perfection stones, cannot convey the full truth, for reality is more obscured, like rough rocks covered with moss and dirt.

If he realized that it was impossible to transmit a real image of one's life, why then write about it? Apparently, he had changed his mind about autobiography as a retrospection of life and tool of self-improvement. He sees it here more as an ideal work of art, which later, in *The Birth of Tragedy*, he will call the Apollonian mode of expression. He dismisses language as useless for describing "reality" but, without an alternative, he continues with the polished notes as mere items of its reference. Otherwise, he would have stopped writing altogether. So, nevertheless in conflict with himself, he continued to write. He writes as painter, rendering images of his childhood, repeating imagery from years back: "Along the highway that runs from Weissenfels through Lützen to Leipzig there lies the village of Röcken. It is enclosed all around with plantations of willows and single-standing poplars and elm trees, so that from a distance only the projecting chimneys and the ancient church tower can be seen peeping through the green treetops. Within the village there extend several largish ponds separated from one another only by narrow strips of land; bright verdure and gnarled willows all around. Somewhat higher up there lies the personage and the church, the former surrounded by gardens and plantations of trees. Close by is the edge of the cemetery, full of sunken gravestones and crosses. The parsonage itself is shaded by three finely formed, wide-branched acacias....

Thus, we had to leave our home; on the evening of the last day, I was still playing with several other children, and then had to bid farewell to them, as I did to all the places I loved. I could not sleep; I tossed and turned on my bed, and towards midnight I got up. Several laden carts were standing in the yard, which was illumined by the feeble light of a lantern. As soon as morning dawned the horses were harnessed; through the morning mist we drove off to Naumburg, the goal of our journey. Here, at first intimidated, afterwards somewhat livelier, but always with the dignity of a thorough little philistine, I began to become acquainted with life and with books. Here I also learned to love nature in its fair mountains and its river valleys, halls and castles, and mankind in my friends and relations."[282]

Then abruptly, he leaves the memories of childhood, jumping straight into the future, demanding from himself to finally "seize the reins of events oneself and step out into life," for, he rationalized, "man outgrows everything that once embraced him."[283]


With still one academic year before him at Schulpforta, he realized that neither the learning institutions nor the system of *Bildung* would be enough to provide him with the desired character to his life. He recognized that life itself is a teacher that offers an experience of reality, of becoming one with the world or—still blasphemously—with God. But Pforta's shortcomings notwithstanding, Fritz was still able to gain something. The gist and rigidity of its education system provided Fritz with the discipline of the reliable valuation of his own skills and didactic matters imposed by the school. "I contained the wisdom of several lexicons, every possible inclination awoke in me, I wrote poems and tragedies, blood-curdling and unbelievably boring, tormented myself with the composition of complete orchestral scores, and had grown so obsessed with the idea of appropriating universal knowledge and universal capability that I was in danger of becoming a real muddle-head and fantasist. It was thus beneficial in many ways as a boarder at Landesschule Pforta to devote oneself for six years to a greater concentration of one's forces and to directing them to firm goals."[284]

Fritz, still a gymnasium student, was already in the future experience zone, ahead of his time. But in the meantime, he was bound to follow the school's educational requirements.

During March-April of 1864, he wrote an essay "Primum Oedipodis regis carmen choricum"[285] as a school assignment, which, Brobjer shows, is yet another plagiarism.[286] Fritz unrepentantly continued "borrowing" from other writers, unmoved by the consequences of being caught just a few months prior. As Brobjer assumes, there were other plagiarisms; the practice would validate to a certain degree future doubts about Fritz's originality. We will refer to this issue, when in early October of 1865, Fritz, a graduate from Pforta and a freshman at Bonn University, visited his schoolmate's father, Eduard Mushacke, in Berlin.

In the interim, we need to address a particular event, which simultaneously ended a chapter of Fritz's life and began a new one.

On June 14, 1864, Ernst Ortlepp, whom Fritz had met earlier in the afternoon at a tavern in Almrich, fell into a trench near Pforta's grounds. He was certainly drunk, so the fall could have been an accident, but it was described by Naumburg's paper as a suicide. He was buried at Pforta, though neither Fritz nor any other students were in attendance. The burial was executed by four workers without a priest, and attended only by Professor Karl Keil, who also paid for it.[287]

Clearly, Fritz was becoming quite nonchalant towards the past, despite realizing that life's events had profoundly influenced his personality. Hence, he began to pay more attention to his frame of mind instead of concentration on his behaviors as an indirect gate to his inner reality, his character.

On March 23, 1864, while spending Easter break in Naumburg, Fritz started working on a different type of autobiography, titled "On Moods" (*Über Stimmungen*).[288] Priming himself by repeatedly playing Liszt's *Consolations*, he focused exclusively on his inner self, on his affective states. As in the past, it was not an attempt to reach the soul by describing his actions retrospectively, but directly addressing his state of mind. Hayman speculates that it was probably written under the influence of Kant's essay "Idea for a Universal History with a Cosmopolitan Purpose" (1784), "which suggests that man wants harmony while nature arranges conflict." Drawing on Kant's methodology, "knowing of no consciousness but his own, and knowing nothing of the outside world except what was in his consciousness, he had an unlimited curiosity about the relationship between the two, and a strong compulsion to trap as much as he could of consciousness into images on paper."[289]

He begins by intimately sketching himself sitting alone in a robe staring at an empty page, trying to sort out thoughts worthy of attention but, at the same time, observing himself as a receptacle for his ever-changing moods and tempers. He analyzes ontological processes underlying behavior in an attempt to find out if he may influence them. The exercise is not merely theoretical but induced by the events of parting with his acquaintances and friends, particularly with an unnamed friend, notorious Erns Ortlepp. Fritz realizes that his moods are instigated by the conflicting emotions and experiences belonging to two opposing camps: the old, established thoughts and feelings, and the new ones, "tempestuous and effervescent like new wine."[290] The inner struggle (*Kampf*) between them seems to be a necessary originator of moods, which, in its potentiality, depends on the responsiveness or unresponsiveness to all the external events and experiences. "It does not lie within the power of the will to make the soul reflect or not, [but] the soul is touched only by what it wants."[291] Fritz wonders further if the will could change the course of events. He concludes it is impossible, for "the soul (*Seele*) is composed of the same or similar stuff as experiences (*Ereignis*), and thus it is that an event (*Ereignis*) which finds no sympathetic resonance can lie so heavily on the soul as a burdensome mood, and can eventually assume such a preponderance that it compresses and constricts the other contents of the soul."[292] Therefore, the soul is an event, thus an experience. Considering the thinker's age and philosophical background, that the soul and experience are of the same staff is a vanguard idea.  The basis for this advanced ontological claim[293]—only recently given proper attention[294]—was later developed into mature philosophical concepts. However, because they lacked a traditional presentation, they were deprived of deserved attention from readers. The soul is of the same or similar stuff as experience of event; struggle is food for the souls; the soul destroys and gives birth to new things *(Die Seele ist aus demselbe[n] Stoff aus dem die Ereignisse gemacht sind oder aus ähnliche[m]; Kampf ist der Seele fortwährende Nahrung,* and; *[Die Seele] vernichtet und gebie[r]t dabei neues)*[295]. These are the budding ideas of Fritz's ontological thought. He developed them relying on an observation of his own conflicting streams of feelings—of love and love lost towards his unnamed friend or lover— attentively being conscious of his changing mood through the sheer process of writing them down. "I no longer love as I loved some weeks ago; I am no longer at this moment in the mood as I was in as I began to write."[296]

This observation prompted him towards the impossible—an attempt to accurately capture the mood he was in at that precise moment. First, he chooses music, then poetry, but eventually finds an appropriate vehicle for the task. It seems like an automatic recording of an involuntary stream of images (the stream of consciousness)[297] coming from his inner soul or his external experiences or, for they are the same, the world. "Take a new sheet, and now pen quickly scribble, ink – quick – here!"[298] Out of necessity for expressing the fluidity of consciousness, he formulates a narrative device spontaneously without naming it, later to be perfected into works of art by James Joyce, Marcel Proust, Jack Kerouac, David Markson, and countless other writers.

After Easter break, Fritz walked back to Pforta via the Kleine Saale River, absorbing the tranquility of rural landscape embraced by a slowly floating river among sloping willows, poplars, and beech trees.

He was back to continue working on school assignments, ideas that personally interested him, and his *Abitur,* the final thesis, which would crown his six-year effort at Pforta. And at last, he had to decide about the field of his further education. At least, Fritz had already decided that he could not follow his father's footsteps of becoming a theologian, freeing himself to realize his unquenchable desire of becoming an artist, to pursue a career in music.

Although the qualitative and imprecise notions of feelings and emotions ruling arts were becoming the main ingredients in his development of thought, contrary to the rigid and mechanical approach of the sciences, he decided to pick something entirely against himself. In contrast to his self-development, which was progressing through primarily emotional experiences, he considered to study ossified and cold classical philology at Bonn University.

However, his choice was not wholly sterilized of original thinking. By choosing philology, he was also exposing himself to philosophy. "The fact [was] that classical philology in Germany was suffused with philosophical speculations (inspired variously by Kant, Schlegel, Schleiermacher, Schelling, and Hegel). [Nonetheless] philosophy and philology were not traditionally part of the same pedagogical matrix in the German curriculum. So, the two pursuits tended to remain separate ingredients of Nietzsche's initial formation," until years later, they converged when he encountered a pre-Socratic philosopher, Democritus of Abdera,[299] James Porter clarifies Fritz's decision.

Later, in 1869 he justified this decision-making process by citing the need for structure in his endeavors. "Only at the end of my Pforta life, having achieved proper self-knowledge, did I give up all artistic life-plans: into the resulting gap stepped philology. I needed, that is, to achieve equanimity in the face of the flux of disquieting inclinations, a discipline (*Wissenschaft)* that could be pursued with equanimity in the face of the changeable and disquieting flux of inclinations, a discipline which could be conducted with cool level-headedness and logical coldness— routine work— without its results stirring the heart."[300]

Was this in the spirit of his recent findings to follow the natural order of things provoking conflict? Or, to masochistically immerse himself in a perpetual struggle (*Kampf*)?

Almost immediately after, or simultaneously with these revelations, as usual against himself, he rushed into work on conflict and struggle, based on its quintessential expression, the Greek tragedy.

During April and May of 1864, at Pforta, Fritz wrote an essay titled "Thoughts Concerning Choral Music in Tragedy" *(Gedanken über die chorische Musik in der Tragoedie),*[301] as a part of a much larger piece titled, "The First Choral Song of Oedipus Rex"[302] written in Latin, Greek and German. Carefully considering its topic, one may conclude that it was a harbinger of his first book, *The Birth of Tragedy from the Spirit of Music*, conceived eight years in the future.

The main argument of the work is that the original Greek tragedy arose not from the historical narrative of "epos, the epic tale of religious content," but from the expression of emotions and lyricism combined with musical elements of the ancient Greek tales. In its mode of perpetual struggle, tragedy was rendered through "the great pathos scenes, broadly conceptualized expressions of emotion, for the greater part musical, in which the action played only a minor role, the lyrical feeling, however, was everything."[303] The parts of the performance were intertwined into a chiasm of perpetual conflict. Simultaneously, the harmony of songs' strophes and anti-strophes (for music was supposed to spark feelings and emotions) pushed action and narrative to a secondary, background-position. Fritz, not only reading but adoring Greek playwrights like Aeschylus, Sophocles, Empedocles, and Plato, experienced the surrounding world through the prism of his feelings and emotions, not through the rationality of scientific knowledge. He saw in the concept of the tragic a reflection of the true nature of the world.

As early as six years before the explicit conceptualization of the antagonistic dichotomy of "Dionysian *versus* Apollonian" in *The Birth of Tragedy*, Fritz came up with its precise formulation in an interpretation of a choral song as a generator of tragic emotions.

"Thus, its three main parts first express a frightened flight, in search of help, then deep suffering and pain, and finally lively and increasing damnation of the plague and a yearning for the arrival of the merciful Gods, well, the finale even reaches a dithyrambic fire, at the end of the third strophe and anti-strophe. Of these three parts, the first one is most intricately sequenced and comprised of the most varying meters, the second one maintains the most uniformity in its sad rhythms, the third one accelerates to the greatest liveliness of emotion, something that is peculiar to the final parts of the first choruses in tragedy. Often, Bacchus is mentioned in them, and here, allusions of Bacchian dithyrambs have been preserved,"[304] Fritz dissected tragedy with great precision, hence, providing himself with the foundations to build upon it his future thought.

He further anticipated the Greek tragedy as a model to redeem "the nonsense (*Unsinn*) in which our opera—not considering the ingenious revolutionary plans of Richard Wagner—finds itself.... The great discrepancy between music and text, between sound and emotion (*Empfindung*)."[305]

He saw in the composer and his ambitions to create a total artwork (*Gesamtkunstwerk*) a genius reformer, savior of opera, the arts, and the German culture. "The 'artwork of the future' (*Kunstwerks der Zukunft*) in which the noblest art forms harmoniously unite, in which one art form serves to allow the other one to appear in the right light, and in which all work together in order to leave behind a uniform enjoyment of art, thus we would have, in them, such fortunately and divinely organized people that the rays of all art forms meet in the prisms of their minds."[306]

He concludes with the claim that human nature (*menschlichen Natur*) cannot comprehend naturally the contradictions of emotions and feelings rooted in intrinsically tragic events of one's life. However, the choral music of Greek tragedy, which provokes conflicting emotions in its choruses and pathos scenes, is the gateway to an authentic experience of the actual world of Dionysian fire, the gateway to the feeling of being alive in the world.

Later, in *The Birth of Tragedy* and subsequent works, he saw it from the perspective of the salient role of choral music. "For what the ancient chorus—this self-entranced mass of sound that no longer *represents* Dionysus but *is* Dionysus—had wanted to indicate is expressed directly and affirmatively in Nietzsche's aesthetic-metaphysical work, and especially in the presentation of Zarathustra–to wit, to hell with deeper meanings! To hell with the higher truths! Let's call a halt to the idea of the preexistence of meaning with respect to its expression! Long live the signifier! Long live smoke and noise! Long live the sound and the image! Long live the illusion of autonomous symbol, the absolute dramatic representation!"[307] – writes Peter Sloterdijk, not afraid to emphasize the spectacularity of presentation.

Roughly at the same time, probably testing his ability to withstand struggle, he confronted his old friends, Krug and Pinder, almost a year after his unceremonious break-up with them. On June 12, 1864, he wrote a long letter, which begins with a sort of apology, but quickly turns to his old writing mode. The premise of the letter was a Fritz's request for a favor: to send him a copy of a doctoral dissertation by a young philologist at Münster University concerning Theognis of Megara, the theme of his planned final work at Pforta. Then unapologetically, he begins to brag about his school performance of reading Shakespeare's Henry IV. "I read Henry Percy with a great deal of excitement and anger,"[308] he writes about his role as Hotspur. The part which is "prone to rage, rebellion, and hyperbolic rhetoric," notices Andrew Lanham, "was the perfect character for a future polemicist like Nietzsche, [who] seems to have embraced his dramatic role."[309] Nevertheless, Fritz boasted pitiably about his role delivery, which Deussen described as "performed in mellifluous and pleasant voice but not without false pathos."[310]

Perhaps others saw it as a failure, but Fritz was quite serious about theatricality and acting tragedy and drama, mainly Shakespearean plays. Enchanted with theater throughout his entire life (some of his acquaintances even suspected that he was not ill during the last ten years of his life but merely acted it out)[311] introduced a method of play-acting into his writing by wearing an ever-changing mask. "The dramatic context of Nietzsche's maskings"[312] is to lose himself to find himself, continuously, "in the process of expanding the stage for his great play, exposing its antiquated foundation and properly determining what masks the actors [and he himself] will wear."[313] In theater and opera he found yet another means to access the sort of self-introspection he had been seeking since his earliest years, expanding his toolkit beyond autobiography.

He put on different masks, but Shakespearean heroes[314] were so natural to him that he assumed from the plays' characters the poet himself.[315] As a budding philologist, he considered the Shakespearian dramas a continuation of Greek tragedies. He viewed—as many German thinkers—Shakespeare a quintessential German poet, which, in a sense, connected him with Wagner, the "savior of German art." However, he was not the originator of the idea. "With respect to this nationalistic appropriation of Shakespeare, Nietzsche was merely following in the footsteps of a great many earlier Germanic writers over the previous century,"[316] writes Duncan Large. As Large proves, citing the original notes to *The Birth of Tragedy*, Fritz appropriated Shakespeare to quite an extent but later did not use those notes. Nonetheless, "on the one hand, [he] envisage[d] Shakespearean drama as the consequence of Greek tragedy and its authors as the fulfillment of Sophocles. But, on the other, [by bringing] Shakespeare and Wagner together stress[ed] the Germanic musicality of Shakespeare's writing.... It is the Germanic mission to perfect the art form—music—which is the true fulfillment of the tragic knowledge that inspired Socrates' misguided scientific enterprise and that Shakespeare stands in direct relation to this mission, as the poet of tragic knowledge; the *music-making Socrates.*"[317]

The volume of Shakespeare that Fritz had received from Aunt Rosalie was at that point heavily annotated.[318] Evidently, he began using the plays to pursue the ideas of self-analysis by identifying with the plays' characters.

To appreciate Fritz's utter devotion, I should mention that for the occasion of his participation in the celebration of the 300 anniversary of Shakespeare's birthday, he commemorated it by composing a poem in ten *ottava prima* stanzas dedicated to the poet.[319] He depicted the changing fortunes of Shakespeare's popularity in the last stanza, boldly comparing Shakespeare with resurrected Jesus, continually living among us. Had Fritz, twenty-five years ahead of time, foreseen his own self-incarnation as the Crucified?


On July 4, 1864, back in Naumburg, he wrote again to Pinder, a long, casual but cheerfully-toned letter, talking about his daily routine, work, and the book he had asked for but never received. Then, quite unexpectedly, at the end of the letter he unconcernedly mentions that his long-time friend, mentor, and possibly romantic interest, Ernst Ortlepp died in a tragic accident or suicide. "By the way, the old Ortlepp is dead. Between Pforta and Almrich, he fell into a ditch and broke his neck. Early in the morning, when it was raining dreadfully, he was buried at Pforta; four workers carried the rough coffin; Professor Keil followed with his umbrella. No priest. We spoke to him on the day of his death, at Almrich. He said that he was on his way to rent lodgings in the Saale valley. We wanted to set a small tombstone for him; we have collected money; we have about 40 Thalers."[320] Evidently, he definitely put an end to Ortlepp's influence on him. He closed that chapter in his life, leaving all the experiences behind turning forward with the expectation of new ones. It is hard to say if he was doing it deliberately because this relationship has ended. Although, there were always intense amounts of emotions intertwined as with any of those acts of leaving, which were incessantly happening throughout his productive life. The period 1863–1864, finishing his schooling at Schulpforta, was a phase of experimentation of parting with the past in expectation of the forthcoming future.

The summer of 1864 was unusually hot. Fritz spent July *Hundsferien* at home in Naumburg. It was the end of his six years of education, but still, he had so much to do before parting with the school. Having performed poorly in a few classes, he was under pressure to write an excellent final essay with an attached autobiography, and prepare for the final examination, and finally choose a field of study at a suitable and prestigious university.

As he had begun earlier in his essay "On Moods," he continued self-consciously observing his modes of temperament, contemplating surroundings and their influence on the change of his frame of mind. As previously, he tried to capture this process through piano improvisation or writing poetry but failed at both. He realized that the only thing he could do was to spontaneously write, nearly like listening to dictation, about what he was experiencing at any given moment—write about experiencing (*Erfahrung*) events (*Ereignisse*) and, at the same time, how his soul (*Seele*) responded to it. He tried to consciously discern a moment of mood creation and its reciprocal influence on experiencing events that in turn impacted his idiosyncratic psyche.

*Mild summer evening, twilight streaked with pallor. Children's voices in the lanes, in the distance noise and music. A fair: people are dancing, colorful lanterns blaze, wild animals growl; here a shot rings out, there a rattle of drums, steady and insistent.*

*Inside the room it is darker. I light a lamp, but the eye of the day looks inquisitively through the half-drawn curtains. It would like to see farther, right into the middle of this heart which – hotter than the light, duskier than the evening, more animated than the voices in the distance – reverberates deep within, like a huge bell sounded in a storm.*

*And I implore a thunderstorm; does the tolling of the bell not attract the lightning?*

*Now, you approaching thunderstorm, clarify, purify, blow fragrances of rain into my dull nature; welcome, at last, welcome!*

*There! You first bolt of lightning, there you flash, right into my heart; and from it arises something like a long, pale column of mist. Do you know it, the dark, treacherous one? My eye is already brighter, and I stretch my hand out after it, as if to curse.*

*The thunder growls, and a voice rang out: "Be cleansed!"*

*Heavy sultriness; my heart swells. Nothing moves. There – a light breath, on the ground the grass trembles – welcome, rain, soother, my saviour! Here it is desert, empty, dead: plant anew!*

*There! A second bolt! Dazzling and two-edged, right into my heart! And a voice rang out: "Hope!"*

*A gentle fragrance rises from the ground, a wind comes up, and the storm follows, howling in pursuit of its prey. It drives broken-off blossoms before it, as the rain swims joyfully after. Right through the middle of my heart. Storm and rain! Thunder and lightning!*

*Right through the middle! And a voice rang out:*

*"Become new!"*[321]

Fritz writes on the spur of the moment with many errors, trying to capture his frustration and the turning on his mood from an inquisitive calmness to a fury of a thunderstorm, crushing into each other.

Regardless of his seeming ease at rapid experimental writing, and probably because of the onslaught of work, he had difficulties with producing required schoolwork to match his own high standards.

In his progression from the age of fourteen, as writing was increasingly becoming the salient creative act of his life, he was becoming more consciously aware of writing's central position in his process of self-cultivation.[322] In his first autobiographical essay, "From My Life" (1858), he already paid a lot of attention to the process of writing itself, which, later on, developed into a necessary experience, the essential method in pursuit of self-formation. Alexander Nehamas aptly postulates that "what for Nietzsche was a necessary but consistently overlooked feature in all philosophy become in his own case, through a life of effort, a self-conscious achievement: he showed that writing is perhaps the most important part of thinking. And since he also believed that thinking '*is* an action,' we might with some appropriateness attribute to him the hyperbolic view ... that writing is also the most important part of living."[323]

Fritz was developing a spontaneous writing style—which later he attributed to the ability to access the genius of the world[324]—but paradoxically, one necessarily expectant of a particular form and content. He complained about it, of course in writing, in a draft letter to an imaginary friend or his *Doppelgänger* titled, "To a Friend," in early July: "Satan! Ink, Pen – Can't I write without scribbling and blots? Without the words running amok into the puddles, on their own?"[325]– frustrated and vexed by the heat of the summer, that he is not producing what he wants, he writes to himself, probably to break a spell of his ill production. But then, just within a few days, on July 8, 1864, he completed his final school essay, "Theognis of Megara."

Immediately afterwards, he wrote about his achievement to Deussen: "It's Friday, 5 o'clock in the afternoon, I just wrote the last page of my work about Theognis, I put all the pages together and weight them in my hand. Then, I pull out the best piece of paper to write you about myself.

If whenever, I really need you now, perhaps you have a similar feeling.

On Monday morning, I started my work full of doubts and wrote 7 pages, on the second day in the evening I had 16 pages, on the third 27; isn't there a beautiful progression in these numbers 1.7, 2.8, 3.9? On Thursday and today I wrote the rest; together, there are 42 tightly written pages which would make at least 60, or more pages with a fair copy. …

Am I happy with it? No, no. But, even if I tried harder, I couldn't have said anything better. Some parts are boring. Others, stylistically awkward. Here and there some things are stretched a bit, like a comparison of Th[eognis] with Marquis Posa! For the most part I have copied my previously notes about Theognis. I am annoyed that I had to copy so much. I have quoted Theognis so often, that the greater part of the fragments is certainly cited by me."

Then, without any explanation, and regardless of his self-criticism, he turned to describe his daily routine in Naumburg, which is a repetitive expansion of a fragment from the "Letter To a Friend." It seems that the practice of making notes and copying them later into a final manuscript had become Fritz's *modus operandi* throughout his writing life.

"Now hear about my life," he writes casually. "I get up early, but not too early, then I have my coffee. Afterwards, I go to my room, there is a large table, completely covered with books, which are mostly opened; a comfortable grandfather chair; I am dressed in my beautiful dressing-gown. I write. Around one in the afternoon, I eat with my mother and sister, drink my hot water, and play a little piano and drink coffee. Then, I write again. At six, the tea and my supper are brought to my room; I drink, eat and write. It gets dark. I pull myself from work, look at the time: half past eight. I dress quickly, leave the house, and in the gathering darkness of the night, harry into the Saale. Which is cool and cold, therefore refreshing. The river rushes, everything else is silent, the fog and I rest on the water. The wind is blows when I go back. I am surrounded by good things. So far, my somewhat exhausting way of life has not really affected me."[326]

A few days later, following the spirit of his passions, on July 12, 1864, he answered a letter from Rudolf Buddensieg, a nephew of his tutor, writing about the effects of music, the topic he worked on a year and a half before, captured in an essay, "On the Essence of Music." Fritz thought a new idea about the effects of music and the overall influence of all the arts on a human being. He divided the qualities of these experiences as physical, which he attributed to the most people enjoying all sorts of arts, and as spiritual or mental, which concerned only a very few, who were receptive to the "miracle," as he calls it, to the rapture of high art. When previously utilizing the term "demonic" (*dämonische*), Fritz had been confined only to the influence of music. But now, he widened and deepened its connotation as the spiritual intuition (*eine geistige Intuition*) concerning all arts.

"As far as your thoughts about the effects of music are concerned, the observation you have made," Fritz replied to Buddensieg, "is probably more or less inherent to all musically oriented people; meanwhile, this nervous excitement, these shivers (*Nervenerregung, Schauer*), are not the effect of music alone, but of all the higher arts. Remember the analogous impression when reading Shakespeare's tragedies. Sometimes, just a single word, an urgent and moving scene, or a glaring contrast evokes this feeling with these, so quite different musical works create the same impression, the same thrill. Remember that this is just a physical effect; it is preceded by a spiritual intuition (*eine geistige Intuition*) that affects only people with rarity, magnificence, and full revelation, like a sudden miracle. But do not think that the reason for this intuition lies in feeling or sensation (*Gefühl, Empfinden*); no, it lies especially in the highest and finest part of the knowing spirit (*erkennenden Geistes*). Do you not feel that something wide, unexpected is opening up? Do you not feel that you are looking into another realm that is usually veiled to man? In this intellectual intuition (*geistigen intuition*), the listener comes closer to the composer than he can possibly do. There is no such effect beyond art, which in itself is a creative force (*eine schöpferische Kraft*). You find the expression that I chose myself two years ago when I wrote several pages to my friends about this subject inappropriate; I called the effect a 'demonic' (*eine dämonische*). But if there are any premonitions of higher worlds (*höherer Welten*), they are hidden here."[327]

A few years later, Fritz broadened this idea of spiritual sensitivity to art, characteristic to a very few individuals, even further; the arts became the world, and the few individuals, the artists.

He developed his philosophical thinking, transforming the idea presented in his first book, as *a genius*, "the primordial spirit that connects the creative rebirth of the world as the 'art' of nature with the genius of an artist. ... The merging of artistic genius with the primordial artistry of the world is, in a sense, the transformation of an artist into a medium that channels the original artistic plasticity through semblance in the work of art."[328] However, there are very few who have the ability to channel the artistry of the world through their genius, and of course, of which elite Fritz considered himself a member.

Continuing with his tasks while at his mother's house, Fritz wrote yet another autobiographical work as a formal school requirement for graduating students. An attachment to his final essay, devoid of personal perspective, it reads as formal and reserved in contrast with his personal experiments. There also could be an additional, more personal reason for this formality. Underneath the guise of emotional spontaneity and rebelliousness, Fritz was tormented by the possibility of not graduating at all: "I don't know whether I'll pass my exam; I hope, however, that if I use the vacation very efficiently, I will pass it well,"[329] he confided to Buddensieg. He was still undecided about university choice on top of all of this, wavering between Bonn and Leipzig, yet another pivotal crossroads, with all responsibility resting squarely on his shoulders.

In the opening paragraph, he prized Pforta for giving him "the greatest and most characteristic part of [my] intellectual education." Then he proceeds to discern two decisive events in his life: his father's death and the transfer from Naumburg's Domgymnasium to Pforta. He deplored his father's death as a deprivation of paternal support and guidance. But, at the same time, he recognized a silver lining: the loss as the spring of the traits of his seriousness *(Ernsten)* and soul's introspectiveness *(Betrachten)*.

He was not, as before, lamenting his fatherlessness, but on the contrary, was reframing his tragedy an experience of affirmative gain. He came to this conclusion not through theoretical speculation, but the subjective experience. It is an onset of discerning that a personal experience of a tragic event, which, for most people, would result in pessimism born out of pain and grief, for him could open the gates into creative expectations. For Fritz—because he believed himself to be of the minority of uncommon and significant people— his personal tragedy become a necessarily productive force. While detaching himself from his old acquaintances, family and leaving behind the known comforts, he proceeded into the unpredictable future.

If my life is just a chain of tragic events full of struggle, pain, and disappointments, in need of reprieve—he could have thought—I fool myself that there are moments of happiness and fulfillment. They are just an illusion brought through the mechanisms of socially induced self-control.

Therefore, instead of fooling myself that life is beautiful, I should embrace its great tragedy, without any expectation of minute pleasures, and dedicate myself to fulfilling my fate towards becoming an exceptional human. And think of what consequences of this proposition's realization would have for me as for any other person.

First of all, it would require inverting the gaze of my inquiries. Instead of dissecting myself through other individuals' attributes, I should focus directly on finding an abundance of the fertile tragedy in my own life, he could have said.

Instead, Fritz devoted his autobiographical instrument, "My Life"[330] of 1864 to the pursuits of knowledge. He criticized himself as being too intellectually broad and unfocused, interested in all subjects but "too-rational mathematics." He believed that knowing too much would necessarily flatten (*verflachenden*) the quality of his understanding. He realized that to satisfy his irresistible curiosity would require a reductionist approach towards the excess of knowledge (*Vielwissen*). It would only shallow his overall intellectual development, but not enrich him with the in-depth wisdom. He understood that the pursuit on a single path of a precise, a far-reaching inquiry is impossible, as it is aggravated by "a true craving for 'universal knowledge.'" Therefore, the only solution would be the exploitation of the conflict between these two opposite forces, he concluded. "I shall hold on to this as an unbreakable principle for my further scientific pursuits: to fight against the inclination towards a flattening quest for an excess of knowledge, and then to further my propensity to try to trace each detail back to its deepest and farthest-reaching origin.... In the fight with the one, in the promotion of the other, I hope to be victorious."[331]

Before graduation, in September 1864, Fritz had to finally choose what subject and at which university to pursue it and pass his final examinations. He received the highest grades in Religion, German, and Latin; good in Greek; satisfactory in French, History, Geography, and Natural Sciences. However, he received an unsatisfactory grade in Mathematics, Hebrew, and Drawing. Professor Buchbinder, who taught mathematics, did not want to award an *Abitur* certificate to Fritz, contrary to Prof. Corssen, who "called Nietzsche the best pupil he could remember at Pforta."[332] Perhaps fortunately for Fritz, the failure with Hebrew eliminated any prospects of seriously considering theology—knowledge of Hebrew was an essential requirement to become a minister—a situation which spared him awkward decision around whether to follow in his father's footsteps. Fritz did try his hand at drawing and painting, but looking at his attempts, it is hard to find any artistic aptness in his works, despite him being exceptionally sensitive to visual experiences of nature and works of art. In any event, he knew his attempts were pathetic since he made fun of trying to become an artist.

Although his musical skills held more promise, as Hayman claims, "it was self-sacrificial for Nietzsche to abandon all idea of an artistic career, opting for philology. He wanted, he wrote, 'a science which could be pursued with cool reflectiveness, logical coldness, equable effort, and would not yield results that size the hold of the heart'"[333] Fritz wanted an exoneration from his earlier ideas that feelings and sensation were the only way of inquiry. He wanted something palpable, material, something he could control, avoiding overstimulating senses, thoughts, and in the end, headaches.

Since Fritz wrote his final essay in Latin about an obscure Greek nobleman and poet of the 6 century BC, Theognis from city-state Megara, in a certain sense, he determined the path of his future education without actually making any decisions a priori. He followed Deussen in attending Bonn University, where two renowned classical philologists, Otto Jahn and Friedrich Ritschl, were teaching.

The thesis (*Valediktionsarbeit*), "De Theognide Megarensi," was a superb philological work entirely in line with his decision of becoming a classical philologist but, at the same time, in agreement with the ideals dear to Fritz's heart—his quest for self-cultivation and nobleness—embedded within the subject of the essay. As usual, he totally devoted himself to the task, regardless of the prejudice he held against it deep down. "I have involved myself in a great deal of surmise and guesswork, but I plan to complete the work with the proper philological thoroughness and as scientifically (*wissenschaftlich*) as I can. I have already worked out a new approach to this man, and on the most points my judgments are at variance with the usual ones,"[334] he wrote to Krug and Pinder on July 12, 1864.

Considering the essay through a prism of philological scholarship, it was done so well "that, had Nietzsche never written another word, would have assured his place, albeit quite a small one, in the history of German philology,"[335] writes Anthony Jensen. Its subject is a contemplation of struggling nobility versus plebeians, the severe polarization comprising the Greek society of antiquity. The work especially emphasizes the concept of nobleness, which, undoubtedly Fritz's pet subject, appeared under different disguises in his work. Kerr, who translated Fritz's thesis from Latin and Greek, claims in the *Preface*—what incidentally is a premise of this work as well—that "interestingly, the present work demonstrates how many of Nietzsche's later views and preoccupations were already espoused by the adolescent: most noteworthy, the birth of the young genealogist of morals—the notions of 'good' and 'bad' are defined in relation to types of individuals."[336]

Through verses of "Theognis," Fritz presented a detailed identity of nobility, progressing from its flourishing towards its demise. "Theognis hailed from an old and illustrious family and throughout his life was earnestly engaged in the pursuit of nobleness,"[337] he wrote. With elaborate detail, Fritz listed attributes characterizing nobles in contrast with the plebeian class to indicate the former's supremacy over the latter's infirmity. Theognis, Fritz wrote, was "the champion of the class of the optimates, he also separated the population in his poetry in such away that he pronounced one part *the good*, i.e., the optimates: the good men among whom was supposed to be every religious piety to the gods; and towards men, every righteousness and goodness. The other part he called *the bad* or *the lowly*, among whom every moral depravity, irreverence, and ungodliness was said to exist."[338] Referring to antiquity, he showed how much the nobles were prized and valued as superior to the plebeians. Their high values were primarily set through their biological heredity, "when its origins hearkened back to heroes, and even gods, as progenitors," in contrast with plebeian who "sprang up from a useless and pernicious stock, was shrouded in obscurity and his name not remembered beyond his life."[339] Then, to strengthen his claim of bio-heredity as the nobles' distinguoshing factor Fritz cited a few lines of Theognis' poetry in its original Greek, the language of the oracle:

> *But about the bad nobody really cares.*
> *Never do the enslaved go upright,*
> *But the crooked necked are ever gnarled;*
> *As a squill doesn't bear roses or hyacinths,*
> *So neither does a slavette a free child.*[340]

The nobles' social advantage over masses came from their religiosity realized through "a covenant between gods and men which stipulated that provided the gods received honours and rites from men, they, for their part, would confer on them goodness and favours."[341] Being noble was a gods' gift, which was perpetuated through heredity and veneration of deities. The "nobles believed that their authority was ordained: the complete administration of all sacred rites was their sole prerogative. For that reason, they imagined the gods were propitious towards them but irate toward the plebeians." For they, unlike "the plebeians, unrestrained by religion, did not fear the gods."[342]

The same allotment of charges and duties, and therefore power, existed in the other areas of social relations. As the nobles were familiar with the "use of weapons" and possessed a "military understanding," thus military power, so they entrusted themselves with governing public affairs, excluding plebeians from any administrative position. The nobles were educated and knew laws, so they always could rule to their advantage "it is usual for a bad man to enact bad as right, and have no fear of retribution thereafter," because they were in principle corrupt people. The plebeians (the bad, useless and lowly, pernicious stock) were poor, ignorant, criminal, living in miserable conditions, surrounded by the same kind as they were, helplessly perpetuating their wretched lives throughout the generations. While the nobles (the good, optimates), on the other hand, were to be wealthy, virtuous, honorable, erudite, living in luxury and splendor in pursuit of dignity (*dignitate*) and to keep the plebeians "subjected and servile." "The dignity of the nobles, by means of which they were able to keep the plebeians subjected and servile, was based on the fame of an ancient lineage; on the ability to manage military and public affairs; on the administration of the sacra; on the splendour of wealth and luxury; on formation in the most noble arts; [and] ought to have absolutely no dealings with the plebeians."[343] Fritz after Theognis postulates further, that if a nobleman must deal with plebeians, "he should present himself with a most friendly demeanour, while, in fact, an inextinguishable anti-plebeian hatred burns within him."[344] A nobleman should treat a plebeian with distrust and deep contempt while showing polished and cordial countenance to enforce intellectual superiority.

Fritz repeats that the attributes of "good" and "bad" are given by the gods, not something that one could attain. In other words, fate is the ultimate agency assigning these conflicting moral values to people. The fate, which later will become a concept of *amor fati*, where the only intervention one could exercise, is to embrace and love whatever his fate would bring him. "Both good and bad are exclusively allotted by the gods to mortals, and that it lies entirely within their purview. 'No one ... is responsible for his own loss or gain / But rather the gods are the givers of each / No man labours knowing in his heart / Whether 'tis to a good or a bad end,'"[345] Fritz cited Theognis.

However, on the other hand, Fritz complains through his protagonist that some plebeians, by acquiring education and wealth, have trespassed into the nobles' realm. In doing so, they disrupted an ancient order of things and, in the end, corrupted the nobility by engulfing it into its own body, consequently eliminating it. "So, it came about that the nobles no longer separated themselves from the plebeians, but rather by intermarrying, they sought wealth, whilst the plebeians by such means strove after and received dignity."[346] This idea of vulgarization of nobleness Fritz later developed into a criticism of democracy, socialism, and other populous movements. In his opinion, the disappearance of human dignity diluted and flattened, in other words, vulgarized European culture.

Apparently, by discerning this loss, Fritz declared the need for its rein-statement. In the years to come, the concept would morph into and inform the other, the more sophisticated idea of *Übermensch*. Was he looking for a solution to this unsolvable argument of heredity, so he could attribute the nobleness to himself? But how? Or perhaps, he was merely testing his own humanness against the Theognis' measure? There are undeniable similarities between significance, dignity, and nobleness, which he used to determine his apparent uniqueness. Although, contrary to the inexorability of heredity, there clearly is scrolling an intrinsic allusion to his quest for greatness in the attempts at the problem. A cre-ative artistic process, a work of art, he later called it. Or was he merely looking for a meaning of dignity? What it means to become a significant, great, noble, dignified, or *Übermensch*-like person? In both instances, though, he envisioned this quest as a creative process. Not a rational scientific inquiry or scholarly phil-osophical speculation, but a process of creating a work of art, himself.

In the beginning of September 1864, almost by the end of his tenure at Pforta, Fritz, following his thesis' speculation about nobility and, perhaps, prompted by his loneliness and anxiety due to the possibility of not graduating, struck up a relationship with Baron Carl von Gersdorff." At first, Carl and Fritz were drawn together by a common interest in music, meeting each other for the first time in the Pforta music room.... By the time they left school, they had moved from the formal to the familiar 'you' (from *Sie* to *du*)."[347]

Somehow—as there are circulating different versions[348]—after the problems with failed subjects but brilliant achievements in Latin and German, Fritz graduated on September 7, 1864, and was allowed to give a talk to an assembly of students and faculty at the graduation ceremony together with all graduating students. We are lacking the originally written materials regarding the speech, however, as Philip Grundlehner claims, Fritz "obediently concurred so as to fulfill the final requisites of the authoritarian institution. In his remarks, he followed the protocol of humbly thanking God. ('He to whom I give most thanks'), the king ('I hope to bring honor to him and the fatherland'), as well as the school and its masters ('Perhaps I can bring joy to them in my later life').[349] On the same day, however, he wrote a short, untitled poem imploring the un-known God for guidance. It is his last poem before leaving Pforta, heading to a

new life in Bonn. He explored—not for an audience but for himself, he said—
the theme of separation, departure, and a new beginning in the form of expression, dearer to him than a formal Curriculum Vitae or a graduation speech.

> *Once more, before I wander on*
> *and turn my glance forward*
> *I lift up my hands to you in loneliness*
> *you, to whom I flee,*
> *to whom in the deepest depths of my heart*
> *I have solemnly consecrated altars*
> *So that your voice*
> *might summon me again.*
>
> *On them glows, deeply inscribed,*
> *the word: To the unknown god*
> *I am his, although until this hour*
> *I've remained in the wicked horde:*
> *I am his – and I feel the bonds*
> *That pull me down in my struggle*
> *and, would I flee,*
> *force me into his service.*
>
> *I want to know you, Unknown One*
> *you who have reached deep into my soul,*
> *into my life like the gust of storm*
> *you incomprehensible yet related One!*
> *I want to know you, even serve you*[350]

With grammatical mistakes and missing punctuation, this untitled piece was
written in a hurry, in the same way as his stream of consciousness work "On
Moods," a poem known as "To the Unknown God."

Grundlehner considers it as Fritz's most mature poetic work, describing escape from the austerity of institutional life into freedom of the unknown.

In its first line, Fritz looks back, once again (*Noch einmal*), at the moments of his life's turning points. The death of his father and leaving his childhood home at Röcken for Naumburg. The admission to Schulpforta, leaving Naumburg's Domgymnasium and home at 18 Weingarten. The renunciation of all his acquaintances and family while still at Pforta. And now, leaving behind the institution which provided the foundations and fatherly concern for his life. Then, in the same line, he looks into the future (*meine Blicke vorwärts sende*), coupling both, the opposites of past and the future, into one. Through yet another set of opposites—lifting his hands upward in the solemn prayer, and, at the same time, looking inwards into the depts of his soul—Fritz prays to the unknown god in the struggle (*Kampf*) between his deep devotion and fear in escaping his influence, and the break from the bonds and service to Him. But contrarily, he belongs to Him and flees the alliance with Him, simultaneously (*Sein bin ich – und ich fühl die Schlingen*). He is not praying to the Christian God he knew as a child, but the unknown god. It is an "allusion to Acts 17:23, where apostle Paul preaches in his Athens sermon: I found an altar with this description: *TO THE UNKNOWN GOD.* [Our young poet] thus shifts the context from the Christian God to a god of his *Urcharakter*, his rudimentary character, as he did in 'Now and Formerly' *(Jetz und echedem)*"[351] His main issue thus is the struggle (*Kampf*) "in the Old Testament sense of Jacob wrestling with the angel in order to know God (*Genesis* 32:26)."[352]

Through writing this poem, Fritz explicitly declared that the struggle always existed in his works. From the moment he lost his father when his life went out of joint, it took root in his writing life. Though tragic, it did leave him with an ultimately positive outcome, for "the struggle (*Kampf*) between opposite forces, makes possible the achievement of a new level of inner consciousness," Grundlehner reads Fritz's poetry. It became the pivotal element, a *modus operandi* of his entire creative life. Without it, there possibly would be no Nietzsche, he concludes.

The graduation ceremony at Pforta was quite elaborate and pompous. "After the boys' speeches, a valedictory poem was read, the rector delivered an oration and, intermittently, the choir sang songs of farewell. However, the point of graduation was to leave, and Pforta had woven this culmination into the ceremony itself. Once the various addresses were completed, the students adjourned outdoors and waited until the horns of postilions sounded and one or more coaches garlanded with flowers drew up. As the undergraduates cheered, the departing alumni stowed their luggage and ducked inside. The horns then sounded anew, the coachmen snapped their reins, and the horses stepped forward, dragging the wagon from the walled school-state into the world at large."[353]

Fritz, leaving Pforta with Deussen and six other graduates knew from past experiences that severing with the old would always be necessary part of his life, because it would inevitably provide possibilities for the new.

Peter Sloterdijk in *Thinker on Stage* provides a conjecture of an act of leaving, claiming that it is essentiality a path towards oneself, unifying two opposites—leaving and coming back to oneself—into one chiasmic unity.

One begins with a motivational onset for his search, maintaining that only people who can admit that their life is unendurable can start on the path to an art of living (*Lebenskunst*). Acknowledging, however, that this mindset can derail into a merely theoretical search, lacking any concrete transformations and instead allowing for the continuation of the same miserable life under the veil of delusional contentment. If one is genuinely seeking oneself, the act of leaving oneself behind becomes a necessity.

The unveiled and unreleased "true self" is the cause of pain, which induces the potentiality to seek after it. Only people who allow themselves to feel pain would then begin looking for the self, which would alleviate their misery, "cease suffering on its own account (*an sich*)." Therefore, only the people who can "escape" from themselves can "find" themselves in that escape. The "escape" is in itself the path of leaving oneself behind, which, at the same time, is the path of finding oneself–in itself: "the will to a path."

Only in the act of leaving, the seeker is able to find the reason for leaving: to find the cause in the effect. A priori speculations of arranging are futile; only an act of leaving itself reveals the cause post factum, undermining the common assumption of cause-effect succession.[354]

"Through the act of leaving, the wanderer begins to discover what he has taken with him in spite of himself, just when he thought he had left everything behind. The true self clings to the heels of the one who is embarking on the path. But only when the wanderer realizes that he himself constitutes his own heaviest baggage can the 'dialectic of the path' begin. Through the efforts made to flee, and also through the stimuli that accompany any meaningful exodus, his powers increase to such an extent that he can recognize and endure what, in leaving, he had not wanted to recognize and endure: the unendurable self. Only along the way does it become apparent how little of what the traveler has driven out of himself really allows itself to be shaken off."[355] And parting was not as easy as Fritz has imagined.

On September 9, 1864, a day after he departed from Pforta, staying at his mother's house in Naumburg, where he arrived with his classmate Deussen, Fritz wrote a thank you letter to Hermann Kletschke, his last tutor in Pforta. "I do not want to let the first days of a new life pass by without expressing thanks, if only in writing, that I owe you.... I only wish that I can give you joy through my future life, and this way, I can give you inadequate thanks,"[356] Your Grateful Assistant, he signed it.

*Part II*

**Free At Last**

# 3

## MY BONN EXPERIMENT

After a little over two weeks in Naumburg, on September 23, Fritz and Deussen began their journey towards Bonn to commence a new academic year at the Bonn University in the middle of October. Their first stop was in Elberfeld, over four hundred kilometers west of Naumburg, where they visited Deussen's cousins.

After the arrival, Fritz wrote to his mother and Elizabeth, describing his trip and first encounter with Catholic Germany, and the taste of freedom after six years of living under total institutional control of Pforta.

*The trip in itself was not much pleasant and of no interest; first, sleepy, snoring travel companions; then, very talkative, noisy, ordinary factory workers, merchants and demanding old ladies; I could tell a story about each of them. We arrived tired and a little grumpy around 11:00 in the evening; you can imagine how "fabulous" such a trip is. We stayed at Brünings', two not too old women and their brother, bedridden with gastric fever. We refreshed ourselves here with wine and bread and went to bed, slept well, got up late, had breakfast - here as everywhere excellent pastries and slices of pumpernickel – then went to Röhrs. There Johanna and Marie were at home; nice girls, however not for me, a bit tasteless in their clothes. They are under the care of an old, very pietistic lady, with whom I got involved the following day in a lengthy dispute about the theater, 'the work of the devil;' I held my position well but was pitied by her for my views. Today we are invited to her for coffee. On Sunday, I met Ernst Schnabel, a young, ex-*

*tremely amiable businessman; he is Deussen's good friend and romantic rival; then Friedrich Deussen, who has a shop here. In the afternoon, we went together to the hills surrounding the Elberfeld. Imagine a long, beautiful Wuppertal valley, through which several cities without definite boundaries stretch like a long, robust chain of factories, one of which is Elberfeld. The town is extremely commercial; the houses are primarily clad in slate on the outside. The women you can see, I noticed particularly fondness for pious head hanging. The young women dress very elegantly, wearing coats with a very narrow waistline like those of Kösener Polin. The gentlemen wear Havana colors, hats, pants, etc.*

*On Sunday afternoon, we went to several restaurants with Ernst Schnabel until 11:00 in the evening. We drunk an excellent Mosel wine, "Pastors Moselkensas," as Ernst called it. Improvising on the piano has not a small effect; I was given a toast. As Lisbeth would say, Ernst is thoroughly enchanted; where I am, I have to play, it is ridiculous. Yesterday afternoon we drove to Schwelm, a neighboring bathing resort, visited the Rothaar Mountains, a well-known site of the old Vehmic court, we went all over the place. In the evening, I played in a tavern, without knowing, in the presence of a renowned music director who later stood there with his mouth ajar. He invited me to participate in his choral club in the evening. Which I didn't do. We drove back and were invited to dine with Schnabel's family. Nice, good people, splendid women, reasonable, pious, conservative. Merchants. You eat well here and drink still better, but you eat different dishes than ours—Swiss cheese and pumpernickel three times a day.*

*Tomorrow morning, we will start with the Rhine trip to be in Oberdreis the day after tomorrow. Ernst Schnabel travels with us. You will get a message from there soon.*[357]

It seems that Fritz, while letting himself go, was nonetheless attentively observing all the details of this new world. He must have felt like a visitor to an amusement park, where they were having fun as young boys do.

After a short stay in Elberfeld, the boys traveled over one hundred kilometers south to Deussen's family home in Oberdreis. Fritz reported on their travels again to his mother and Elisabeth, naturally omitting certain details, like getting drunk, making a riot while trying to pick up girls, and riding horses with Paul and Ernst.[358]

"I would very much like to give you news about me before my birthday, which unfortunately I cannot spend in Bonn. I will instead celebrate it here since Pastore Deussen's wife has her birthday on the same day.... Afterward, on October 16, we'll leave early for Bonn. So, I don't expect any letters or gifts on my birthday – the delivery to these areas is difficult.

"On the last evening in Elberfeld, I made an interesting acquaintance with a wealthy Parisian merchant, Ingelbach, related to Deussens. Paul, his father Friedrich Deussen, and I were with him in a hotel until late at night, dined exceptionally fine, drank Bordeaux wines, and talked about his favorite subjects, religious matters. It was a joy. Next year he will visit us for a few days in Bonn....

"Our Rhine trip was wonderful. These days, I longed again for this magnificent green current, looking truly forward to Bonn.

"I wish that you got to know the pastor's wife. She is of such learning, the subtlety of feelings and speech, and such diligence, which is rarely seen in many others. All different people praise this woman. Pastor Deussen is entirely under her influence. Although he is an honest, good, and wonderful man, however, is not always consequent. Pastor's sons are all efficient people like most mechanical engineers. But daughter Marie Deussen despite her youth is an attractive, very intellectual girl, who occasionally reminds me of you dear Lisbeth, which is why I cannot deny her my special favor, of course. Like her mother, she is incredibly active."[359]

Fritz played piano with Marie and dedicated some of his compositions to her, like a year ago to Anna Redtel. However, gathering from the letters he sent his mother and sister, he is more interested in *Frau Pastorin*, his friend's mother, Elisabeth Deussen, than Marie. In all letters he sent home to Naumburg during the trip, he did not fail to praise her.

"We arrived in Altenkirchen in terrible weather an hour ago. I went there with Ernst Schnabel to buy a birthday present for *Frau Pastorin*, namely a piano cover because we had once overheard such a wish from her. Unfortunately, the small town offered nothing at all, and we have nothing to bring but our goodwill.

We live here very comfortably. Yesterday was the so-called *Schlör* at the parish, where the flax is broken and rolled. There were over 30 people from the parish. *Frau Pastorin* and her daughter came to visit. You can imagine the trouble, but she always keeps her serene calm, whatever she is doing, and does not allow herself to rest for a moment. Saturday is one of the biggest festivals for the parish and the surrounding area. *Frau Pastorin* Elisabeth Deussen and I have a birthday together."[360]

Fritz wrote about festivals, markets, fairs, and holidays providing a sketchy view of the everyday life of folk in the countryside, which, it seems, he enjoyed. His health also improved because of the long walks amid tiny hamlets and towns, sometimes for four to seven hours per day. "I recover a lot. So, I can start working all the more efficiently,"[361] he wrote, getting ready for his new life at the Bonn University.

On October 15, 1864, was his twentieth birthday which he celebrated with Frau Deussen, and again, he wrote home. "Early in the morning, we sang a four-part chorale "Praise the Lord, oh My Soul" outside Frau Pastor Deussen's bedroom. ... In the evening, we played party games on the grass and did some dancing. ... Early the next morning, we traveled six hours to Neuwied, having taken a moving farewell. We were a little tired when we got to the steamship and arrived in Bonn at about 4 o'clock,"[362] already in his new apartment in Bonn, dedicating rest of the letter to his continuously prohibitive financial situation. His life's next chapter had already begun.

Fritz found an apartment on the second floor of a house at Bonngasse 518. "A very nice house at the corner of two lively streets with a balcony, pleasant and very clean. [The apartment is] spacious, with three large windows, everything elegant, clean, and with a sofa,"[363] he wrote his mother, surely being aware that his apartment in the centrum of Bonn was near the Ludwig van Beethoven's birthplace on the same street, at number 20. After settling down in two separate apartments instead of living together, for it was cheaper, Fritz and Deussen started on making rounds with their letters of recommendations, visiting different professors.

He brought with him references from Professor Carl Steinhart written on September 7, 1864, introducing him as a boy of "a profound, pensive nature, enthusiastically inclined towards philosophy, particularly towards the Platonic one, in which he is already fairly immersed. He still vacillates between theology and philology; however, the latter will very likely win, and particularly, under its guidance, he will turn to philosophy, to which his innermost striving leads him, after all."[364] But the letter did not make much of an impression on the faculty in Bonn. On top of it, he could not register for classes due to his prevalent and humiliating lack of money, which certainly complicated his transition to an independent academic life. He outpoured his frustrations and anger in each of the letters home brazenly reminding about "the old complaint," while listing his expenses and demanding money.

After two weeks that took him to raise the required amount, he finally registered for classical philology classes, as well as, perhaps trying to please his mother, theology. Choosing two majors, he was facing quite a large load of classes. Apart from the circumstances of family expectations and his own developing anti-Christianity, his indecision still showed his lack of independence in the inability to decide on his field of study. Or perhaps it was an intentional move to gather enough information about the subjects to choose the most feasible career path for himself later.

Recounting Fritz's attitude towards Christianity and authority, historian Daniel Blue, rigidly searching for definitive answers, labels Fritz as hypocritical.[365] Except, I think, it is otherwise. Fritz, even as a child, was full of groundless hubris and the tendency to self-promotion. He knew exactly what to do to foster the notion of himself as a different, significant person. Looking at his photographs from the period, I wonder if the little emotive smirk contorting his lips was a pose or an actual display of cynicism mixed with contempt.

Nonetheless, whether it was a roleplaying or an ingrained character trait, Fritz's choices were uniquely geared toward shaping his persona into someone superior to others, with the great men of Greek antiquity, always on his mind.

Enthusiastic about receiving the coffeemaker and other goods from his mother, Fritz, immediately, after moving into his first in life apartment, rented a pianino, bought an oil lamp, and several other essential things. In the same first letter from Bonn to Franziska, he listed other necessities together with a litany of anticipated expenses, not including a penny for entertainment (*Kein Pfennig für eine Vergnügung*). Then he requested a large sum of the allowance money, in the end scolding his mother that the money did not arrive, reminded her about the *Paupertätszeugniß,* proof of poverty needed for a scholarship. He ends the letter with the commanding tone: *Vergeßt das ja nicht!* Don't forget that![366]

After his life in a provincial, medieval town of Naumburg and six years of monastic austerity at Pforta, Bonn seemed such a metropolis, especially when one could participate in the cultural events in nearby Cologne, one of the largest cities in Germany. However, besides the availability of theater, opera, and philharmonic, for Fritz, one of the most disturbing features of the region was Catholicism, which prevailed regardless of the Bonn-Cologne metropolis, being a part of the Kingdom of Prussia. Fritz, who could see from his apartment's window a Jesuit church across the street, complained about the university's observance of the Catholic calendar instead of Protestant, which, on the other hand, is interesting in itself considering he was in the process of becoming an atheist.

When choosing his classes, Fritz did it with an unrestrained excess. He registered for two classical philology classes; one with Friedrich Ritschl and the second one with Otto Jahn on Plato's *Symposium*[367]—both famous philologists although in continuous and escalating enmity; two theology classes, one on the *Gospel according to John* and the other one, thought by Wilhelm Ludwig Krafft, on the history of the early Church; two classes in the history of art with art historian Anton Springer and one course in politics with Heinrich von Sybel, a historian and politician.

Blue claims that Fritz did it against the university's rules; however, he managed to attend all seven classes, because after all, in the German system of higher education, then as now, no one really cared how the students perform.

The students were entirely on their own.[368] In contrast to middle school educa-tion, where the rules are stringent, compared sometimes to a monastic or prison routine, the educational system at the university level is wholly relaxed to the point that some students cannot adjust, get lost and fall out from the system. "In Prussia, these external structures were deliberately withdrawn. Students could study what they wanted. They were rarely monitored to ensure showing up for classes or given neither tests nor grades. Instead, having presumably 'learned how to learn' at the Gymnasium, they were expected to use their new freedom to develop their own compass and to set their course through a self-imposed and self-disciplined pursuit of knowledge. At a Prussian university, one didn't receive an education; one accomplished it oneself, and the school system as-sured this by suspending students in a disciplinary vacuum. As one historian remarked, 'After [the student] has matriculated, and has given his hand to the rector in token of his promise to obey the laws of the university, no official in-quiries about him for several years; he is left entirely to his own devices.'"[369]

For the free-spirited and independent Fritz, it was the most advanta-geous situation. In contrast to the rigid structures of Pforta that he had diffi-culties navigating, at Bonn he felt like an eel finally reaching the see. He could do as pleased to pursue his task of self-development as part of his studies, rather than as a distraction from them. For Fritz, time in Bonn was a contin-uous Dionysian orgy of new experiences, a diverse storm of new and exciting ideas: listening to the greatest opera singers and concerts, improvising on pi-ano, getting drunk, singing in a chorus sacred German music, participating and watching *Mensuren* (academic fencing), reading philosophy, falling in love with actors and visiting brothels, partying at nights on the Rhine in the light of the torches, borrowing money then recklessly spending it, arguing in drunken screaming matches; in other words, experiencing the freedom to have fun, dis-appointments, and sorrows.

In all of his classes, beyond their face value subjects of theology or phi-lology, Fritz searched for buried philosophical content to pursue it independently. According to Brobjer, during the winter semester of 1864-65, Fritz read his first book on the subject of general philosophy by Karl Fortlage, *The Genetic History of Philosophy since Kant (Genetische Geschichte der Philosophie seit Kant, 1852).*

"Fortlage strongly emphasized Kant's importance and can be regarded as a neo-Kantian but also had a strong sympathy for Fichte. The work consists of a thorough discussion of German philosophy from Kant until the middle of the nineteenth century. It begins with a seventy-five-page account of Kant's philosophy followed by a discussion of several major philosophers, most extensively Fichte, Schelling, and Hegel (40-60 pages each), but also Schopenhauer (pp. 407-23). The book ends with four shorter and more general chapters: *The Relation between Philosophy and Socialism* (pp. 456-76), *A Comparison of the Different Systems* (pp. 477-82), *Philosophical Habits and Methods* (pp. 482-84), and *Skepticism as the only True Position of Science* (pp. 484-88)."[370]

Within a couple of weeks of his arrival in Bonn Fritz wrote to his tutor at Pforta, Kletschke, about his courses enrollment. Oddly, though perhaps not too surprising considering his growing interest in philosophy, he wrote that he enrolled in the theology and philosophy classes, omitting his second major, philology. "Perhaps you would like to learn what I have done and what I will do today. At eight in the morning, I listened to church history by Krafft. I am enrolled in theology and philosophy in which, I believe I followed your advice. However, I am not very satisfied with this college at the moment; it does not contain much inspiration....

"At ten o'clock, I attended Springer lecturing about German art history. I am pleased to get acquainted with this witty man by participating in an art seminar he has just started. At 12 noon, I attended Jahn, who began his lectures on the Platonic *Symposium* today. You surely imagine how pleased I must be to hear an excellent philologist talk about a work of antiquity that I particularly love. This afternoon Ritschl is also lecturing for the first time about *Miles Gloriosus*,"[371] he wrote, forgetting of the previously declared break with his past.

It seems that Fritz was not satisfied with the curriculum offered by the university right from the beginning. He criticized it as lacking inspiration (*es enthält wenig Anregendes*), so he supplemented it with his own research, outside his supposedly main subject of study, classical philology. When looking from the perspective of someone interested in contemporary culture, all those lectures contained a kernel of philosophical contemporaneity comprised within them, whether it to be the church's history, history of art, theatre plays, and politics. It all depended on the attitude of the listener. So, it appeared that Fritz was selectively studying only the subjects which could expand his rising interests in philosophy.

Having so much to do at the university and privately in the pursuit of self-advancement never stopped Fritz from partying; he participated in drunken revelries, frequent trips to Cologne to attend concerts, theater and opera, and nightly excursions on the Rhine, lit by torches, with plenty of wine going around.

On top of all those commitments, he joined a student fraternity (*Burschenschaft*), a radical student organization at the University of Bonn, the Franconia. The movement of student fraternities at German universities was originated, not long before Fritz's time, in 1815 "by young Germans recently returned from the 'wars of liberation' against Napoleon's armies of occupation"[372] to promote united and liberal Germany. However, by Fritz's time at the university, they had degenerated to mostly drinking, dueling to get a dueling scar, and networking associations. "Membership usually had (and still has), however, a serious, ulterior purpose: establishing connections with future leaders of industry and politics that would be useful in later life. To his mother, unimpressed by the fraternity phenomenon, Nietzsche put this in more elevated terms: the fraternities were, he wrote, 'the future of Germany and the nursery of German parliaments,'"[373] he writes, never forgetting his aim at reaching the highest echelons of the society. Hayman describes the fraternities' movement in Germany as congregations of young men "singing patriotic songs and parading through the streets in uniforms, behind a military band. During the 1930s, the Hitler Youth would be built up over the tradition of the *Burschenschaften*, taking advantage of the fact that, as in the nineteenth century, boys would join not for political or ideological but social reasons."[374]

During the first, winter semester Fritz was so eager to experience newfound freedom when he slipped out from under the control of family and Pforta that quite often, he was drunk to the point of having a hangover, forgetting his past experiences with alcohol. "Having wrenched myself out of bed, I am writing this morning in a direct refutation of the opinion that I have a *Kater*. You will not know this hairy-tailed animal. Yesterday evening we had a great assembly, ceremonially singing 'Landesvater' and endlessly drinking punch.... Yesterday's *Gemütlichkeit* was splendid, edifying. You know, at assemblies like this, there is a general buoyancy (*exultation*) of the soul. It is not just beery *Gemütlichkeit* (*beer induced sociability*),"[375] he wrote his sister between December 11 and 12, 1864. Perhaps he was not having as much fun as he described it to Elisabeth but was merely playing along with the rest of the boys. Except, Deussen spoke about Fritz and himself as "not taking much pleasure in it. The ridiculous patriotic rituals had a little attraction for us cosmopolitans; we found the mandatory drinking bouts on the tavern evenings disgusting. The pedantic instructions which the pledge master gave us in chapter and verse on the most trivial things seem ridiculous to us, and when on almost all Sunday evenings we had to skip lectures, no matter how interesting they might be, in order to watch Franconians and Alemannians slashing their faces in a faraway barn outside the city, we could not really enjoy that either."[376]

Nonetheless, Fritz still went along and participated in a duel, a type of academic fencing called *Mensur*. Today, it is still popular with fraternities in Germany, Austria, Switzerland, Latvia, Estonia, Belgium, Lithuania, and Poland, a rigidly regulated rapier fight with sharp weapons.

According to Deussen, Fritz described an accidental encounter: "Yesterday, after the tavern evening, I went to the market for a walk. An Alemannian joined me; we had a very lovely discussion on all kinds of topics in art and literature, and upon parting, I asked him most politely to 'hang one' on me. He agreed, and as soon as possible, we will have a go at each other."[377] Within a few days, they met. According to Deussen's testimony, the duel was over within three minutes, providing Fritz with a small scar across the bridge of his nose which, for whatever reason, is not visible on his later photographs.

Still, despite the growing burden of responsibilities, Fritz did not stop there. Although always unsure of his musical talent he joined the community chorus, where he sang bass. Then, perhaps stimulated by improvising and attending opera and concert halls in Cologne, Fritz started to compose again.

Maybe he was unsure about his musical aptitude, but undeniably, he could not live without music. It was an essential element of his life, or better, as Georges Liéber explains it, music was his life. "Music is not just present in Nietzsche's work in an explicit way, in the form of critical analysis and commentaries, [but] it constitutes a constant reference as well as an invisible framework."[378]

At the beginning of December 1864, Fritz knew that he would not travel back home for Christmas due to a disastrous money shortage. And he was not invited to Deussens's. His friend's extended family was coming to celebrate Christmas at the house in Oberdreis. In a letter from December 7-9, 1864, he asked his mother for a Christmas present of Schumann's piano reduction to Byron's *Manfred*, well in advance so it would be delivered on time. "I will spend the holidays alone; I think I will appreciate gifts all the more. [So], don't forget 'Manfred,'" he repeated his request again, signing it with the Franconia emblem.[379]

Under Schumann's spell (Fritz already paid homage at his tomb by laying a wreath there), he composed Schumann-inspired eight *lieder* as Christmas presents for Elisabeth. "He bound the manuscript for her in lilac-colored morocco with a silhouette of himself stacked to the front"[380] and attached a letter with very detailed instructions on how to play the pieces.[381] Almost immediately afterward, he wrote home again. He instructed Elisabeth not to open the package before Christmas or ask for a reason for his image on it. Then, becoming deeply nostalgic, expressed his deep yearning for home: "I do hope you will have a Christmas tree with lights ...We will light a tree in the tavern, but naturally that's only a pale reflection of how we celebrate at home, for the main thing, the family and circle of relatives, is missing.... Do you remember what wonderful Christmases we had in Gorenzen? ... It was so lovely; the house and the village in the snow, the evening service, my head full of melodies, the togetherness ... and me in my nightshirt, the cold, and many merry and serious things. Altogether a delightful atmosphere. When I play my *Eine Sylvesternacht* (New Year's Eve), it is this that I hear in the sounds."[382]

Fritz became ecstatic when *Manfred* score, a present from Aunt Rosalie, arrived on Christmas day. He played the four-hands score with one of the frat boys.

It was his first Christmas spent outside his family—or any other family, in that case—alone. He was alone because of circumstances beyond his control. However, he immediately rationalized it as a necessary locus for his endeavor: only by being alone could he set foot through Schumann's music on the Byron-Manfred's path of *Übermensch*. But mere physical loneliness was not enough. It had to embody longing for disappearing refuge of faith, comforts, and familiarity of tradition, the homeliness of family life. Only within a contradiction—the collision of refuting and hankering for the Christian tradition, simultaneously—could Fritz begin his quest for a springboard onto the trajectory of self-fashioning.

During the week between Christmas and New Year's, he was planning to write a New Year's wish to his mother in verses, as he used to do, but he got sick again. "It may be that I now demand much more of a poem. It may be that I am slightly more sober and practical, which would not be a bad thing. It may be that the diabolical toothache which tormented me is driving out any possibility of rousing enthusiasm. ... I love New Year's Eve and birthdays, for they allow us hours – which admittedly we can often create for ourselves, but seldom do – in which the soul can stand still and review a phase of its own development. Crucial resolutions are born in such moments. I am accustomed on these occasions to bring out the manuscripts and letters of past years and to make notes. For a few hours, one is raised above time and almost steps outside one's own development. One secures and documents the past and receives the courage and resoluteness to resume traveling along one's path. It's lovely when the blessings and wishes of the relatives fall like a mild rain on these resolutions and decisions, the first seeds of the future,"[383] he writes to his mother and sister, at the end of 1864, preparing them for the expected changes in his life.

Fritz's mother Franziska did not spend Christmas at her home in Naumburg either but traveled to the nearby town, for—as she wrote to Fritz—"to stay here is almost impossible without you." As for Elisabeth, she had begun to discover in her brother's absence that her friendships with Naumburg's upper crust were shallower than she had realized. Neither she nor her mother were invited to several social events (including a dance hosted by the Pinders), and apparently, she was both surprised and hurt by this ostracism. Franziska had counseled, 'Don't count too much on friendship; rank and class prevail,'"[384] which succinctly reflects their compliant and an accepting attitude towards the matters of social standing—entirely contrary to Fritz's inflated views of his provenance.

During the gloomy and lonely last night of the year 1864, Fritz wrote a short essay, "A New Year's Eve Dream" (*Ein Sylvestertraum*), inspired by Schumann's music. He resurrected the old ideas conceived three years ago, almost to the day, in "On the Dramatic Works of Byron."

*It is quiet in my room; every now and then, coals crackle in the hearth. I turned down the lamp. There is no light in the room, only the flickering glow of the stove's fire slipping on the floor and mahogany of my pianino.*

*It is the last hours before midnight; I have rummaged through my manuscripts and letters, drank hot punch, then played the requiem from the Schumann's Manfred. Now, I want to leave everything behind and only think of myself.*

*So, I kindle the fire again, then returned to the sofa, laid my head on my left hand, close my eyes and think. The spirit quickly flies over to the sites it loves in Naumburg, in Pforta and Plauen, then finally returns to my room. My room? But what do I see on my bed? Someone lies there – he moans softly and wheezes – a dying man! And not alone! Shadows seem to hover around. Yes, the shadows speak.*

*"You bad year, what did you promise me and what promises you did not keep? I'm more miserable than ever, and you told me I should be fortunate (Glück). Be cursed! Dear year, you looked at me with the sinister eye, but your May comforted me, and your autumn was the nostalgic trace of May. Be blessed!*

*Old year! You have brought so much pain (Mühe), but you also rewarded (entschädigt) me. So, we owe ourselves nothing. Farewell! I have eagerly waited, looking out when you will fulfill my wishes (Wünsche). Do it now, in your last hour. Help me!"*

*But everything was silent. The old year wheezed quietly and steadily. It sounded like sighing.*

*Suddenly everything grew bright. The walls of the room flew back, the ceiling floated up. I looked towards the bed, but it was empty. Then I hear a voice:*

*"You fools! Fools of time that is not, and nowhere, but in your mind! I ask you, what have you done? If you want to be and have what you hope for, what you are waiting for. Do what the gods have laid in front of you as the price for your struggle (Kampfpreis). When you are ready, the fruit*

*will fall, but not before!"*
*Then the hand of a clock moved into an upright position.*
*Everything disappeared. The clock struck twelve. On the*
*streets, people loudly cried: "Happy New Year!" – [385]*

What a picturesque, romantic dream! Or, perhaps a daydream, or a vision induced by music: a nostalgia after the family tradition celebrating the New Year. Although, as these are all the attempts at elucidations, one thing cannot be overlooked: it is again an autobiographical piece projecting the task of interpreting the past to prevision the future. And, it is without a doubt, a premonition of Fritz's future literary style, when words would invoke—instead of dry and soulless descriptions—a range of sounds, smells, and images.

Then again, the breaking with the past, "leaving the past behind" to concentrate solely on the author's own future. But the egocentric approach to his project was essential to sustain its budding conditions: to cultivate oneself, one must necessarily focus on oneself only. The only way to do it is through a struggle, wherein lurks a solution; but still, one must take on a fight: "what are you waiting for, do what the gods have laid in front of you as the price for your struggle."[386] It is the way of bringing not mere consolation, but planting the seeds of creativity as a product of pain, ever-present death, and lost love. It is quite unlike the ordinary people, who are desperately clinging to the passing of time, seeing in its elapsing the release from their ills. They console themselves with hope that without doing anything, something "better" will always come along.

But Fritz was standing on the completely opposite site from the others: everything concerning himself was about literally doing. The piece is about the beginning of Fritz's serious ontological concerns, social critique, and a modus operandi of the project of himself as a subject dressed splendidly with the images from his past.

On January 11 he wrote the first letter of 1865 to Aunt Rosalie about putting back some discipline into his life. He started getting up at six in the morning instead of 8, which was quite frequent before Christmas of 1864.[387] Shortly after the letter, he returned his rented piano, probably to save some money. Nonetheless, he frequently traveled to Cologne, only 30 kilometers away from Bonn, to attend theater, operas, and concerts. He heard such singers like Adelina Patti, an Italian who was considered the best opera singer who ever lived, and a German soprano Jenny Bürde-Ney. He saw on the stage such actors like Marie Seebach and Friederike Goßmann. "We Franconians were naturally in love with them. We shouted their songs across the beer-table, and drunk toasts,"[388] Fritz wrote to his mother on February 2, 1865. Next, he described planned changes concerning his education and future career. First, because Bonn was too expensive, he decided that the summer term will be his last semester there, listing all the expenses as a justification for his decision. Next, Fritz wrote that he has shown his songs he sent her for Christmas to the choir director, Caspar Brambach, to whom he "spoke in detail" and who was probably negatively critical of the works, for he suggested taking lessons in counterpoint. Fritz could not afford lessons, so instead, he gave up composition again, ipso facto giving up on any prospect of musical career:[389] "I really don't have the opportunity to [train myself in music] in Bonn. Perhaps on New Year's, I wrote to you that I didn't want to write or compose this year,"[390] he confessed to his pen pal von Gersdorff. Although, "having renounced theology, music tempted him more than ever," claims Liébert, "yet even though he is flattered to pass for 'an authority' on such things among his fellow students, he was aware of his shortcomings. 'I am becoming a bit too critical to be able to deceive myself about my possible talent any longer,' he writes [again] to his friend Gersdorff in August 1865."[391] Thus, he "has made a firm decision not to compose anything this year." Then, he announced, without any further explanation, that he decided not to take theology classes in the summer semester but concentrate on a single major, classical philology.[392] It was a prelude to what would occur within a couple of months, during the Easter break, at home in Naumburg.

Two months before Easter, on February 18, 1865, he traveled to Cologne again, but this time for a reason other than sightseeing or attending a performance or concert. Instead, he planned to indulge in a not so cultural activity: he tried to lose his virginity at a brothel. If we to believe Deussen—the only source in that matter—this was Fritz's exploit against his new principles. It appears, that he was trying rationally to fit-in. The decision to visit a brothel was in agreement with Franconians' devotion to having a good time. Still, the whole endeavor was performed against his own will, for Fritz was most of the time implicitly critical of Franconians' conducts.

According to Pletsch, "he objected to the clause that no longer required strict sexual abstinence of fraternity members. Apparently, it was no secret to Nietzsche that fraternity brothers 'who wanted to sin went secretly to Cologne,' and that disturbed him. [His] efforts to be a dashing member of the Franconia were not very successful. One of his fraternity brothers later recorded that Nietzsche had not given a very jovial impression; he seemed unable to loosen up. And in fact, Nietzsche never did have a sense of humor in social situations; his wit was reserved for his writing or was so ironical as to seem unpleasant. He knew that his fellows were only partially convinced. Fritz wrote to his mother that, while he was not disliked, he was best known for being satirical and mocking. He was often unhappy, too moody, and frequently bothersome to himself and to others. He wanted very much to be liked but recognized that he was neither successful nor happy doing what it took to be well-liked by other members."[393]

So, he lived in a continuous dissonance between trying to be one of the frat boys and becoming a significant person, although, the latter was a pose as well, a mask he wore throughout his entire life. Fritz's multiplicity of attitudes, of objecting to the lack of compliance with chastity rules, but, at the same time, going along with the typical attitude towards losing virginity and, entirely outside the standard norms, self-cultivating his own greatness, were just a tip of entanglements in his many disguises. As one of his fellow students later noted, it reached the point of such a multi-identity that he concealed "a complete man and woman, oddly coupled inside a single body."[394]

Deussen claimed that Fritz, like Plato, *mulierem nunquam attingit* (he never touched a woman). This character trait was exemplified by Fritz allegedly telling Deussen about his visit to Cologne's brothel. "I found myself suddenly surrounded by half a dozen apparitions in tinsel and gauze, looking at me expectantly. For a short space of time, I was speechless. Then I made instinctively for the piano as being the only soulful thing present. I struck a few chords, which freed me from my paralysis, and I escaped."[395]

As no one from the fraternity brothers accompanied Fritz, why had he told Deussen the story of his unsuccessful attempt at getting laid? Was it a repulsion or fright of the "soulless apparitions" he encountered for the first time in his life, which, at the moment of storytelling, morphed into a condemnation of the entire enterprise of visiting brothels as an unwritten, although fraternity's *a must* rule? Or was he a supercilious man, beyond sexual urges and corporeal gratification?

Torn in all directions, in mid-April of 1865, Fritz traveled to Naumburg for the Easter vacations. He brought several books (over twenty) to read during the break. He listed them in order of importance: David Strauss's *The Life of Jesus*, August Reissmann's book on German music history, Adolf Bernhard Marx's *Ludwig van Beethoven: Leben und Schaffen*, and Karl Fortlage's *The Genetic History of Philosophy Since Kant*. The rest of the books concerned poetry, music, theology, and philology.[396] Of this large haul, the most critical position was held by Strauss's volume.

Fritz was introduced to David Friedrich Strauss' *The Life of Jesus* (1835), probably in the class of Professor Krafft. As the book was quite popular, Strauss republished it under a new title, *The Life of Jesus, Reworked for the German People* in 1864. Fritz, who certainly knew the work as most of Germany, purchased it and persuaded Deussen to buy it as well. Though, the second version, addressed to a broader readership, was not as good as the original, the main idea was as perturbing as the one in the initial release. Strauss refuted two predominant schools of theological thought concerning the notion of miracles by characterizing them as mythical and trying to prove their invalidity through science. He explained the problem by claiming that the gospel was mainly a myth, invented by people like any other literary production.

Strauss's work was not the only influencing factor on Fritz's decision to break with Christianity. Still, it became a pivotal turning point of openly repudiating the church's doctrine, although not the faith itself. After reviewing the list of readings, it becomes apparent that Fritz's interest in music and poetry, regardless of his assurances, did not evaporate overnight. As well as one may notice a significant and consistent interest in reading philosophy, including new ideas regarding Christianity's social implications.

He arrived at home laden with books and a boisterous attitude to put the record straight. In the first words, he notified both his mother and sister that he dropped theology and will continue solely with philology. In one drastic gesture, he outright rebelled against the long-standing family tradition of becoming a clergyman. Brandishing the Strauss's book in front of their noses, he refused to participate in the Easter services or take the Holy Communion. Both mother and sister were devastated, but Fritz was transforming himself in front of their eyes. It transpired only at the family's micro-level; however, it was the first explicitly displayed step towards social criticism and contemplative conduct of life, unceasing throughout his lifetime.

As Fritz decided to leave Bonn for it felt unwelcome, foreign, and unaffordable, he considered an alternative, the University of Leipzig where he could feel at home—Leipzig is only 50 kilometers from Naumburg. "He was trying to live in the same style as before coming to Bonn – 'that is to say without being extravagant, but without setting narrow limits of being parsimonious. It would have been wrong to give the impression of being a poor man,'"[397] he concluded that money his mother could provide him with was simply not enough for his expenses.

During his second semester at Bonn, Fritz attended six lectures and seminars, only one class fewer than during the first semester. Although his major was classical philology now, he took only two courses on the subject, one by Jahn and the other by Ritschl. He continued with Springer's art history and took one class by Karl Joseph Simrock on a medieval poet, Walther von der Vogelweide. The additional two classes, "Plato's Life and Teaching" and "Outline of the History of Philosophy" were taught by philosopher Karl Schaarschmidt.

Thomas Brobjer, in *Nietzsche's Philosophical Context*, lists the paraphrased philosophy lectures' themes from Fritz's unpublished notes he took during the studies. They were primarily introductions to Indian philosophy; Greek philosophy from the sophists to Hellenistic times; Greek and Roman patristic writings; thinkers like Spinoza, Locke, Berkeley, Hume, Condillac, Bonnet, Condorcet, Buckley, and the Scottish school of common sense; and Schopenhauer's critique of Kant's philosophy. There is an absence of notes, Brobjer notices, concerning German philosophers aside from Schopenhauer and Kant. Nevertheless, it is worthy to note that Fritz came across Schopenhauer's thought long before he "discovered" and read his works.[398]

It is intriguing that Fritz, a philology major now, did not replace theology with philology but choose two philosophy classes instead. So, it seems that philology was becoming a necessary emblem to access concrete, although never major goal in his life. Fritz's religiosity and devotion to God were replaced with reason and individualistic self-recognition—an egocentric faith in yourself. It seems that his Janus performance was being enacted, to adapt to the ever-changing needs and circumstances Fritz found himself in.

Fritz was factually studying philosophy but declaring complete dedication to philology. At the beginning of the summer semester, in the letter to Franziska from May 29, 1865, he justified leaving Bonn for Leipzig University.[399] He has pleased that he studied philology in Bonn, for it had the most advanced classical philology department in Germany. But he found out that professor Ritschl, after a long and vicious quarrel with professor Jahn, had to leave Bonn, and decided to move to Leipzig. Taking it into account, Fritz concluded that Leipzig will become the center of classical philology in the country. Besides, he repeated, he never felt comfortable in the Catholic city. Moving back to protestant Saxony, closer to home and friends, would make his life comfortable and less lonely. His acquaintance from Pforta, Carl von Gersdorff, who, through an exchange of letters, was becoming a close friend, was also moving to Leipzig from Göttingen.

"I very much admit to you that similar experiences as you have had to a certain extent also occurred to me, that the expression of the conviviality at the pub evenings often displeased me to a great extent, that I could hardly stand certain individuals because of their beer materialism. Also, to my greatest annoyance, that I was judged by them with outrageous presumption and with an *en masse* opinions about people."[400] Fritz shared his disdain for the *Burschenschaften* with Gersdorff ending the letter without an emblem of Franconia and with the words of a true friendship – *Dein treuer Freund*.

At the same time, the long-standing companionship between Deussen and Fritz (or more like a servitude on the part of Deussen) was disintegrating due to Fritz's extravagant, truculent, and always demanding fraternity lifestyle, which he continued despite loathing it.

"I thought I was enslaved by a demonic power, and my admiration for him was like a kind of pain," Deussen writes about Fritz while distancing himself from him. However, Fritz did not despair much. He turned around and found yet another candidate for a friend, a fraternity brother, Hermann Mushacke, who also planned to leave Bonn for Leipzig; the new friends started to spend most of their free time at Hermann's apartment.

A week passed from Fritz's Easter outburst, but Elisabeth was still tormented and shocked by the events of her brother's display of such implicit rebelliousness against Christianity. She sought consolation with uncle Edmund who himself, as a young pastor, displayed doubts concerning the faith. Unable to find a compelling explanation, Elisabeth wrote Fritz, arguing beyond her usual conforming nature to Fritz's high-minded attitude he displayed at home. "With your views," she wrote, "which are actually depressing, you have found a too-willing student. As Mamma says, I too have become overly clever, but since I can't forget my lama– [conformist] nature, I am full of confusion … This, however, is certain: it is much easier not to believe than the opposite, and the difficult is likely to be the right course to take ... Anyway, I really regret your bringing the unhappy Strauss with you on holiday, and that I've heard so much about him from you. For to hear that it is possible to doubt and criticize what are (at least to believers) the loftiest things is the first step towards a new belief or unbelief. And when that happens, it is for me as though the firm protective wall has fallen, and one now stands before a broad, map-less, confusing, mist-enshrouded desert where there is nothing firm, with only our own poor, miserable, and so often fallible spirit to guide us."[401]

A thought of being sheltered by the wall of faith, preventing one from facing reality, was obviously in agreement with his ideas of confronting it in order to overcome it. Quite surprised by Elisabeth's comprehensive argument, he took the letter seriously and answered it on June 11, 1865, as he would answer any of his ever-changing pen pals.

> *This time, you have provided me with rich material which I enjoy very much 'chewing over' in an intellectual sense. In the first place, however, I must refer to a passage in your let-*

*ter which was written with as much pastor-coloration as with a lama's heart. Don't worry, dear Lizbeth. If your will is as good and resolute as you say, our dear uncle won't have too much trouble. Concerning your basic principle, that truth is always to be found on the side of the more difficult, I agree in part. However, it is difficult to believe that 2X2 does not equal 4. Does that make it, therefore, truer? On the other hand, is it really so difficult simply to accept as true everything we have been taught, and which has gradually taken firm root in us, and is thought true by the circle of our relatives and many good people, and which, moreover, really does comfort and elevate men? Is that more difficult than to venture on new paths, at odds with custom, in the insecurity that attends independence, experiencing many mood-swings and even troubles of conscience, often disconsolate, but always with the true, the beautiful, and the good as our goal? Is the most important thing to arrive at that view of God, world, and reconciliation which makes us feel most comfortable? Is not the true inquirer totally indifferent to what the result of his inquiries might be? When we inquire (Suchen), are we seeking for rest, peace, happiness? Not so; we seek only truth (Wahrheit) even though it be in the highest degree ugly and repellent. Still one final question: if we had believed from our youth onwards that all salvation issued from someone other than Jesus, from Mohammed, for example, is it not certain that we should have experienced the same blessings? It is the faith that makes blessed, not the objective reality that stands behind the faith. I write this to you, dear Lisbeth, simply with the view of meeting the line of proof usually adopted by religious people, who appeal to their inner experiences to demonstrate the infallibility of their faith. Every true faith is infallible, it accomplishes what the person holding the faith hopes to find in it, but that does not offer the slightest support for proof of its objective truth. Here the ways of men divide: if you wish to strive for peace of soul and happiness, then believe; if you wish to be a disciple of truth (Wahrheit), then inquire (forsche)."*[402]

He began his argument with a series of questions delineating the concepts of truth and faith from a purely philosophical perspective, choosing a primacy of rational objectivity over subjective faith. He dismissed uncritical acceptance of general knowledge as an impairing factor in search for truth. He identified the omnipresent attitude of confusing the faith with seeking happiness as false, stressing again the necessity of truth. He summarized his argument by emphasizing the search for the platonic principle as the majority's only acceptable path of life, understanding that most people would seek peace of mind and happiness. In that phase of his development, apparently, he was an idealistic truth-seeker, where struggle, hardship, and disappointments were a part of the philosophical endeavor he chose to pursue. He ended the letter with the words, which would become one of his often-repeated quotes.

What seems a piece of discourse for Elisabeth's benefit was yet another bit of his budding attempts at self-inquiry. Fritz was becoming a lab specimen of his own experimental vivisection of himself.

Next, to elaborate the subject farther, he sent Elisabeth a German translation of *Life Thoughts* (1858) by Henry Ward Beecher, the American Abolitionist with an inscription: "Dear Lisabeth, take this book as an answer to the 'religious' lines of your last letter."[403]

It was yet another pivotal moment in Fritz's life: he turned inwards to see the world through the prism of his own becoming, thus opening himself to the world's fortunes and accepting them as his own – Pletsch speculates.

"From the time Nietzsche put theology and the phantasies that he had associated with fraternity life behind him, his inquiry would be into himself. Instead of trying to become a *flotter Student,* which he now felt he could never be, he set about finding out who he really was. After that, he was never to turn from the pursuit of his true self, no matter how unpleasant the search might become. It is from this point in his life that the intellectual quest that he was later to use as the subtitle of his autobiographical *Ecce Homo* dates: 'How One Becomes What One Is.' He accepted the fact that he could not fulfill expectations of others but would have to come to terms with himself and what fate had decreed for him. From this time on he was tacitly living by the motto, *amor fati,* loving his fate."[404]

Even though Julian Young's interpretation seems of a simplified determinism with which Fritz would have had disagreed, it is still worthy to accept it as a description of yet another turn in Fritz's life, although with few adjustments.

Fritz's life was not a continuous flow of events with one or two turning points. He had no such luck. Fritz's life was full of unexpected turns, bumps of different highs, dead ends, and slips into inadvertent depths. There were no signpost, flows, or continuity, but an accidental cacophony of events combating each other, without any plans, strategy, or goals. Fritz was a novice composer trying to create a musical masterpiece out of chaos.

In the second part of the letter, Fritz picturesquely describes his trip on June 2 to Cologne with the Bonn Municipal Choral Society to participate as a choir member in the Lower Rhine Music Festival. The choir of 182 sopranos, 154 altos, 113 tenor, and 172 basses, with an orchestra, made up of artists consisting of 160 men, including 52 violins, 20 violas, 21 cellos, 14 contour basses, and seven solo singers, was directed by Ferdinand Hiller (1811-1885). They performed Handel's *Israel in Egypt,* which brought Fritz back to his Saxonian upbringing, the time of his first epiphanies in the Naumburg's Cathedral, listening to Handle's Messiah when he decided to become a musician. Fritz's enthusiasm for the celebration of Christian music did not rule out his antireligious attitude, instead strengthening his particular type of faith—the refutation of a traditional yes-or-no approach towards religion in favor of a nontraditional entanglement of faith and rationality, simultaneously contradicting and antagonizing each other, as a springboard to further discoveries. His love for sacred music satiated his nostalgic tendencies towards the protestant tradition and ideals of family life, which he knew were lost irreversibly for him.

## LEAVING BONN FOR LEIPZIG

Although Fritz's "official" reasons for leaving Bonn were expenses, following Ritschl to study philology, and the reunion with his two friends, Mushacke and Gersdorff, there was, although, undisclosed to his family the other cause—his hidden desire to study music. "I'm not going to Leipzig now just to pursue phi-lology there, but I want to train myself primarily in music. I have virtually no chance for that in Bonn. Perhaps I wrote you around New Year's that I wanted neither to write poems nor to compose this year. Up to now, I achieved the for-mer— sufficient reason to believe that this vein is drained—I offended against the latter just quite recently by again producing a song. [In July 1865, Nietzsche wrote "*Junge Fischerin*" for voice and piano.] I am becoming a little too critical to be able to deceive myself any longer about possible talent. Therefore, I seek above all to develop my critical faculty,"[405] he wrote to Gersdorff on August 4, 1865. Overcoming his pride, he admitted to himself that, having a relatively poor formal training in music (apparently confirmed by a suggestion from the choir-master Caspar Brambach), he would not be able to become a great musician. Still, he had a deeply rooted passion for music and hoped to become an artist, instead of a fossilized academician, a hope which he could not share with his family.

But why he could not perceive himself already an artist, an unrestrain-able compulsive writer who had to write, forming not only artistic but philosoph-ical ideas, and cultivating himself as an artist and a philosopher, or an artist-phi-losopher. Possibly because, he was still infested with the traditional, common thinking of how one becomes an artist, and as a person, he was not able to see it.

The end of the semester was approaching, and the departure from Bonn was closer too. As always, before or during drastic changes in his life, Fritz got sick again: "I have, incidentally, been suffering from severe rheumatism in my left arm since the last vacation,"[406] he wrote his sister on June 11. Between the end of July and beginning of August, he fell seriously ill and stayed in bed for days. "The rheumatic pains had spread from his arm to his neck, his jaws, and his teeth, joining forces with the headaches, which renewed their attacks. For much of the time, consequently, he felt apathetic about work, though there was much to be done,"[407] Hayman describes Fritz's ailments.

These bouts of illness, coincidental with crucial decision points in his life, somatized and intensified his internal suffering, reflecting his conflicting state of mind. In some sense, he was provoking them by following up upon his decisions, consequently finding himself in a conflicting situation, which, if we follow his thought, could produce something unexpected and different from the choices that created it in the first place. The illness, and of the body manifestation of his internal struggle, crystallize a state of mind that enabled the discernment of new possibilities.

On August 9, 1865, Deussen and Mushacke accompanied a barely convalescent Fritz to the night steamship on the Rhine, on which he began his journey back home to Naumburg. Deussen, as he wrote, apparently relieved that Fritz was leaving, confessed with reprieve after the ship disappeared in the nightly fog of Rhine. "I also breathed a sigh of relief like one from whom a heavy pressure is removed. Nietzsche's personality had exerted a strong influence during the six years of our life together. He had always shown a sincere interest in my situation, but also a tendency to correct, criticize, and occasionally torment me, as was shown perhaps even more clearly in our continued correspondence."[408] But Fritz, expecting to be healed by mere departure, was still tormented: "[As I] stood on board of the steamship in the dump, rainy night and watched the few lights which marked the riverbank at Bonn slowly vanish—everything gave me a sense of flight,"[409] he wrote in his notebook. Although, "everything" did not seem to include the loss of a friend. In his reminiscence of Bonn's time in a letter to Mushacke, he did not mention Deussen. It seems it was a repetition of previous engagements: yet another abandonment of now useless acquaintance.

"Bonn had left a nasty taste in the mouth. Eventually, I hope to look back on it as a necessary link in my development, but at the moment, this is not possible. It still seems to me that in many respects, I have culpably wasted the year. My time with the Fraternity seems to me, to be frank, a *faux pas*, particularly the last summer semester. In doing so, I transgressed my principle of devoting no more time to things and people than is necessary to learning them... I'm annoyed with myself... I am by no means an unqualified fan of Franconia. To be sure, I think back on good comradeship. But I find its political judgment minimal, only active in a few heads. I find the face they present to the world plebeian and repulsive, and not being able to keep my disapproval to myself have made my relations with the others uneasy... With my studies, I must also be fundamentally dissatisfied, even though much of the blame must be ascribed to the Fraternity, which thwarted my best intentions. Right now, I am aware of what wholesome relief and human elevation is to be found in continuous, urgent work … I am ashamed of the work I did there … It's junk. Every single piece of schoolwork I did was better,"[410] he wrote to Mushacke but, in fact, summarized his Bonn experience for himself.

Nevertheless, as he was able to see positive elements even in the most hopeless situations, he recognized that he could turn the wasted year to his advantage. As he revised through this clownish period of his life, he knew that he has learned something about himself. Later in the letter, he outright explained that he had learned to understand himself better through a need of a close friend because the two were interdependent and essential factors in his life. "In my estimation, the greatest profit of the year is that I have learned better to understand myself. And, not least, that I have won an intimately sharing friend. For me, these necessarily go together. That I with my complex inner conflicts, with my throwaway, often frivolous judgments, could draw such a dear human being as you, sometimes surprises me, but I hope for the same reasons,"[411] Fritz wrote sincerely to Mushacke. He conducted himself toward Mushacke with a polite mannerism of self-criticism, hoping that his new friend would benefit from the relationship somehow, but in the end, it was only about our hero.

While recuperating in Naumburg from his ailments and reworking his "Theognis" paper which would qualify him for philology seminar at Leipzig University, Fritz was invited by Hermann Mushacke to visit his family in Berlin.

He responded to Hermann as in anticipation of subject matters that would be brought in conversations during the Berlin visit: "My current life is filled with preparation for Berlin, like our earthly existence is for future heaven. At the coffee time, I eat a little piece of Hegelian philosophy, and if I have a bad appetite, I take Straussian pills." He was apparently expecting to meet one of the champions of post-Hegelian philosophy, Herman's father, Eduard Mushacke. Although, Blue claims that Fritz met Hermann's parents in late July of 1865,[412] possibly in Bonn, so he knew what to expect.

He arrived in Berlin at the Mushackes on October 1, 1865, where he was introduced again to Hermann's father. It must have been quite a pleasant surprise for Fritz, who, with *The Life of Jesus* in hand, found out that the senior Mushacke was an acquaintance of Bruno Bauer and knew Max Stirner (pseudonym of Johann Caspar Schmidt, 1806-1856) as "a good friend." Although Fritz perhaps knew that already and was motivated to meet someone who took part in the philosophical movement before the wave of revolutions of 1848. "Humans, who can be loved and esteemed, still more, humans, who understand us, are ridiculously rare. But that's our fault, we arrived around 20, 30 years too late in this world,"[413] he wrote to another Pforta friend Raimund Granier in September before leaving Naumburg for Berlin. He apparently yearned for yet another historical period he did not experience.

Bauer and Stirner were Young Hegelians, an association of Hegel's students, which included in their ranks among others, Ludwig Feuerbach, Karl Marx, and David Friedrich Strauss with whose work Fritz was smitten at the moment. They represented a radically leftist interpretation of Hegel's works reflected in Stirner's book, *The Ego and Its Own* (*Der Einzige und sein Eigentum, 1844*; recently translated by Wolfi Landstreicher as *The Unique and its Property*) considered, at the time, as the most infamous book of philosophy published. According to Bernd A. Laska, in all probability, Mushacke senior had a copy of Stirner's book in his library which he lent to Fritz. Furthermore, Fritz and Hermann's father had many conversations concerning Left Hegelians' ideas and drank champagne on Fitz's birthday till they became so acquainted as to address themselves per "*Du*," despite their age difference.[414]

"It is hardly conceivable that old Mushacke did not tell Nietzsche, who showed a keen interest in the pre-1848 intellectual epoch, of his friend Stirner; that he did not have Stirner's *Der Einzige* on his bookshelf; that Nietzsche did not devour this book on the spot. Immediately after, he had struggled towards atheism with the help of critiques of religion written by Feuerbach and Strauss; perhaps also Bauer's critique of the Gospels,"[415] Laska claims. This argument is also used by one of the prominent Nietzsche's biographers, Rüdiger Safranski, who dedicates seven pages to Stirner in his *Nietzsche* biography.[416]

Stirner portrays God and other faith-based ideas as products of man, deprived of reality. He acknowledges man's creative potential by refocusing from the subject of man's creation, God, to the man's inexhaustible ability to create. He recognizes that we are able to destroy the "*other world outside of us*" though we can't help but replace it with the "*other world in us*," namely, the other illusions like mankind, humanism, progress, liberalism, freedom, equality, fraternity, etc. "They brought the work of the Enlightenment, the overcoming of God, to a victorious end. They didn't notice that the human has killed God in order to now become 'sole God on high.' The *other world outside us* is indeed swept away, and the great enterprise of the men of the Enlightenment is accomplished; but the *other world inside us* has become a new heaven and calls us forth to storm the heavens once again: God has had to make way, but not for us, rather for humanity."[417]

There is no such a thing as "mankind," for there are only countless individuals. "Mankind" is an empty notion. There is no "equality" among mankind, either, as one person cannot experience another person's experiences. There is no mankind's "fraternity," as a person cannot extend his feeling towards all the members of mankind. "'Freedom' is another prominent general concept that took the place of the idea of God. With biting irony, Stirner describes the process-oriented thinkers who construct a societal and historical machine that is expected to conclude its clattering business with the production of 'freedom' as though it were a commodity. Until such time, however, we remain slaves of this machine of liberation in the capacity of party workers. The will to freedom thus turns into a willingness to stand in the service of logic,"[418] Safranski interprets Stirner.

Stirner's solution to these and other phantoms, as he calls them, is to "break up thoughts with thinking," in other words, to rise beyond thoughts and become a creator: "This is why, beyond each moment of your existence, a fresh moment of the future beckons to you, and developing yourself, you get away 'from yourself,' i.e., from your current self. As you are in each moment, you are your own creation, and now in this 'creation,' you don't want to lose yourself, the creator. You are yourself a higher essence than you are, and you outdo yourself. But that you are the one who is higher than you, i.e., that you are not mere creation, but likewise your own creator."[419]

For Fritz, who had tried for a while now to form an idea of Self with the help of similar notions, seeing them laid down explicitly in front of him with such impudence, viciousness, and humor, must have been shocking. Laska claims that it was a moment of revelation in Fritz's life to such an extent that it made him a philosopher. He even suggests that Fritz, as a sensitive person, went through some kind of spiritual breakdown, going from a state of elation to depths of depression.

After meeting with old Mushacke, Fritz recognized "his insights concerning the administration of higher education, his scorn of Jewish Berlin, and his memories from the era of the Young Hegelians.... The completely pessimistic atmosphere of a man who has seen much behind the scenes," wrote in his notes. And it changed him: "At that time, I learned to like seeing the dark side of things when—through no fault of my own, as I thought—dark things happened to me."[420]

Because of the notoriety of Stirner, the always self-restrained Fritz could not have mentioned his ideas in his writing. He was always quite a prudent and conservative person counting on recognition by German academia. Admitting to value Stirner's work would have expunged any hopes for it. In his book *Nietzsche,* Safranski, using words of Wolfgang von Rahden, succinctly explains Fritz's salience about Stirner throughout his entire life. He "would have been permanently discredited in any educated milieu if he had demonstrated even the least bit of sympathy for Stirner, a coarse and ruthless man who insisted on naked egoism and anarchism; the censorship in Berlin, which was a general source of embarrassment, allowed the publication of Stirner's book for one reason alone: the thoughts it presented were so exaggerated that no one would concur with them."[421]

After the visit, Fritz wrote a letter from Leipzig to his new friend Eduard Mushacke, seeing in him his absent father. However, all the notes from that period were either lost or burned by Fritz or, later by overprotective Elisabeth, that there is no reference or even allusion of Stirner or his work in the entire oeuvre. Furthermore, Fritz himself avoided any comments or discussions concerning the subject of *The Ego and Its Own*. He wanted to be a recognized, cherished, and respectable genius philosopher of his epoch, far from any subversive, revolutionary, obscure authors. From the beginning, with his childish poems dedicated to his mother, letters, notes, essays, and music, and later his books, he was always in control of his output, in the expectation of specific—although, always changing—image of his person and work, which would persist after his demise. He was consistently either producing or destroying his work, always with a future reader on his mind. It seems, that the legacy he was creating was everything.

# 4

## LEIPZIG: THE HAPPIEST
## DAYS OF MY LIFE

On October 17, 1865, the two friends arrived in Leipzig. "First of all, we wandered about the city center quite aimlessly, enjoying the sight of the lofty houses, lively streets, and constant activity. Then we adjourned for a little rest about midday to the Reisse restaurant … It was on this occasion that I first read the newspaper at midday, which thereafter became a regular habit. But all we did that morning was to note down the various advertisements for respectable or even elegant rooms, with bedroom etc.,"[422] Fritz recalled a couple years later.

The town was not unfamiliar to him, for he had visited it as a teenaged boy. "I went to Leipzig for the whole day and visited book and music stores there; I also saw remarkable things, like Auerbach's Cellar, which I really liked a lot. It was so nice to wander around aimlessly without knowing the streets, wherever chance led me. Then come across the beautiful park, the charming gardens, the bathhouse. Isn't all of this quite pleasant?"[423] – he reminisced in his first autobiography.

They found lodgings next to each other in a working-class neighborhood. Fritz's apartment was in an annex to the main building at Blumengasse 4 (today Scherlstrasse) and Mushacke's at the neighboring house, under number 3B, fifteen minutes' walk from the university. Their apartments were located near cash registers and safes' factory, and Fritz's building was "full of his landlord's screaming children." For his entire life thus far, Fritz was isolated from the lower classes, living at the parsonage, boarding school's dormitory, or isolated by the exclusivity of the university walls. With his congenital tendency to exaltation and grandiosity, he appears to have been at least annoyed by his new living arrangements, if not downright distraught. "The rain drips quietly on the zinc-covered roof under my two windows. A lot of people live around me, and I can see into their rooms. Nothing but hideous faces! And in the gardens that spread out on both sides, everything is yellow, as if mummified, desolate. That is now my world,"[424] he writes to his mother on October 22, 1865, still shaken after the Berlin experiences. In addition to his mood of vulnerability and hopelessness, he could not register for Ritschl's seminar due to a lack of qualifying materials. The "Theognis" essay, he was rewriting during summer in Naumburg with other necessary reference works, was lost in transit.

Perhaps, through losing grip on his affairs motivated him to write a letter to Franconia, breaking all the ties with the fraternity, aggravating his plight even further. Realizing at the same time that he felt, as Hayman names it, an "ambivalence" toward, not just the *Burschenschaften* but towards the German people in general, he wrote: "I do not cease to value the idea of the fraternity highly. I will simply confess that to me, its contemporary manifestation is something I am dissatisfied with. It was hard for me to bear a full year as a member of Franconia. But I held it to be my duty to get to know it. Now nothing binds me to it. So, I say farewell. May Franconia soon overcome the stage of development in which it finds itself at present,"[425] he posted it on October 20, 1865, attempting to conclude yet another period in his life. It almost seems that being a frat boy had been just another research project, yet another experiment he needed in his attempts at self-cultivation.

But Fritz's grim mood was not as overwhelming as it might seem. There were moments of elation of which he enthusiastically noted or wrote letters. As Young claims, "the student years in Leipzig were the happiest of his life."[426]

Having an excuse for not attending the lectures and seminars, Fritz went to opera and theater and wandered through Leipzig's many bookstores, spent many hours in coffeehouses, and on hikes with his cousin Rudolf Schenkel. Spending too much, he asked his mother for money again.

At last, on October 19, Fritz and Herman went to register for classes, convinced that it was the hundredth anniversary to the day that Goethe had registered for classes, though, it was not so, "he was off by a day."[427] Nonetheless, considering it a good sign, Fritz wrote presumptuously to his new friend,

Eduard Mushacke: "We have the modest hope that after another hundred years, our matriculation will also be remembered."[428]

A few days later, on October 25, Ritschl had his inaugural lecture, which was attended not only by academics but the entire intellectual elite of Leipzig. With this occasion, Fritz made an enthusiastic entry into his notebook: "Everyone was generally excited at the appearance of this renowned man whose conduct during the Bonn affair had put his name in the newspapers and in every mouth. As a result, the academic citizenry was fully in attendance, but number-less non-students also stood to the rear."[429]

"Ritschl made his way into the hall in his large felt slippers, though otherwise he was faultlessly attired in evening dress, with a white tie. He looked with good-humored cheer at the new world before him and soon discovered faces that were not strange. While going from group to group at the back of the hall, he suddenly cried, '*Hallo*! There is *Herr Nietzsche*, too!' and he waved his hand gleefully to me"[430]—Fritz must have been thrilled to be recognized in such a large gathering of people. It was "his first happy experience in Leipzig," writes Blue.

## ARTHUR SCHOPENHAUER
## AND MAX STIRNER

One day, by the end of October 1865, Fritz was browsing through the old collections in his landlord Herr Rohn's antiquarian bookshop. He stumbled across a book—an event which he described as a truly turning event in his developments as a philosopher. It was a copy of Arthur Schopenhauer's *The World as Will and Representation*, published in 1819.

"I took it in my hand as something totally unfamiliar and turned the pages," he confesses, almost in ecstasy. "I do not know which demon was whispering to me: 'Take this book home.' In any case, it happened, contrary to my principle of never buying a book too hastily. Back at the house, I threw myself into the corner of the sofa with my new treasure and began to let that dynamic,

dismal genius work on my mind. Each line cried out with renunciation, negation, resignation. I was looking into a mirror that reflected the world, life and
my own mind with a hideous magnificence,"[431] he wrote to capture the moment,
however not immediately after the event, but more than two years later.

And there is yet another small issue with this statement. The Schopenhauer's work, as already mentioned, was familiar to Fritz. On at least two occasions, he had come across the philosopher's principal work. During the winter
semester at Bonn University, Fritz read a book by Karl Fortlage, *Genetic History of Philosophy since Kant,* where a section was dedicated to Schopenhauer.
Then, during the summer semester, he took a course, "An Outline of the History
of Philosophy" that Professor Schaarschmidt lectured, among other things, on
Schopenhauer's critique of Kant. It is impossible then that during his tenure in
Bonn, Fritz did not hear about Schopenhauer's major work, which, at that time,
was becoming very popular after years of obscurity. Why was Fritz trying to
conceal his knowing of Schopenhauer and his major work three years later?

By treating it as revelation, he was covering yet another event. A salient discovery, of which he could not speak about, with Max Stirner's *The Ego
and Its Own,* which, in many respects, was comparable with Schopenhauer's
opus. Arthur Schopenhauer, a freelance professor at Berlin University, who had
recently died, during the 1860ties, had had his grand opus becoming widely
popular. In contrast, Stirner was a despised, obscured pariah in academic circles—admitting to deriving ideas from that author would not help in Fritz's
young career. By elevating Schopenhauer to an almost messianic importance,
he simultaneously concealed his own knowledge of Stirner. His "discovery,"
accidental or intended, created an illusion of removing the subject of Stirner's
book from Fritz's intellectual priming.

Nevertheless, both works, Schopenhauer's and Stirner's, left an irre-
vocable impact on his thought. As both encounters happened within one month,
they should have been seen as a single turning point in Fritz's development,
especially since there are striking similarities between these two authors, regardless of Fritz's ostentatious pointing towards Schopenhauer's influence only.
And any speculations on this subject are unsubstantiated, for there is a lack of
evidence, one way or another. According to Bell, Fritz or his sister, Elisabeth,

burned a notebook from that period. There are only suggestions that he read Stirner in the nuances of his letters.

On November 5, 1865, Fritz wrote enigmatically to his mother and sister, referring more to an abstract state of mind than to a concrete event: "Do you really take it so lightly, this existence in which so much is contradictory, and nothing is clear except that it is not clear? It seems to me that you always evade the point by joking," he asked scoldingly. "'Do your duty!' All right, my revered dears, I do it or strive to do it, but where does it end? How do I know at all what is my duty? And, if we set the case and I lived according to the obligation, is the beast of burden more than a human being if it fulfills more precisely what one asks of him? Has one done enough for mankind to satisfy the demands of the circumstances into which we are born? Who tells us to be determined by circumstances?

"But if we did not want to do that, if we decided to just look after ourselves and force people to recognize us as we are now, what then? What do we want then? Is it necessary making a life as bearable as possible?

"There are two ways, my dears: one strives and gets used to being as limited as possible, then, while screwing one's mind wick as low as possible, one seeks riches and lives with the pleasures of the world. Or one knows that life is miserable. One knows that the more we want to enjoy it, the more we become slaves to it. So, one gives away to the goods of life and practice abstinence. One is barren against oneself and love for all others because we are compassionate to the comrades of misery—in short, one lives according to the strict demands of the original Christianity, not of the present, sweet and fuzzy. Christianity cannot be 'joined in' *en passant* (in passing) or because it is fashion.

"And, is life bearable now? Well, yes, because its burden is getting smaller and smaller, and no ties bind us to it anymore. It is bearable because it can then be disposed of without pain."[32]

Within a week, he wrote again, but this time just describing his daily routine, showing his mother that he was back on track with his education, realizing perhaps, that sharing his observations concerning his new discoveries of Schopenhauer and Stirner was a bit too much for his family.

Schopenhauer, favoring a clear and direct style of writing, critical of his German predecessors, "Kant, Fichte, Schelling, and particularly of Hegel, whom he described as a charlatan, humbug and windbag,"[433] began his philosophy with a declaration of Kantian persuasion: "The world is my representation,"[434] as the first line of his breathtaking work. This statement turns away from the general attempt at objectivity towards inward subjectivity, putting the reader squarely into the Kantian realm of reality as a subjective illusion, or better, representation of the real as the *thing-in-itself* (*Ding an sich*), never accessible to human cognition. Consequently, we humans are living in a constructed reality of the world. Our experiences, because they are narrated exclusively by our illusionary cognition which enables us to communicate with each other, are reduced to a construct which may or may not reflect the real thing. According to Kant's model, we would not know how closed or far our constructed reality is from the real thing, for we are intrinsically oblivious to it, the *thing-in-itself.* By turning the view on reality from out-there to a singular subject, reversing the trajectory of inquiry from outward bound into inward bound, enabled the feasibility of accessing the real, otherwise unveiled the Kantian inaccessible. He proposed an alternative of introspection into oneself, the subject.

"If we attend, first, to our own bodies, and if we look inwards rather than outwards, [Schopenhauer] suggests, we find a kind of experience that is veil free. And what we find in this experience is, in a word, 'will.' That which presents itself to outer perception as bodily action presents itself, in introspection, as 'will' (feeling, emotion, desire, and decision). This provides a vital clue to the nature of reality in general. That which, from the outer perspective, appears as a physical body is, Schopenhauer announces, in its inner reality, will. So, the Kantian problem is solved. Take away the veils and what is left, as the thing in itself, is will: 'What Kant opposed as the *thing in itself* to mere *appearance*, this *thing in itself,* this substratum of all phenomena and therefore of the whole of nature, is nothing but what we know directly and intimately and find within ourselves as *the will.*'"[435]

The will as feelings, emotions, and desires, an essence of the true reality, accessible through the introspection—the body of a subject as a mirror of the world—was a philosophical breakthrough for Schopenhauer. Introspection, Wolfgang Schirmacher describes succinctly, is "the inside what is in me, accessible to me alone, and protected by the sovereignty of *being there* (Heidegger's *Dasein*) is the authentic path of the will itself in me."[436]

The same subjective point of departure is demonstrated in the first sentence of Max Stirner's *The Ego and Its Own*. Stirner begins his philosophy with reversing Hegelian starting point of Being, *"Being, pure Being,* without any further determination. In its indeterminate immediacy, it is equal only to itself.... Being, the indeterminate immediate, is, in fact, *nothing,* and neither more nor less than nothing"[437] – with the first line of Goethe's poem *"Vanitas! Vanitatum Vanitas!"* – "I have based my affair on Nothing."[438] Nothing has become a point of departure for Stirner's philosophy. Not an empty nothing but nothing embodied in the I: "I am not nothing in the sense of emptiness, but I am the creative nothing, the nothing out of which I myself create everything as a creator."[439] This creative power of I has been gradually expunged throughout centuries of human existence to the point that we are ashamed of what we really are. Or better, we actually do not know who we are. Stirner calls for awakening from this nightmare of becoming someone else in perpetuating this construct we call civilization but concentrating wholly on becoming ourselves. "Thousands of years of civilized culture have obscured what you are to you, have made you believe that you are not egoists, but are called to be idealists ("good people"). Shake that off! Don't seek for freedom, which just deprives you of yourselves, in 'self-denial'; but rather seek yourselves, become egoists, each one of you become an almighty I. Or more clearly: recognize yourselves again, recognize what you actually are, and let go of your hypocritical endeavors, your foolish addiction to be something other than what you are. I call them hypocritical because you have still remained egoists all these thousands of years, but sleeping, self-deceiving, crazy egoists, you *Heauton Timorumenos*, you Self-tormentors."[440]

Stirner postulates becoming an egoist as a self-master in relation not only to the outside world but as well to the inner passions. He shows the danger of submitting to one's drives and needs to the point of being subjected and dependent on them. Becoming a slave to them. To avoid these dangers, one must become a Stirnerian egoist and liberate oneself completely from inner or outer dependencies and passions. In this context, Stirner introduced the term of ownness (*Eigenheit*),[441] as a self-mastery. "I am *my own* only when I am in my own power, and not in the power of sensuality or any other thing (God, humanity, authority, law, state, church, etc.); *my selfishness* pursues what is useful to me, this self-owned or self-possessing one."[442]

The ownness or self-mastery, in a sense, could have been an answer to Schopenhauerian destructive power of the will. And, perhaps as Stirner wrote his magnum opus over twenty years after Schopenhauer's *The World as Will and Representation* was published, he was responding to it. But, as Schopenhauer was utterly unknown at the time, and he was never mentioned directly by Stirner, it could have been a coincidence. According to Schopenhauer, the will is an unveiled *thing-in-itself*; otherwise, the world is an unceasing experience of suffering: "Willing and striving are its [nature's] whole essence and can be fully compared to an unquenchable thirst. The basis of all willing, however, is need, lack, and hence pain, and by this very nature and origin it is therefore destined to pain. If, on the other hand, it lacks objects of willing, because it is at once deprived of them again by too easy a satisfaction, a fearful emptiness and boredom come over it; in other words, its being and its existence itself becomes an intolerable burden for it. Hence its life swings like a pendulum to and fro between pain and boredom, and these two are in fact its ultimate constituents. This has been expressed very quaintly by saying that, after man had placed all pains and torments in hell, there was nothing left for heaven but boredom.

But the constant striving, which constitutes the inner nature of every phenomenon of the will, obtains at the higher grades of objectification its first and most universal foundation from the fact that the will appears as a living body with the iron command to nourish it. What gives force to this command is just that this body is nothing but the objectified will-to-live itself. Man, as the most complete objectification of this will, is accordingly the most necessitous of all beings. He is concrete willing and needing through and through; he is a concretion of a thousand wants and needs. With these he stands on the earth, left to his own devices, in uncertainty about everything except his own need and misery. Accordingly, care for the maintenance of this existence, in the face of demands that are so heavy and proclaim themselves anew every day, occupies, as a rule, the whole of human life."[443]

Schopenhauer thus builds his system upon suffering, where the human or human body is a quintessential expression of this suffering. In other words, if one looks deep enough, one will find not only his own pain as an individual experience, but the pain of the world. A human, then, is an embodiment of the world as absolute struggle and suffering.

An individual goes through life trying to avoid pain by satisfying his needs. However, constantly aware that if he would reflect with cold rationality on his life, he could realize the ultimate unavoidable failure he is unable to dodge, his death. Except in our constructed reality, we live with the illusion of a wonderful life. We conduct our lives as they have no end, in absolute denial, through building sophisticated mechanisms of hiding the ubiquitous suffering—like sweeping dirt under the rug. We live in a Hollywood dream, producing stories featured in the theaters of sociocultural, scientific, and religious systems.

Max Stirner approaches this problem adequately: all institutions that make up our modern world are generators of human alienation. People fool themselves that their ideal life will eventually emerge, continually striving to be different, better, perfect, unable to face the truth that this new life will never come. We live in an illusion reinforced by a web of institutions, not resolving our expectations but numbing our despair.

"I can never be happy with myself as long as I think that I first still have to find my true self, and that it must come to this, that not I but Christ or some other spiritual, i.e., ghostly, *I*–for example, the true human being, the human essence, or the like–lives in me,"[444] Stirner makes us aware of reality, with the proviso that we have done away with God. Thinking that we are at liberty to pursue the greatness of man, not realizing that we created a new god, the tyranny of ourselves over ourselves, of being better, smarter, prettier, stronger, happier. "At the entrance of the modem era stands the 'God-man.' ... The *other world outside us* is indeed swept away, and the great enterprise of the men of the Enlightenment is accomplished; but the *other world inside us* has become a new heaven and calls us forth to storm the heavens once again: God has had to make way, but not for us, rather for–humanity. How can you believe the God-man has died before the man in him, as well as the God, has died?"[445] We have trapped ourselves in the futile exertion to become the ideal man, creating, at the same time, a new god, man *as* God. Why do we not want to see the tyranny—instead of facing it, continually ameliorating it? We must be spineless masochists who feel good as slaves, without any hope for freedom.

Meanwhile, state institutions utilize suffering by shielding or laying bare its impact on us to enforce its control attempts in the scheme of righteousness and liberty.

"Every state is a despotism, whether the despot be one or many, or, as some like to imagine a republic, all be lords, i.e., play the despot over each other. This is the case every time when a given law, the will expressed perhaps in the opinion of a popular assembly, should be from then on law for the individual, to which he owes obedience, or towards which he has the duty of obedience."[446] Therefore, the state's authority focuses on the individual: particularly on his behaviors and thoughts. The individual is the material on which the states exercises its power: "The state always has the sole purpose of limiting, taming, subordinating the individual–of making him subservient to some universality or other; it lasts only so long as individuals are not all in all, and is only the clearly marked *limitation of me*, my restriction, my slavery. Thus, the state has never aimed to bring about the free activity of individuals, but always that bound to the *state purpose*."[447] Through this molding and squeezing into the state's ready-made expectation, the individual is therefore becoming … civilized. This process is being repeated throughout the centuries in all the so-called civilizations. When each of them is self-sustained by producing its sustenance of new individuals for whom the positions vacated by the manure of aged ones are waiting to be fulfilled. The never-ending circularity of birth and death, perpetuating the state.

Ironically, it is a creation of man but, instead of being in service of its creator, it has become its master, with the submissiveness of its creator, the slave. "Whoever has to count on the lack of will in others in order to exist is a shoddy product of these others, as the master is a shoddy product of the slave. If servility ceased, it would be all over for lordship. My own will is the destroyer of the state; the latter therefore denounces it as 'self-will.'"[448]

To create this self-imprisonment the masochistic attitude is indispensable. A prison created on the foundation of faith, specifically the Christian

166 HOW I BECAME WHAT I AM

faith, in Stirner's words, was a core expression of institutionalized suffering. His comrades, the New Hegelians proclaimed the absence of God and consequently freedom from His tyranny, but Stirner showed that God, with its organized faith, was still at the foundation of modern, secular culture. "After the annihilation of faith, Feuerbach imagines entering into the supposedly safe harbor of love.... But actually, only that God has changed, the Deus; the love has remained: there, love for the superhuman God, here, love for the human God, for homo as Deus. Thus, the human being is to me—sacred.... Who is his God? The Human Being! What is the divine? The human! So, the predicate has indeed only changed into the subject, and, instead of the phrase 'God is love,' one says 'love is divine,' instead of 'God has become human,' 'the human being has become God,' etc. It is just a new—*religion*."[449]

If we reintroduce Schopenhauer into this schema of the metamorphosis of God into Man as God, we still could see the same features of our existence. For, no matter from which perspective we look at it from, our life is a bundle of suffering because, after all, we ourselves are the reinforcers of that pain, either through God or a man-god. "In the New Testament, the world is presented as a vale of tears, life as a process of purification, and the symbol of Christianity is an instrument of torture.... Here everyone is punished for his existence and indeed each in his own way. For one of the evils of a penitentiary is also the society we meet there.... A fine nature, as well as a genius, may sometimes feel in this world like a noble state-prisoner in the galleys among common criminals.[450] Let no one imagine that Christian teaching is favorable to optimism; on the contrary, in the Gospel world and evil are uses almost synonymous expressions,"[451] Schopenhauer normalizes suffering as the world's status quo.

Is the inexorable logic of the seething *will-to-live*, the relentless, mindless force of suffering, only emphasized by the illusion of control over it, here to show us that it should have been otherwise? In our relentlessly vain rationality, we ask immediately; is there a solution to this misery, or at least, a hope for it? A release from suffering that comes from nothing?

Considering the present state of things, we may speculate that there are two possibilities. With the benefit of technology, we may create a brave new world of such an advanced illusion that it could effectively make any attempt of penetrating it impossible. There is no way to differentiate it from the real thing. In other words, an illusion of illusion which becomes the actual thing in itself, an alternative to the *thing-in-itself,* would in fact (although, still illusionary fact) be extinguished through the second negation (illusion) of the *thing-in-itself* and its illusion simultaneously.[452]

Or, immediately go for the release from pain and commit suicide, individually or *en masse,* thus destroying the world and, at the same time, the evil. However, both instances are merely different ways of doing away with humanity, in other words, self-extermination and, in it, returning to our point of departure.

Suicide, seemingly a gesture of liberation from the bandage of incessant will, comes down to just getting rid of one's own body, leaving the real source of suffering, *will-to-live,* untouched. A person may feel that after so much suffering beyond his control, finally, he is taking his fate into his own hands. Ironically, it is not just a simple repudiation. Contrary, it is an affirmation of the *will-to-live* through simple destruction of its manifestation, "the will's phenomenon, the body."[453] Contrary to expectations, and "far from being a denial of the will, suicide is a phenomenon of the will's strong affirmation.... The suicide wills life, and is dissatisfied merely with the conditions on which it has come to him."[454]

Schopenhauer, dismissing suicide as an ineffectual relief from pain, albeit the most easily accessible, did not stop in his search. He went back to the beginning of his philosophizing, again to Immanuel Kant's *thing-in-itself.*

"Kant," Safranski points out, "left behind him a well-appointed house for rational cognition, except that the thing in itself was like a hole letting in the draught."[455] Schopenhauer appreciated Kant's humbleness, who, while organizing his system from a purely rational point of view, invited a paradox beyond explanation into it: "Human reason has this peculiar fate that in one species of its knowledge it is burdened by questions which, as prescribed by the very nature of reason itself, it is not able to ignore, but which, as transcending all its powers, it is also not able to answer."[456] But, he could not restrain himself from entering an open path, which became his philosophy. Schopenhauer justified Kant's limitation as a lack of awareness of contemplation: "It is perhaps the best description of Kant's shortcomings if one says: he did not know what contemplation is." Nonetheless, Safranski claims, contemplation, as a state of mind which young Schopenhauer self-experienced climbing mountains, is an escape from the everyday routine of life's realities, "the race-rat [of] self-assertion." Therefore, Schopenhauer understood Kant, who left the opening of *thing-in-itself* as "the reverse side of all our imagination," as "the great theoretician of human freedom."[457] But he did not enter this path himself; he acquires help from another philosopher, Plato, and his allegory of the cave in the *Republic.*

Unchaining oneself from the illusions of the will and walking into the sun of the perfect world of the Idea is the way to free ourselves from the bandage of the *will-to-live*, to find ourselves in the realm of denial of the will. Schopenhauer walked into that path of will-less, timeless, spaceless, and causeless contemplation, postulating that "the transition is possible, but to be regarded only as an exception from the common knowledge of particular things to knowledge of the Idea takes place suddenly, since knowledge tears itself free from the service of the will precisely by the subject's ceasing to be merely individual, and being now a pure will-less subject of knowledge. Such a subject of knowledge no longer follows relations in accordance with the *principle of sufficient reason*; on the contrary, it rests in fixed contemplation, of the object presented to it out of its connexion with any other, and rises into this."[458] Experiencing the world detached from the will is possible only through the viewer's aesthetic contemplation when the will is momentarily refuted. In other words, by employing an artistic attitude borrowed from disinterested contemplation of works of art or objects of nature that can suspend for a moment an incessant influence of the will on his life, an individual experiences reality as an aesthetic phenomenon. "The peace always sought but always escaping us on the first path of willing, comes to us on its own accord, and all is well with us. It is the painless state, prized by Epicurus as the highest good and as the state of the gods; for that moment, we are delivered from the miserable pressure of the will. We celebrate the Sabbath of the penal servitude of willing; the wheel of Ixion stands still."[459]

However, this concerns only visual arts, the world as representation. Schopenhauer wanted to go deeper, so he distinguished a different art as the most adequate for his purposes, music. More specifically, music that does not represent the *world of appearance* or anything, but rather is a direct copy of the *thing-in-itself.* Therefore, he distinguishes music from all other arts as the most adequate way to temporarily suspend the will. "Music differs from all the other arts by the fact that it is not a copy of the phenomenon, or, more exactly, of the will's adequate objectivity, but is directly a copy of the will itself, and therefore expresses the metaphysical to everything physical in the world, the thing in itself to every phenomenon."[460]

Then, going even further: "philosophy is nothing more but a complete and accurate repetition and expression of the inner nature of the world, [and] music is an unconscious exercise in metaphysics in which the mind does not know it is philosophizing."[461] Philosophizing is composing, performing, or listening to music, in other words expressing the inner world of *thing-in-itself.* Why does music, then, with its source in the will and as the will-in-itself, bring us so much joy, rather than misery? Why is music not harmful if it is "a direct copy of the will itself"? It must be that music temporarily affects the change of our attitude by suspending the hold of the will to live and everyday shallow rationality, inducing a state of mind which allows us to enjoy—albeit without realizing it—the truth of becoming. It is not a mere change of an object of experience, which would seem obvious, but the transformation of an inner attitude of a subject into a renewed state of a cognitive mind deprived of the will.

The idea of a change in the subject's attitude towards the world exposes an essential aspect of the relationship between the world and its individuality. "Every individual, completely vanishing and reduced to nothing in a boundless world, nevertheless makes himself the center of the world, in order to maintain his own self, a drop in the ocean, a little longer. This disposition is *egoism*, which is essential to everything in nature. [And it is] the objectification of the will and has for its form the *principium individuationis.*"[462] Every one of us thinks that he is the center of the world, which, with our demise, would cease to exist. But, after facing the deaths of others around us, we continue to go about our business with indifference. We occasionally perform our grief rituals to satisfy customary obligations unless connected to the deceased on a deep emotional level. We see ourselves through the prism of the *principium individuationis* as separate, distinct, egotistic individuals who suffer alone. Even if we recognize our egocentrism and assume an altruistic attitude ready to sacrifice our own individuality to benefit others, becoming good and compassionate individuals, we still ultimately benefit ourselves, with the ego boost of feeling how great we are for helping others. Even, if like Jesus Christ, we took the world's suffering onto our shoulders, we still would not deny the will: it would merely add an illusion of meaning to our suffering.

Continuing this thought, which appeared to be leading towards hopelessness, Schopenhauer nevertheless called for a solution: "If we compare life to a circular path of red-hot coals having a few cool places, a path we have to run over incessantly, then the man ensnared in delusion is comforted by the cool place on which he is just now standing, or which he sees near him and sets out to run over the path. But the man who sees through the *principium individuationis* and recognizes the true nature of *things-in-themselves*, and thus the whole, is no longer susceptible of such consolation; he sees himself in all places simultaneously and withdraws. His will turns about; it no longer affirms its own inner nature, mirrored in the phenomenon, but denies it. The phenomenon by which this becomes manifest is the transition from virtue to *ascetism*."[463] It is not enough to appropriate our own and the others' suffering but to turn towards it and willingly embrace it. In other words, Schopenhauer suggests one defies the will by willingly bearing more than one could seemingly handle. Thus, he proposes chastity, poverty, and fasting as remedies for sovereignty from the will. "It may be that the inner nature of holiness, of self-renunciation, of mortification of one's own will, of ascetism, is here for the first time expressed in abstract terms and free from everything mythical, as *denial of the will-to-live*, which appears after the complete knowledge of its own inner being has become for it quieter of all willing."[464]

The ultimate denial of the will is, according to Schopenhauer, suicide by willing starvation. "This kind of suicide is so far from being the result of the will-to-live, that such a completely resign ascetic ceases to live merely because he has completely ceased to will."[465] It is so close to eliminating the fear of death, which, as an ultimate ingredient of human suffering, was an instigating force for the emergence of philosophy. "Death is the real inspiring genius ... of philosophy, and for this reason, Socrates defined philosophy as a 'preparation for death.' Indeed, without death, there would hardly have been any philosophizing."[466]

Again, we have arrived at the notion, accessible only through renunciation of the *will-to-live*, while looking through the prism of the *principium individuationis*. In other words, the so-called philosophy practiced by academics has nothing to do with true philosophy, for philosophizing can only be achieved by accepting the life-death process of continuously becoming and passing away. The realization of becoming as swaying on the edge between life and death. It seems that this process of coming to be and passing away is equally balanced on both sides. However, when we are born, at the exact moment, we began to die, fall apart, together with the world as it is inevitably falling towards a state of entropy. Our lives are merely failed attempts at stopping it, blinding us with an illusion of growing, developing, getting better. But in truth, we can evolve only through death.

Perhaps, only from that perspective, the Kantian *thing-in-itself* would unveil itself, only to be buried with us. Ivan Ilyich never talked about his death-bed experiences. Tolstoy merely imagined it contemplating the event as the work of art.[467]

Stirner, on the other hand, has a less fatalistic approach to this problem. Instead of postulating the kenosis of individuality as Schopenhauer, he elevated it to idealistic proportions.

He compares the idea of freedom, the most glorified value, with ownness (*Eigenheit*),[468] which "is not at all an idea like freedom, morality, humanity, etc. It is only a description of–the *owner*."[469] He asserts that in the literal sense, to achieve the freedom–"the whole of *freedom*, for a piece of freedom is not *freedom*–"[470] for which we yearn is impossible. There always is an element of economy involved in social interrelations, for a genuinely unconditional relation is impossible: "because the human being is *hungry for gain* and does nothing 'gratis.' But what about that 'doing good for the sake of the good' without the prospect of reward? As if here too, the reward was not contained in the satisfaction it would grant. Thus, religion is also founded on our egoism and exploits it; calculated on our desires, for the sake of one of them, it stifles many others."[471] The idea of complete freedom from all dependencies, conditions, and exploitations is unattainable. It always positions the individual as the central, indispensable element who would profit from these relationships throughout its performance. And this profit feeds our ownness or egoism. "*Freedom* rouses your rage against everything that is not you; *egoism* calls you to joy over yourselves, to self-enjoyment. *Freedom* is and remains a longing, a romantic lament, a Christian hope for otherworldliness and the future; *ownness* is a reality that, from itself, removes just as much unfreedom as hinders you by barring your own way."[472]

According to Stirner, egoism, the concentration of the exclusively individual self, is a ubiquitous characteristic of our relationship with other human beings, our environment, the world.

In most instances, egoism denounced—though hypocritically—social interdependencies, religion, politics, etc., which it denies as nonexistent or diminished irrelevant. On the contrary, egoism is immanent within our existence, Stirner claims. Whatever activity we perform, it is, in the end, for our own benefit, even if we claim completely otherwise. Instead of denying and fooling ourselves, we should enhance and bring to the surface what is, and always been, our intrinsic quality.

"Thousands of years of civilized culture have obscured *what you are to you*, have made you believe that you are not egoists, but are *called* to be idealists ("good people"). Shake that off! ... The own one is the free-born.... He recognizes nothing but himself; he does not need to free himself first, because from the start he rejects everything outside himself, because he prizes nothing more than himself, deems nothing higher than himself–in short, because he starts from himself and '*comes to himself*.'"[473]

But one must be vigilant that his egoism's object would not become his master, like dependency on desires, passions, wishes, or satisfactions could. If that would be the case, then "they are egoists in the usual sense, selfish people, looking out for their advantage, sober, calculating."[474] They are not people who know or trying to find *what they are*. They are not *coming to themselves*, to *what they always been*, but artificially, on the surface, satisfying their immediate urges or numbing their pain. But they are people whose actions, activities, and interventions would always seem artificial. A bitter taste of insufficiency in engagement with art, literature, work, creative pursuits, or even career will creep out to the surface. They are never deep enough to experience complete fulfillment.

All these characteristics are concerning humanity as a general idea, however, according to Stirner, this does not count. What is relevant is an individual, not the concept of the individual, but I as a single, separate individual who can influence himself. Humanity, human beings, are the ideals of an illusion to exercise others' power and control over myself. And when the individual sleeps out from under the authority of others, "if the individual raises himself above the limits of his individuality, this is rather just he himself as an individual.... *The* human being is only an ideal.... To be *a* human being doesn't mean fulfilling the ideal of *the* human being, but rather showing *oneself* the individual. It is not how I realize the *generally human* that needs to be my task, but how I satisfy myself *I* am my species, am without norm, without law, without model, etc. Perhaps I can make very little out of myself; this little, however, is all, and is better than what I allow the power of others to make out of me, through the training of custom, religion, law, the state, etc."[475]

Although we do not have any notes of Fritz's response or reaction to Stirner's work, we can assume that his reading of *The Ego and Its Own* have clarified, if not consolidated, his convictions toward Christianity, God, the state, humanity, and individuality. Anyhow, the reading had provided him with the foundations for planned but inhibited by progressive illness in the last year of his productive life, hence never completed the central idea of his thought, revaluations of all values.

As foundations of European civilization, the Christian church, promising an illusionary idealism of the afterlife, has introduced the anti-life, anti-human system of values, which Fritz almost instinctively refuted from the moment of his father's death. The church and state's doctrines claim that our existence on earth, the actual, concrete suffering, is merely a preparation for an illusion of life after death. In that context, an individual human being—a slave to Christian rule, the state, and his desires to become something better according to the imposed external models—has refused the ability to create himself in harmony with his own intrinsic but lost to reach value system. The objective proposed by Stirner is not to become an extension to human as a better or super-human man, a superman or Godman but to overcome our own humanity, produced by the "thousands of years of civilized culture." To recreate ourselves as over-man—an outside the continuum of civilization's evolution, a self-created entity, the *Übermensch*.

These readings, especially Stirner's book, as I said, were kept under wraps by Fritz. Albeit, they must have caused an epiphany for him. The ideas contained in the readings were the confirmation of his budding philosophy. "I hung suspended in those days alone with certain painful experiences and disappointments ... Now imagine the effect in such circumstances of read-ing Schopenhauer's chief work ... Here I saw a mirror in which I beheld the world, life, and my own nature in a terrifying grandeur ... Here I saw ... sickness and cure, exile and refuge, Hell and Heaven,"[476] Fritz made a note in November of 1865. He interlaced these readings with sightseeing at nearby towns attending concerts to digest all those revelations. "Leipzig was a splen-did place for culture—first of all, for music. One of the great centers of Ger-man music, Leipzig had been Bach's workplace in the eighteenth century, and Schumann's and Mendelssohn's a couple of decades before Nietzsche's arrival in the nineteenth. It was also the birthplace of Richard Wagner. In addition to offering a rich concert-life centered in the famous Gewandhaus Orches-tra, it was also a center of—usually vigorously polemical—theorizing for and against 'modern music.' Founded by Schumann in 1834, the *Neue Zeitschrift für Musik* (to which the Germania Society had subscribed) was published in Leipzig and had become dedicated to the defense of 'modern,' that is to say Wagnerian, music."[477]

Apparently under the influence of Schopenhauer's recommendation of asceticism, and Stirner's idea of ownness, "for a period of two weeks, Nietzsche forced himself to go to bed no earlier than two in the morning and to get up no later than six. He prescribed himself a strict diet, created his own cloister, and lived like an ascetic."[478]

## *VATER* RITSCHL

By the end of 1865, Fritz was invited among three other students for tea on December 4 at Friedrich Ritschl's house.[479] The gathering at Ritschl's involved an incitement to form a philological society, the Leipzig *Philologischer Verein*, where member-students could present their work, a similar enterprise to Fritz's Germania initiative. During the afternoon, Fritz was introduced to Ritschl's wife, Sophie. Who became his "first 'motherly woman' to whom [he was] inordinately close"[480] despite the twenty-four years age difference. She was a baptized Jewish woman, nee Guttentag, a daughter of the chief physician at Breslau Jewish Hospital, whose Jewishness Fritz indeed recognized.[481]

The first organizational meeting of ten members of the Philological Society took place on January 11, 1866, "in a pleasant, vaulted room in a restaurant on *Nikolaistrasse*."[482] Then, shortly afterward, on January 18, 1866, they met when Fritz presented his paper on "Theognis", "The Latest Edition of the Theognidea,"[483] on which he was working during the last summer vacation. The presentation was received with great enthusiasm, of which he did not fail to make a note:

"After overcoming my initial shyness, I was able to express myself forcefully and with emphasis and had such success that my friends expressed the greatest respect for what they had heard. Astonishingly elated, I came home deep in the night and sat down right at my desk to write bitter words in the book of observations [the Schopenhauerian notebook] and suppress the enjoyed pride from the tablet of my consciousness."[484] But he could not suppress it. Contrary, it gave him the self-confidence to give a copy to Professor Ritschl. Within a few days, he was summoned to Ritschl's office, who prized his work for its rigorous research and refined composition. He even proposed to help Fritz to publish it as a small book. It was more than he would ever expect: "For some time I went about under a spell, it was a time I was born as a philologist,"[485] he wrote. But the book project was never realized. Ritschl found out that two French philologists are about to publish their work on Theognis. Thus, Ritschl opted to publish the paper in *Das Rheinische Museum für Philologie*, a prestigious journal that he edited.

During that time, while Fritz was working on the ancient catalogs of Aristoteles' writings,[486] he stumbled across a book by Diogenes Laertius, which kindled his interest. When Ritschl learned that Fritz—now was visiting Ritschl's house regularly—was interested in the author of *Lives and Opinions of Eminent Philosophers*, the third century AD biographer of ancient Greek philosophers, he encouraged Fritz to write an essay about the historian. Coincidentally, shortly thereafter, the department announced a competition for the best essay on Diogenes Laertius. Whatever one could infer from this coincidence, one thing was certain, Professor Ritschl was looking after Fritz as his protégé, and Fritz, in return, viewed him as a father-figure, affectionately calling him among his fellow students, *Vater* Ritschl.

"I went twice almost every week to see him at lunchtime," Fritz records in his notebook, "and on every occasion found him ready to indulge in serious or frivolous conversation. As a rule, he sat in his armchair and had the Cologne newspaper in front of him, which, together with the Bonn newspaper, he had long been accustomed to read. Amid the vast medley of papers, there stood a glass of red wine. When he was at work, he always used a chair which he had upholstered himself.... In his talk, he showed no inhibitions; his anger with his friends, his discontent with existing conditions, the faults of the university, the eccentricities of the professors were all expressed.... He likewise poked fun at himself, at his elementary idea of managing his affairs and would tell, for instance, how, formerly, [he] had been in the habit of concealing the money he received in notes of ten, twenty, fifty or a hundred Talers in books so as to enjoy the surprise of their discovery later on.... His eagerness to help others was simply splendid, and for this reason, many young philologists, in addition to being indebted to him for their advances in scientific knowledge, also felt themselves bound to him by an intimate and personal debt of gratitude."[487]

Though occupied with his intellectual endeavors, Fritz did not fail to attend lots of concerts in the company of Karl Franz Brendel, who was an editor at the *Neue Zeitschrift*, succeeding its founder, Robert Schumann. Brendel, a musicologist, and music critic coined the phrase *Neudeutsche Schule* to describe the progressive musical movement in Germany headed by Richard Wagner and

Franz Liszt. Being on the receiving side of the musical performances reawakened Fritz's dormant desire to actively participate in this cherished art.

Fritz joined the Leipzig choral society conducted by Carl Riedel,[488] where he rehearsed Beethoven's *Missa Solemnis*. But he was unable to participate in its church performance on Friday, March 2, 1866 due to a cold, but instead was in the audience, described the event to his mother and sister as the most glorious experience. "Yesterday the *Missa Solemnis* was performed by the Riedelschen Vereine, I could not yet participate, but I listened. A large crowd of many strangers filled the church. The soprano solo was performed by Emilie Jauner-Krall, whom you love Lisbeth, and know from Dresden. The performance was excellent and extremely uplifting. It was one of my most beautiful musical enjoyments."[489] Exploiting Leipzig's cultural opportunities, Fritz also attended the theater, sending flowers to actresses, especially to the famous "blond angel," Hedwig Raabe. In other words, Fritz's life in Leipzig was full of excitement and extraordinary discoveries.

In letter of March 4, 1866, Fritz announced an early arrival for Easter holidays to his mother and sister, which—he revealed—would be his working vacation dedicated to his new project of publishing a book on Theognis, suggested by Ritschl. He asked for secrecy about the project and, as always, for "the old complaint," money.

He arrived in Naumburg probably around March 10 but did not rush to work on the project. Instead, he was "taking pleasure in almost nothing but Schopenhauer, Schumann, and solitary walks," he summarized his vacations to Gersdorff in a letter from April 7th, 1866. He began under the spell of Schopenhauer and ever-present Emerson: "Sometimes there come those quiet meditative moments in which one stands above one's life with mixed feelings of joy and sadness, like those lovely summer days which spread themselves expansively and comfortably across the hills, as Emerson so excellently describe them. Then nature becomes perfect, as he says, and we ourselves too; then we are set free from the spell of the ever-watchful will; then we are pure, contemplative, impartial eyes. In this mood for which I long above all others, I take my pen to answer your friendly and thoughtful letter."[490] Fritz experienced philosophy corporeally.

He desired and achieved a contemplative mood not rooted in rationality, but conflicting feelings, moments when he could free himself from the will, the inextinguishable, mindless drive to live. He attained this disinterested, meditative, and unspoiled by reality state of mind through spiritual openness to nature. He freed himself through the contemplative reading of Schopenhauer, who shows that experience of art, nature, and music could open the gates of reality, hiking outside the town, and listening to Schumann's *Scenes from Goethe's Faust.*[491]

"Three things are my relaxation, but infrequent ones: my Schopenhauer, Schumann's music, and then solitary walks. Yesterday a magnificent storm was in the sky; I harried out to a nearby hilltop, called *Leusch* (perhaps you can tell me what that means), found a hut up there, a man who was slaughtering two kids, and his young son. The storm broke with immense force, with wind and hail. I felt an incomparable elation, and I knew for certain that we can rightly understand nature only when we have to run to her, away from our troubles and pressure. What to me were man and his unquiet will! What were the eternal 'Thou shalt,' 'Thou shalt not!' How different the lighting, the wind, the hail, free powers, without ethics! How fortunate, how strong they are, pure will, without obscuring from the intellect!"[492] Fritz, pulled into the realm of philosophy proper, for which he was looking during his young life, was indeed in his element. But he did not come to it from the outside, as an intellectual, naming it, but he was becoming, experiencing it through his emotions. While working on Theognis essay solicited by Ritschl, Fritz understood the difference between the scholarly routine of classical philologists and the exultation of living philosophy. Nevertheless, it seems that he did not know why he repeatedly decided against his own instincts: "There is of course no denying that I hardly understand this trouble which I have imposed upon myself, which takes me away from myself (from Schopenhauer also—it is often the same thing), which will result in exposing myself to the judgment of people and will perhaps compel even me to put on the mask of a learnedness that I do not possess. One loses something, in any case, by getting into print."[493] Then he explicitly lamented over the difference between theory and practice of Schopenhauerian thought – the divide, which he tried to eliminate during his life as an anti-philosopher. He was apparently ready to pursue philosophy as his vocation but, despite himself, continued with philology as his career, bearing a splintered lifepath.

Before going back to Leipzig, Fritz placed an advertisement in the *Leipziger Tageblatt* for a new apartment on a grand floor in a non-commercial area. He wanted to get away from the screaming children and the Jews.[494] He tried to change the apartment for some time, for apparently, Jewish merchants in the area were annoying to him.

He rented a room at Elisenstraße No. 7, which he described to his mother and sister as "very high, cool and quiet—so far as I can tell—beautiful carpet, large mirror, large oil painting in gold frames depicting an old man as the room decoration. In addition, secretary, vanity table, oven, bed, book shelve and 2 chairs. The owner is a machine manufacturer, people who live very elegantly and are obviously wealthy. The house itself is beautiful and not at all old."[495]

In the same letter, he complained about health—since he suffered from a cold again—but, thanks to his walks through the streets of Leipzig, he was getting better. With Gersdorff, they were looking for a new place to eat, for "the food that you get in the restaurants is hardly appetizing at present. Moreover, everywhere it is teeming with revolting, insipid apes and other merchants. So that I really long for the termination of this intermezzo. Finally, Gersdorff and I found a tavern where we did not have to countenance oily butter and Jewish mugs (*Judenfratzen*) but were regularly the only customers. This is the restaurant that was already recommended to me by the old Mushacke"[496] Then, within just a few days, he wrote with a change of heart about Leipzig to Hermann Mushacke in Berlin: "Everywhere the food is terrible and just as expensive; in the theater, *The African Woman* is still plying; and everywhere you look, there are Jews and associates of Jews (*Juden und Judengenossen*)."[497]

What Robert Holub indirectly interprets these comments as an acceptance of anti-Semitism by Fritz. He elaborates that it was a typical and unconcealed attitude amid Germans, at the time, and Fritz's "likely exposure for the first time not only to a significant number of Jews in one place but also to anti-Jewish slurs and comments from his university colleagues." Then, he contends it by invoking Fritz's "great respect and admiration"[498] for Sophie Ritschl, a converted Jew who belonged to the elite of German society to which he aspired, and what had blinded him into acceptance of her Jewishness.

Fritz exhibited contempt for the lower classes from a young age, which later progressed to repulsion towards grubbiness, ugliness, greed, stupidity, narrow-mindedness, vulgarity, and loutishness in German society. As he indeed scorned plebs, he was not an anti-Semite or, in that matter, an anti-Catholic or an anti-German. Throughout his life, however, he demonstrated clear ethical and aesthetical priorities.

Instead of building upon his contentment with new surroundings, Fritz, in contrast to his usual discipline of hard work, fell into a lethargy of inactivity. He was not happy with philology and stopped attending Ritschl's seminar, who felt offended. "Such people overvalue themselves prodigiously,"[499] Fritz wrote, rationalizing Ritschl's taking offense to Hermann Mushacke, who did not come back from the Easter holidays, but stayed at home and entered Berlin University. Then, in June 1866, as political tension between Austria and Prussia grew, Gersdorff, his last friend also departed from Leipzig for a military training camp in Spandau, a borough in Berlin.

When Mushacke and Gersdorff, his fellow Schopenhauerians, were gone, Fritz was again all alone. "All in all, I am somewhat lonely in Leipzig despite my many colleagues.[500] Who is there in the whole world I could really confide in? With the bulk of my acquaintances, it is truly impossible, though there are likable, decent people among them.... But the days are over when one could quickly make a friendship—which really means more than friendship,"[501] he complained in letter to Gersdorff.

Fritz was dejected, albeit almost immediately after Gersdorff left, he began a new friendship. He approached Erwin Rohde, a fellow enthusiast of philology who followed Ritschl from Bonn to Leipzig and was also a Philological Society member.

By the summer, the two were inseparable. They both were smitten with Schopenhauer, loved music, poetry, and Greek antiquity. Rohde, "the most handsome of all the young men in the class,... was deep down," as Curt Paul Jantz describes, "almost feminine in nature, with a craving for love,"[502] ready for a new relationship after he split with a fat, aggressive, pro-Wagnerian, bland boy.

By the end of June, politically aware Fritz wrote to his mother and sister about the political situation they were all in, basing newspapers as a source.[503]

Fritz, a Saxon by birth, living in Leipzig and Naumburg, thus being a subject of Prussia, seemed quite patriotic and clear about his political affiliations. Looking always ahead into the future, he wrote to his friend Herman Mushacke in Berlin, delighted with changes taking place around them: "Who would not be proud to be a Prussian in these times? Don't you have the strange feeling that an earthquake made the apparently unshakable ground unsafe, as if history had started rolling again after years of stagnation and crush down countless linkages with its force? And in reality, the only mind of one individual, of one significant man, has set the machine in motion. If we look backward, we could have sensed the coming thunderstorm was in our guts for years. I don't mean that higher evil forces have their hand in the game. First, rotten buildings would have collapsed in a trifle, even if only a child would shake their foundations. In any case, one has to be careful not to crash with their fall."[504] He finishes the letter with courteous but impersonal greetings to Hermann's father, who had been his greatest friend just a few months ago.

He celebrated the collapse of the multistate German domain, glorifying a strong man, Otto von Bismarck, whose "audacity, courage and ruthless consistency" lead to unified Germany under the rule of Prussia. Like many times before, he was once again besotted with a strong, uncompromising individual who strived single-mindedly to accomplish his goals.

Fritz wanted not only to proclaim his alliance to the Prussian cause but actively participate in it. He expected, at any moment, to be drafted, walking many a time to *Landamt* (administrative and judicial authorities) to ask when the one-year voluntaries would be recruited. He was clear about his responsibility towards the fatherland. "Our situation is quite simple. When a house is on fire, one does not ask first whose fault it is; one puts it out. Prussia is on fire. It is now the matter of saving what one can. This is a general feeling,"[505] he succinctly informed Franziska and Elisabeth of their situation.

Even though he was not drafted during this time, nonetheless, something, perhaps even more relevant than patriotic duty, has happened in his life. In August 1866, Fritz came across a work by Friedrich Albert Lange (1828-1875), titled *History of Materialism and Critique of Its Meaning in the Present (Geschichte des Materialismus und Kritik seiner Bedeutung in der Gegenwart, 1866)*, published in the same year. It is not clear how he "discovered" the book, but as Brobjer reliably speculates, he was sent a copy by one of the Leipzig or Naumburg bookstore owners, with whom he had a very close relationships.

In the same period, as he was finishing the "Theognis" essay, which became a burden—regardless of being quite a significant addition to the field—for he was steering away from the discipline of classical philology. He believed that he was "lacking the requisite faith and [was] wasting his talents as a philologist."[506] Or perhaps, he did not wanted to invest into the field irrelevant in the schema of profound political, scientific and socioeconomical changes going on around him. "I have never written with such displeasure,"[507] he admitted to Gersdorff. It became apparent that he was becoming confident that philosophy was precisely the way of life for him. So, as usual, he got eagerly down to reading Lange.

"Finally," he continued to Gersdorff, "Schopenhauer should also be mentioned, for whom I have every sympathy. What we possess was recently made quite clear to me by another work, which is excellent of its kind and very instructive: F. A. Lange's *History of Materialism and Critique of its Meaning in the Present*. Here we have a highly enlightened Kantian and natural scientist. His conclusions are summed up in the following three propositions:

> *1) the world of the senses is the product of our organization.*
> *2) our visible (physical) organs are, like all other parts of the phenomenal world, only images of an unknown object.*
> *3) our real organization is, therefore, as much unknown to us as the real external things are. We continually have before us nothing but the product of both.*

Thus, the true essence of things, the thing-in-itself, is not only un-known to us; the concept of it is neither more nor less than the final product of an antithesis which is determined by our organization, and the antithesis of which we do not know whether it has any meaning outside our experience or not. Consequently, Lange thinks, one should give philosophers a free hand as long as they edify us in this sense. Art is free, also in the domain of concepts. Who would refute a movement by Beethoven, and who would'find an error in Raphael's *Madonna*?

You see, even with this severely critical standpoint, our Schopen-hauer stands firm; he becomes even more important to us. If philosophy is art, then even [Rudolf] Haym should submit himself to Schopenhauer; if philosophy should edify, I know no more edifying philosopher than our Schopenhauer."[508]

Fritz evidently began to shape his ontological concerns regarding the impossibility to form a picture of Kantian *thing-in-itself.* He was more than en-thusiastic about his recent discovery of Schopenhauer's thought—confirmed by the most recent discovery of Lange's materialistic approach—that philosophy through art can develop and improve one's moral judgment. By citing Lange, he explicitly consolidated philosophy with art, concluding that art, in its highest forms of expression, is philosophy in its purest and most natural state—perhaps still yearning after his own pathway of becoming an artist, which by that point he had abandoned. Although, it was still not evident to him then that philosophy is itself a form of art.

He prized Lange's work in letters to his friends, but for whatever reason, he never mentioned its influence on his thought in the later published works. It is not as drastic an omission as the treatment of Max Stirner's *The Ego and Its Own* which incidentally was mentioned in Lange's work, and to whom Lange dedicates more space than to Schopenhauer—although connecting both philosophers through the concept of the will.[509] Fritz, a staunch admirer of *The World as Will and Representation,* would not simply ignore Lange's remark that "Stirner emphasizes will so much that it appears as the basic force of the human being. It can remind of Schopenhauer."[510] Therefore again, he would, most like-ly have read the work, or at least flip through its pages, as he frequently did.

Like most German philosophers, Friedrich Albert Lange begins with the Kant's *thing-in-itself* as a starting point of his argument. He dismissed the metaphysical and speculative approach of Schopenhauer, associating it with poetry and generally artistic inquiry, postulating materialism as the only plausible way to cognize reality. As he tells the story of materialism, beginning with the opening statement "Materialism is as old as philosophy, but not older,"[511] he offers "a quite detailed account of natural sciences (*Wissenschaften*) and their relation to philosophy,"[512] retelling the history of philosophy through the prism of natural sciences.

In "Nietzsche's Reading and Knowledge of Natural Sciences" Brobjer speculates that: "Although Schopenhauer's philosophy is, of course, fundamentally metaphysical and speculative in character, throughout his writings, he discusses, takes issue with, and appeals to a whole host of contemporary scientific theories to underpin his system. He even published a treatise called *On Vision and Colors* in 1816, which was almost entirely a work of physics. Schopenhauer is, therefore, likely to have been a significant pervasive influence on Nietzsche's attitude towards science and the philosophy of nature. Moreover, ... Lange's *History of Materialism* contains a quite detailed account of the natural sciences and their relation to philosophy. It seems as if Lange was as crucial in introducing Nietzsche to, and awakening his interest in, various scientific debates and theories, as Schopenhauer was for his engagement with philosophy a year earlier."[513]

For Fritz, Lange had proposed something innovative and bold—he had consolidated metaphysics with materialism. Through arts enhanced by the materialism of natural sciences, which does not dismiss works by artists and composers, the speculative approach provides a perfect probe of inquiry into the self and the world as one universal modus operandi. So, there was not a mere chiasmus of philosophy and art, but a triad of interrelations between philosophy, art, and science—an entanglement as a unified whole, which most adequately validated and supported Fritz's interests.

Lange's work also reintroduced Fritz to Kant for he read Karl Fortlage's *The Genetic History of Philosophy since Kant* in 1864-65. However, Curt P. Janz claims that *Geschichte des Materialismus* was Fritz's "first image of Kant's works."[514]    Additionally, Brobjer also claims that Fritz did not read anything original by Kant, only about Kant in Kuno Fischer's *Geschichte der Neuern Philosophie*. Nonetheless, during 1867–1868, inspired by *History of Materialism*, Fritz probably read *Critique of Judgment*, the third critique dealing with aesthetic and teleological judgment.

Therefore, during the second half of 1866 and on to 1867, Fritz was quite busy. He read Schopenhauer, Lange, Kant (or about Kant), Stirner, work for Ritschl on the Aeschylus lexicon, and researched Diogenes Laertius' *Lives and Opinions of Eminent Philosophers* for a paper due to enter competition, on August 1, 1868. And it was an onset of his arousing interest in yet another Greek philosopher whose life was a part of Laertius' work, Democritus. Additionally, he attended few lectures at the University, preferring to enjoy outings to the theater, concerts, and opera, and spending time with his new friend Rohde.

Officially, he was studying classical philology but as clearly evident from his task choices, longed for philosophy. Despite his fading interest in classical studies, he nevertheless indoctrinated his colleagues, specifically Deussen, to switch from theology to philology, although never to philosophy. He prized the profession of the philologist, perhaps to rationalize and assure himself, that he was on the right track. "We humans have only a few really productive years: these will inevitably escape with advanced age. The original views, which we carry out throughout later life in events and experiences, are born in these years in their support and reinforcement. But since our profession accompanies us through our lives, it is necessary to find ideas and deeper meanings. However, our philological studies have the peculiarity that recognizing something new or finding a groundbreaking method requires a simultaneous degree of learning and routine, experience, and practice. The more I learned and absorbed, the more I searched, connected, and developed. The more and clearer I see, standing in the courtyards of philology peering into its sanctuary, the more I seek disciples for it. This is a course of study that takes a few drops of sweat but is really worth the effort. The real philologist soon finds the strong and invigorating sensation of a life's work. We shouldn't, dear Paul, depend on a life insurance company and timely benefices. We both long for the expulsion out of that melancholy state, where the young spirit has not yet found a fitting path on which he could walk."[515] Omitting all this praise, it is quite clear that the necessity of sacrifice in hope of finding something valuable is not an alternative in life that could satisfy Fritz. He pretended that he made his choice under the pressure of slipping time. However, in reality, he was hesitant, still searching for his own vocation and, for an audience to bring it under his spell. He did not know where he was going, but he was certainly looking for followers. I am sure he had realized for quite some time already that he was swaying between careers, depending on the moment's circumstances. But being already twenty-two, with enough experience behind him, under the influence of lectures by Lange and others he was anxious to finally find something concrete, tangible, which could launch his career.

"I longed for a counterweight to the shifting and restless nature of my earlier inclinations for a field (*Wissenschaft*) that could be advanced with cool sobriety, with logical iciness, with steady work, without the results directly touching the heart. All of this I then thought to find in philology,"[516] disappointed Fritz wrote in his notebook. In fact, he was becoming more and more attracted not only to philosophy, but to wandering in search of himself as a way of life, the creative process of self-cultivation as a form of philosophy.

But in the end, Fritz was glad to be in Leipzig. According to Julian Young, he spent the happiest moments of his life there. "The last year in Leipzig has been very dear to me. Whereas in Bonn, I had to accommodate myself to rules and forms I didn't understand, had pleasures forced on me that I couldn't bear, and lived a life without work among crude people [in the Franconia fraternity] who put me into a deep, bad mood, Leipzig has unexpectedly reversed all that. Delightful, dear friendships, unearned favors from Ritschl, numerous co-workers among my student colleagues, good taverns, good concerts, etc. Truly they all combined to make Leipzig a very dear place to me,"[517] he wrote Gersdorff in October 1866. He was enjoying good health; was a protégé of an influential professor; had a company of good friends and acquaintances; in a close relationship with a Leipzig socialite Sophie Ritschl and, in an intimate friendship with fellow student Rohde who was in love with him. He was a member of a prestigious and exclusive philological society; had Schopenhauerian friends with whom he could discuss philosophical ideas; was relishing in a vibrant cultural life of Leipzig.

So, for Fritz, life was good. He was busy producing and acquiring a lot, although, in the same letter, he wrote about the cholera epidemic that was spreading along with the moving troops. He had to move out from Leipzig to Kösen, where, with his mother and sister, they remain in quarantine. At least seven of his friends, relatives, or acquaintances died, but, judging by his letters, he seemed not to be much moved by those events. Restless, he even cracked a joke about lazy professors who postponed their lectures for three weeks, citing the plague as an excuse.

In November 1866, Fritz decided to share the circumstances regarding the "Diogenes Laertius" competition. In a letter to Mushacke, he writes about a mysterious incident while visiting Ritschl. "I have to tell you about his special kindness (*eine besondere Liebenswürdigkeit*). You know that I have dealt with Laertius Diogenes, what, here and there, I shared with Ritschl. A few weeks ago, he asked me very mysteriously if I would, if a request came from another party, write about the sources of Diogenes Laertius. What, of course, I happily affirmed. A few days ago, the university competition's theme appeared. The first thing that caught my eyes was the title, "*De fontibus Diogenis Laertii*."[518] It would be his second major work after the "Theognis" essay, which he worked on together with many other tasks related to his course of study. However, he could not resist ending the letter with evoking his real passion: "The most significant philosophical work that has appeared in the past few decades, of which I could write a great eulogy, is undoubtedly Lange's *History of Materialism*. Kant, Schopenhauer and this book by Lange — I don't need anything else,"[519] Fritz succinctly delineated his interests. Passion for philosophy was formulating his one and only vocation.

Christmas and New Year's season Fritz spent, in Naumburg waiting for his friends to answer his many letters. But he waited in vain. None was writing him back, but Herman Mushacke, to whom Fritz described yet another sad event. The passing of his beloved aunt Rosalie Nietzsche on January 3, 1867, which he witnessed and did not failed to describe. "A thoroughly painful illness and hemorrhage for several hours before her death. It was dusk. Snowflakes swirled outside. She sat upright in bed when death slowly arrived with all its sad manifestations. This peculiar experience, once seen with full consciousness, does not leave your head quickly,"[520] he described the event with melancholy poetics.

Within only a couple of weeks, he wrote another letter pondering suffering and death. His friend's brother, Ernst von Gersdorff, passed away after injuries he received during the battle at Königgrätz. "Now, dear friend, you have experienced first hand—I noticed it from the tone of your letter—why our Schopenhauer exalts suffering and sorrows as a glorious fate, as the δεύτερος πλοῦς [*deuteros plous – second best*] to the negation of the will. You have experienced and also felt the purifying, inwardly tranquilizing, and strengthening power of grief. This is a time in which you can test for yourself what truth there is in Schopenhauer's doctrine. If the fourth book of his chief work makes on you an ugly, dark, burdensome impression, if it does *not* have the power to raise you up and lead you through and beyond the outward violent grief, to that sad but happy mood which takes hold of us too when we hear noble music, to that mood in which one sees the earthly veils pull away from oneself—then I too want to have nothing more to do with this philosophy. He alone who is himself filled with grief can decide on such things: we others in the midst of the stream of things and of life, merely longing for the negation of the will as an isle of the blessed, cannot judge whether the solace of such philosophy is also enough for times of deep mourning."[521] Fritz directly applied what he learned from *The World as Will and Representation* into an actual, physical event, noticing that the experience was exclusively subjective and non-transferable. He tested the validity of Schopenhauer's claim which—if we take into account a reply from Gersdorff that "of the letters that I read during this difficult, tearful time, none made such a soothing impression on me as yours"[522]—proved to be correct. Fritz was beginning to consciously live his philosophy which was becoming his way of life. He was gazing inwards, towards his inner subjective self as the authentic, accessible realm for his experiments.

Continuing with this idea, he consoled Gersdorff again, explicitly raising the matter of self-improvement built upon an unpredictable fate. "Pious people believe that all the suffering and accidents which befall us are calculated with the precise intention of...enlightening them. We lack the presuppositions for such a faith. It does, however, lie in our power to use every event, every small and large accident, for our improvement and efficiency (*Besserung und Tüchtigung*) to derive benefit from them. The intentional character of the fate of the individual is no fable if we understand it as such. It is up to us to make purposeful use of fate, for events in themselves are empty shells. It depends on our disposition: the worth that we attach to an event is the worth it has for us. Mindless and amoral people know nothing of such a purposefulness of fate. Events do not adhere to them, but we want to learn from events. The more our knowledge in moral matters is increasing and completed, the more the events which have affected us would form or appear to form a closed circle."[523]

Fritz saw society divided into the mindless, unprincipled, ignorant, religious rabble and the knowledgeable, ethical, atheistic elite. Considering the latter, he proposed to utilizing each and every life event—whether evoking pleasure or suffering—towards the purpose of enriching and improving himself. He implied that one should open oneself to fate, not merely thinking about it, but absorb it into one's existence, the experience brought by it. In his later life of philosophy, these experiences crystallized into the concept of *amor fati* and willing the eternal return.

Up to this point, Fritz saw the acquiring of a professional career as a mode of ascent to society's higher echelons. He saw a profession as an extrinsic attribute, acquired by learning purposeful skills, contrary to an inherited, given social standing, such as aristocratism. In Fritz's eyes, the significance of one was defined by the professional position, which was attainable, sustainable, and changeable, thus socially defined and generated. With an unfolding of the idea of self-improvement and utilizing of fate, one is a sculptor of self in the process of self-development.[524] Through his latest readings, he formulated the process of making himself, employing the Schopenhauerian method—contrary to the heredity and the learning skills—as a self-focused, intrinsic act of self-agency.

## BECOME WHAT YOU ARE

During the Easter break in Naumburg, Fritz received a letter from Erwin Rohde, with whom he was getting acquainted quite closely, or at least, Rohde seemed to think so. "May [this letter], my dear friend, serve as a pledge of the unwavering love with which I always think on [sic.] you. To you alone, I owe the best hours of my life. I wish you could read in my heart how inwardly thankful I am to you for all you gave it. You have tapped in me the happy country of the purest friendship in which I, with a heart thirsty for love, glanced at earlier like a poor child in a lush garden,"[525] Rohde confessed his love, acknowledging that the relationship between Fritz and himself was evolving into deep affection. Unfortunately for Rohde, it was a one-sided exuberance. Fritz, now the mentor and the "giver," as Köhler portrays him,[526] was more restrained.

When Fritz met Rohde in Ritschl's inspired philological society, they quickly discovered that they had a lot of in common, and from that moment become inseparable.

"A fellow student reports that 'when the couple entered the room, gracefully and glowing with health and intellectual eminence, all the other students looked at them in amazement as thought they were two young gods'"[527]— Greek gods come to mind.

At the beginning of April 1867, Fritz, still in Naumburg, wrote to his on-and-off friend Deussen—who was about to move to Berlin—persistently pressing him to relocate and study philology in Leipzig, so they could reunite again. Then, perhaps expecting that his pleadings were in vain, he bragged in vengeance that he planned to move to Paris next year to work with Paris library collections. But Fritz neglected to mention that the trip idea came from Rohde and that they were seriously considering living together in Paris for a year. It seems that Deussen always has been one in Fritz's entourage whom he needed only as an obedient admirer but never a friend. Anyway, at that time, he was genuinely looking forward to living in Paris.

Within a few days, on April 6, he wrote Gersdorff about the move but again not a word about his friend and future roommate Rhode, regardless of Gersdorff a closer friend than Deussen. Instead, he wrote a self-critique about his own lack of writing style, lamenting "that it is difficult to write well, that no man has a good style by nature, that one must work at the uphill job of acquiring one. ... It would be a very sad state of affairs," he continued effusively, "not to be able to write better and yet warmly to want to do so. Above all, a few gay spirits in my own style must be unchained; I must learn to play on them as on a keyboard, but not only pieces I have learned by heart—no—but also free fantasias (*freie Phantasieen*), as free as possible, yet still always logical and beautiful (*logisch und schön*),"[528] he describes his aim.

Fritz wanted to replicate his talent in piano improvisations—a skill highly prized by many of his listeners—into a facility of spontaneous writing, in which he would be able to express himself with full rational precision and formal beauty. He wanted to achieve, with the first draft of impromptu writing, excellence in both form and content. And this ability, he claimed expectantly, was not given, but achievable with hard work. It was the culmination of an issue he had long had on his mind—the seeking of a style, which, once found in the form of spontaneous writing, he could refine for the rest of his productive life. However, "the most important elaboration [concerning style] comes in 'The Doctrine of Style,' ten notes presented to Lou Salome in 1882,"[529] adds Tracy Strong.

Then, as if the necessity of writing was seriously obstructed by his current study, he began to criticize the field of classical philology. First, he focused on the field practitioners, blaming them for a myopic viewpoint that lacked a whole perspective of, and passion for, antiquity. Then, he turned to the process of philologists' work itself, finding it lacking independent thought, in doing so reproving yet again his mentor, supporter, and champion of his own achievements, Professor Friedrich Ritschl.

"We would not deny that most philologists lack the elevating total view of antiquity," Fritz lashes out, "because they stand too close to the picture and investigate a patch of paint, instead of gazing at the big, bold brushstrokes of the whole painting and—what is more—enjoying (*genießen*) them. When, I ask, do we ever have that pure enjoyment of our studies in antiquity, of which we, unfortunately, speak often enough? ... Our whole way of working is horrible. The hundred books on the table in front of me are so many tongs which pinch out the nerve of independent thought (*selbständigen Denkens*)."[530]

At the end of the letter, Fritz turned to the Schopenhauer–Stirner brew for corroboration regarding independent thought floating on the outside of established institutions. Attestation, it seems, not as much for Gersdorff as for himself: "In brief, my friend, one cannot go one's way independent (*selbständig*) enough. Truth seldom dwells where people have built temples for it and have ordained priests. We ourselves have to suffer for the good or foolish things we do, not those who give us the good or the foolish advice. Let us at least be allowed the pleasure of committing follies on our own initiative. There is no general recipe for how each man is to be helped. One must be one's physician but at the same time gather medical experience at one's own cost. We really think too little about our own well-being; our egoism (*Egoismus*) is not clever enough, our intellect not egoistic (*egoistisch*) enough,"[531] Fritz explicitly stressed the importance of self-formation. Not through rigors of conventional models, but through acceptance of one's own egoism, embracing own positive and negative outcomes—a very Stirnerian idea. He was not formulating precise ideas in his letters, but definitely signaling their hatching. Despite all this, although he complained about the academic philology, he still worked on Diogenes Laertius project, simultaneously complaining and boasting about it.

Fritz spent the summer of 1867 with Rohde, who was far more forthcoming and garrulous about their relationship than Fritz. Their friendship embraced all aspects of their lives, writes Julian Young in his *Nietzsche* biography. They read Schopenhauer together, took lessons in riding and in pistol shooting. That summer, they spent the two weeks in *Böhmerwald* visiting the village of Klingenbrunn and the nearby towns of Zwiesel and Regen, near the Bohemian border.

Rohde remembered it as "a time of joy and informality.... What a bliss it is to enjoy the friendship of this profound and sensitive man. We spent the entire summer together living as though in a magic circle – not brusquely cutting ourselves off from the outside world yet almost always alone together."[532] Rohde was infatuated with Fritz's piano playing, which opened up his soul when he heard the magic sounds that Fritz produced in the twilight of those summer evenings, listening for hours to his improvisations at the keyboard.[533] He was grateful for being admitted to a tight circle of Fritz's friends and "for having opened up before me the promised land of pure friendship, a land of which, eager for affection, I had formerly only caught a brief glimpse, like a poor child who peeps into a sumptuous garden.... I am a thirst for beauty, for the guidance of a spirit that will free us from ourselves,"[534] he wrote to Fritz like a dreamer astray.

Whereas Fritz, although yielding to the idyllic moments with Rohde, never forgot his tasks. The deadline of August 1, to enter for the Diogenes Laertius competition was quickly approaching. The essay, titled *"De Laertii Diogenis fontibus,"* investigating sources used by Laertius in his *Lives and Opinions of Eminent Philosophers*, Fritz wrote in two language versions: in Latin,[535] as the requirements for the competition, and in German.[536] It is perhaps puzzling why he would bother with an additional German version. Although, it was apparent that Fritz recognized that the majority of people did not understand Latin or classical Greek, and, like any other writer, he craved readership and appreciation.

While gathering materials for the paper on the surviving catalogs of Aristoteles' writings, he encountered the work of Diogenes Laertius, a biographer of the Greek philosophers. According to a historian of ancient philosophy Jonathan Barnes, Fritz was immediately attracted to Diogenes' work,[537] what is based on Fritz's testimonials in notes and letters, although, Barnes does not explain what explicitly attracted Fritz to the material.

The reasoning may have been that Diogenes wrote about philosophers, and philosophy was becoming Fritz's passion. Diogenes' book, *Lives of Philosophers*, is the only surviving work compiling ancient Greek philosophers from Thales to Epicurus into a single source, used by all academics dealing with philosophy, before the twentieth century. And Fritz was fascinated not just with the philosophy of antiquity as the kernel of his emerging thinking but lives of all the significant thinkers as models to follow.

Fritz criticized Diogenes' work for its unreliability, for mixing facts with fiction and extensively copying from other authors without crediting them – a known practice among ancient writers. But, at the same time, he was fascinated with Diogenes' frivolous method and style of dealing with the history of philosophy. Diogenes considered not only dry philosophical speculations, like Kant or Hegel, but the inclusion of living and breathing personalities within the scope of his description, for example as of Zeno of Citium:

"It is stated ... that [Zeno] consulted the oracle to know what he should do to attain the best life and that the god's response was that he should take on the complexion of the dead. Whereupon, perceiving what this meant, he studied ancient authors.

Apollonius of Tyre tells us how, when Crates laid hold on [Zeno] by the cloak to drag him from Stilpo, Zeno said, 'The right way to seize a philosopher, Crates, is by the ears: persuade me then and drag me off by them; but, if you use violence, my body will be with you, but my mind with Stilpo.

The story goes that Zeno of Citium, after enduring many hardships by reason of old age, was set free, some say by ceasing to take food; others say that once when he had tripped, he beat with his hand upon the earth and cried, I come of my own accord; why then call me? Whereupon Zeno died on the spot through holding his breath."[538]

So, Fritz found in Diogenes a confirmation for the old method he practiced as a teenager. When studying at Schulpforta, he was fascinated with and wrote about characters in mythical and historical tales, focusing not only on their influence on the course of history but the protagonists' inner struggle to overcome their own weaknesses and misfortunes of fate on the path of becoming the great tragic heroes of their age. Fritz was developing an anecdotal style that injected the spirit of life into philosophical concepts, which was becoming his own unique style of philosophizing.

In a similar sense, Paul Swift, while discussing Diogenes's style, confirms Fritz's emerging form of writing:

"What is interesting about Diogenes Laertius is he gives us details of the biographies and characters of the ancient Greek philosophers, a strategy which preserves a story of philosophy told from a different (non-Platonist) perspective. The details he provides about the ancient Greek philosophers open a context for interpreting their thought and *who they were as real persons* in their psychological struggles during their lives. Diogenes Laertius's preservation of the details about what philosophers actually did for love and money, whether they drank alcohol, and whether they enjoyed tragedy, offer a glimpse into who they were psychologically, a type of narrative which influences Nietzsche's reflections on Greek tragedy and its significance for Socrates and Plato."[539] "The personalities or character typologies of the ancient Greek philosophers," Swift continues in *Becoming Nietzsche*, "are something that is irrefutable. Such aspects need not be thought of as mere trivia but may be viewed as important for understanding whether there is a personal relation between a philosopher and a philosopher's system.... The larger issue of the connection between what a thinker thinks and what a thinker is need not be rejected as a spurious psychologistic concern."[540]

I should also add that Fritz probably was more interested in "what a thinker is" than in a thinker's system. In Fritz's opinion, a description of a system was an indirect way to reconstruct an image of a thinker's personality, or character as he called it. Fritz transfigured the concern of what one is, into the imperative of becoming what one is. In the initial part of the Diogenes Laertius essay, he included his transcription-interpretation of Pindar's Greek epigram, γένοι' οἷος ἐσσί (Genoi' hoios essi),[541] *Having learned, become what you are*, which, in his subsequent interpretation become – *Become the one you are*,[542] then, – *Become what you are*, which has developed into one of the central claims of his philosophy, one of his concepts not easily yielding to interpretation.

Fritz wrote without qualms that he borrowed it from Pindar, then applied his take on it.

Fritz attempts to go a bit further than mere identifying with Pindar's directive of *becoming*—becoming as an a-teleological perpetual motion of change, contrary to a static being. It is a simultaneous a-teleological process in two opposite directions: stripping oneself of the sociocultural excrescence, and—as one is brought into the natural, true potential of oneself—building upon it or transforming it or utilizing one's potential into a higher level of over-human qualities. In other words, creating oneself anew. One can succumb to the imperatives of our civilized life, mainly relying—if not entirely—on the mindlessness of numbing consumption, avoiding, as much as possible, any challenges and suffering, becoming a fat, bitter blob of mindless flesh. Or one can experiment with one's body and mind, embracing his fate and putting oneself to the test of life's suffering and hard labor of learning, thus sculpting one's body-mind into an ideal of the Greek hero.

Additionally, there is an interesting issue with the pronoun *what* instead of *who*: as the latter connotates a belonging limited to a sociocultural schema, sociocultural affiliations, whereas the former acknowledges the subject as a part of the world as a unity. Through that simple *what*, Fritz is reaching into the subject of the ontological concerns sparked by the ongoing lecture of Lange's *History of Materialism*.

The third issue is contained within the already realized presence of *what one is looking for*. The statement lacks a literal declaration of *what one will be* but proclaims that one already *is*, nonetheless, pushing its status quo into history. Colligating what already passed (*is*) with an expectation of becoming (*will be*) in concurrence within (*as*) the world's chiasmic unity, the statement announces the perpetual production of one's (*the world's*) transformation. Without any teleological expectation, but instead, with anticipation of self-creation, the ontology of *is* reveals itself as a force of one's incessant self-becoming.

Therefore, without a doubt, Fritz implicitly signals interest and a way to proceed towards the concept of radical anthropocentrism, which he later experimented with repeatedly in his productive life.

## DEMOCRITUS OF ABDERA

While working on sources of Diogenes Laertius' *Lives*, Fritz encountered an obscure pre-Socratic philosopher Democritus of Abdera (ca. 460–380 B.C.E.), whose obscurity was not due to a lack of relevant thought but the absence of his writings, for most of his output was lost, but not to an accident.

Democritus rejected Plato, who, still to this day considered the most influential thinker of antiquity, in turn downright dismissed Democritus' work, likely out of revenge. The philosopher was not mentioned even once in Plato's oeuvre. Consequently, his writings, rendered irrelevant by Christianity, were therefore not copied throughout the centuries, and disappeared from the philosophical discourse. His works survived only as secondhand testimonials.

Initially, Fritz came across Democritus probably reading Schopenhauer and then Lange, though he could have also stumbled upon his ideas through Aristotle. Fascinated by the person of the philosopher, whose importance was placed by Lange over Plato's, Fritz started to make notes for an essay that would reconstruct Democritus' life and thought, with emphasis on his system of atomism.

Owning to Lange's *History of Materialism*, where "Democritus is featured as a cornerstone of the Western philosophical tradition down to Kant and into the nineteenth century,"[543] claim James Porter, Fritz at last encountered an idea which allowed him to move his concentration from philology to philosophy. However, his essay—like many of Fritz's projects—was never completed, although, never abandoned either. As Porter implies, Fritz's career is "best viewed as dotted not by false starts but by false endings. In a real sense, Nietzsche never decisively renounced any of his plans. He simply found another way to give them expression."[544]

Fritz was familiar with Plato from the early stages of his engagement with classical philology, beginning in Schulpforta and at the Bonn University. With the stipulation that apart from "having a good knowledge of Plato's writings [he had] little *engagement* with his philosophy." In other words, he was concentrating only on the philological aspects of the philosopher's writings, paying no attention to his ideas. Plato, the second philosopher after Emerson whom Fritz read, never had a big impact on him, compared with Emerson, Schopenhauer, Democritus, Kant, Lange, and Stirner. In a letter to Deussen, who planned to write his dissertation on Plato, Fritz wrote—"dating Plato is like cuddling up to a cloud"[545]—advising him to give up the idea.

Throughout his life, Fritz read Emerson and Lange, criticized Schopenhauer and Kant, and never explicitly admitted knowing Stirner. Still, Democritus probably influenced Fritz to such an extent that, regardless of his continuing with philology, the young scholar had utterly transformed himself into a self-determining thinker. Despite his complete dedication to work on Democritus, Fritz did not mention the philosopher to almost anyone. Except, in September 1867, when he wrote to Ritschl, citing his interest with Democritus as an excuse for the delay in completion of yet another project the professor forced on him, the *Rheinische Museum* index. "Incidentally, I cannot say that I had advanced further in the preparation of the index because another research (Democritus' fake writings) is currently keeping me occupied,"[546] Fritz defiantly informed his mentor. His new interest was of more worth to him than any earlier promise or obligation he owed out of courtesy or as a returning favor. In the summer of 1867, Fritz "embarked on the project that in many ways would prove to be a decisive turning point in his career."[547] He completely submerged himself in reconstructing the thought and person of Democritus, at the same time discovering a new way for his own growth.

Democritus, an exceptionally prolific philosopher surpassed only by Aristotle, was well-known in antiquity but had many adversaries, especially Plato and his followers. In his notes, times and times again, Fritz brought an anecdote about Plato itching to burn all the works of Democritus. "Theologians and metaphysicians had heaped their deeply rooted resentment (*Groll*) against materialism; the divine Plato held that his writings were so dangerous that he thought they should be annihilated in a private *auto-da-fé* and only through reflection would he be dissuaded, that it would already have been too late, since the poison itself would already have been disseminated too far."[548] Thus—as Plato's wish was eventually achieved through Christian censorship—Fritz set himself upon a challenging task of reconstructing philosopher's life and thought.

From the first projects taken on in classical philology, Fritz recognized its ossification and tried to bring an innovative approach to it. As Porter asserts, Fritz had a distaste for the field's stasis as an exemplar of harmony, beauty, and cheerfulness—the recognition of the Greek culture prevalent within the circles of classical scholars at the time. Taking on the Democritus project as an escape from classicism, he confirmed his deeply rooted passion and indulged in an always subcutaneously present intrinsic capriciousness.

Why would Fritz, who considered suffering and chaos as the modus operandi of human existence would embrace a culture which glorified idealism, beauty, and tranquility? "One may wonder how deeply he could possibly have been impressed by this tradition since he would apparently repudiate what the Greek skeptics described as the very goal of their skeptical practice: namely, *ataraxia*, commonly understood as 'freedom from disturbance' or 'peace of mind.' Nietzsche, as we know, has little patience for those who place the highest value on the avoidance of suffering."[549]

However, in his fragments instead of *ataraxia*, Democritus proposes *euthumia* (cheerfulness, good mood)*,* which, according to his reader Jessica Berry, may lead to *ataraxia. A* view that was more compatible with Fritz's ideas. "For men achieve cheerfulness by moderations in pleasure (*terpsios*) and by proportion (*summetria*) in their life; excess and deficiency are apt to fluctuate and cause great change in the soul. And the soul which changes over great intervals is neither stable nor cheerful. So, one should set one's mind on what is possible and be content with what one has, taking little account of those who are admired and envied, and not dwelling on them in thought, but one should consider the lives of those who are in distress, thinking of their grievous suffering, so that what one has and possess will seem great and enviable, and one will cease to suffer in one's soul through the desire for more.... Therefore, one should not seek those things [e.g., wealth, fame], but should be cheerful at the thought of the others, comparing one's own life with that of those who are faring worse, and should congratulate oneself when one thinks of what they are suffering, and how much better one is doing and living than they are. For by maintaining that frame of mind one will live more cheerfully and will avert not a few evils in one's life, jealousy and envy, and malice."[550]

Within this fragment—a bit of a naïve maneuver to feel better—lies the concept of continuous change, fluctuation, and suffering as the attributes of reality. On the opposite, inner realm, there is also quite an interesting reflection about the soul (*psuche*), because Democritus has a materialistic conception of the world with the soul as a part of it, an atomic structure that continually changes. The soul is not a closed entity, separated and insulated from the rest of the world. It is therefore susceptible to any external or internal influences, in other words, the flow of experiences. The Democritean conception of the soul—materialistic and ubiquitous—is an astonishing revelation and reinforcement of the ideas Fritz was absorbing from Schopenhauer, Stirner (as an interpreter of Hegel), Kant, and Lange, so he could have built the conception of an interpretation of inner-outer reality of his own, anew.

Lange's *History of Materialism*, where Democritus takes a central position, was a pivotal moment in Fritz's development as a philosopher, when he recognized experience in materialistic terms, as a tool in one's process of self-cultivating development. "Lange himself occupies an unusual role in the panoply of post-Kantian thinkers since rather than reinterpreting the transcendental in an idealist way, he refers all questions of experience directly to our physical makeup. It is the 'physical-psychical' organs of our bodies that transcendentally frame the way things like 'matter' appear to us. These frameworks are thus material, but their precise origin is unknown to us. In this sense, the question of the thing-in-itself stops here for Lange. He argues: 'for the thing-in-itself, we must *substitute the phenomenon,*'" Nina Power construes. Then she further expounds on Lange's position towards materialism: "'Materialism is as old as philosophy, but not older,' [writes Lange] thus simultaneously establishing the historical importance of materialism as a series of postulates about the nature of things but also denying it the privilege of being outside the status of philosophical speculation, and thereby opening it to all of the criticisms and critique that this entails. ... Lange, therefore, presents his history, *as well as experience in general,* not only from the perspective of materialism but also from the position of the *critique* of materialism."[551]

Consequently, through Democritus and Lange's work, Fritz began to develop his own theory of "will and force" which, in the later stadium of his intellectual development, became the *will to power.* In the process, he rejected Schopenhauer's substitution of the Kantian *thing-in-itself* with the still the same transcendental idealistic *will* and discarded his critique of materialism in favor of "materialistic atomism."

Democritean atomism as "the ultimate composites of all reality," which reveals itself to us through our senses, had, therefore, a human dimension in itself. It was not mechanistic, primitive materialism, but it had a component of illusion in the relationship between matter and sensation. Therefore, the illusionary part of perceiving reality necessitates an artistic approach towards it, a creative, aesthetical realization of the world around us. In this artistic approach, Nina Power writes, Democritus coupled "skepticism about the world" with "a drive to a hypothesis about nature." In that sense, and what attracted Fritz the most, was that Democritus was "an aesthetic thinker, a *poet.*"

"Democritus, in going *beyond* materialism even in one of its first inceptions, offered above all a *method* of philosophizing that allowed for both critical, skeptical thinking *and* the construction of hypotheses about the world. Democritus, arguably much more than either Lange or Schopenhauer, *united* Nietzsche's scientific and aesthetic sensibilities, and it is this *overturning* of the disjunction between art and science, perhaps more than anything else he learns from his work on Democritus, that will remain at the heart of Nietzsche' s own philosophy."[552] Therefore, if we accept this claim, then scientific hypothesizing becomes a form of art or—agreeing that the contemporary artistic production is merely entertainment, decoration, or a source of pleasure—the only form of art worthy of consideration. "The aesthetic dimension for Nietzsche is neither an accessory to philosophical inquiry nor is it ontologically suspect but serves as a condition for the possibility of identity and ontology,"[553] writes Swift.

Fritz, breaking with a traditional approach to the practice of philosophy, sees ontology and epistemology as types of artistic expression. He adopts the view that human understanding is a process of imaginative creation similar to artmaking. Under the influence of Schopenhauer, he speculates that teleological judgment—Kantian reflective a-cognition—allows a thinker "to 'see' things in the world that are not really 'out there,' independant from the human perspective."[554] He fully reversed the traditional mindset of identifying reality along with the mechanistic point of view where the artistic consideration is hegemonized by science, into the perspective where the artistic attitude determines the scientific perspective of seeing the world: "Rather than considering the aesthetic dimension from the perspective of science, Nietzsche attempts to consider the significance of science from the perspective of the aesthetic condition of life."[555] This, quite radical adjustment in the prevalent worldview would come to fruition in his later writings, but there remains a question: how can one manage to change one's way of perceiving the world to such a dramatic extent? As Fritz's thinking was never merely theoretical but continually re-applied to his own person, with the attitude of experimenting with one's body, there arises yet another question: was he ever successful in his endeavors? Could he really experience his own postulate of the world as a work of art in its becoming?

The other idea which haunted Fritz even before he read Kant, Schopenhauer, Lange, and fragments of Democritus was a concept of teleology he most likely encountered reading Plato and Aristotle. However, his interest in it arose after denouncing the Christian faith he needed to fill the void left by refuting belief. He was particularly concerned if there was purposiveness (*Zweckmäßigkeit*) independent of human inventiveness in nature. He rejected metaphysical explanations of cosmic order, then the suggested presence of intelligent designer. He did not hesitate to ask if there was a degree of rationality and intelligence in nature independent of the human experience, but at the same time, dismissed any "discursive intentions" in its emergence.

These questions were probably instigated by Fritz's profound antipathy towards Platonic idealism[556] and were assertively addressed with Laertius's and Lange's Democritus readings. "Democritus's interpretation of teleological causes had an impact on Nietzsche's entrance into philosophy, since Democritus appears to have rejected the idea of an order bestowed upon nature by an external intelligent designer,"[557] Swift proposes.

Augmented by his prolific readings throughout the years, the question of identity continued to recur, and acquired new philosophical significance after his encounter with Democritus. "Where do identities come from? To what degree are identities, in general, a function of the representing subject?"[558] – Fritz posed these questions in reference particularly to Democritus, the central subject of his inquiry. However, he perceived them in a much broader sense, beyond the prism of himself or any one individual. While reading the *Lives of Eminent Philosophers*, he was trying to reconstruct the personalities of the philosophers in conjunction with their philosophical systems.

He saw these two dimensions as one reciprocally interdependent unit. While recreating Democritus' character and thought, he realized that his research was becoming a method of philosophical inquiry which he could apply introspectively to himself, which he did. "A kind of inquiry that asks *who one is* is a viable ground to evaluate the thinker as a person. The larger issue of the connection between what a thinker thinks and what a tinker is needs not be rejected as a spurious psychologistic concern.... [Susan] Neiman, accentuating the irony of how Kant, Hegel, and Wittgenstein all are determined to avoid 'merely' psychological, writes: 'the hostility against psychologism in a field concerned with self-knowledge is deep and striking. For all the great differences between them, one thing uniting Rousseau and Nietzsche is disdain for other philosophers' distinction between philosophy and psychology.'"[559]

But for Fritz, Swift claims, these concerns were not just valuable by themselves but necessary as an additional perspective in his epistemological attempts. Fritz asked himself—was the philosopher's worldview a psychological coping mechanism? What he was investigating in Democritus and Schopenhauer—pursuing their work outside the academic institution—was the "powerful masculine seriousness,"[560] the autonomous and self-sufficient "real men" of thought. He admired Schopenhauer—regardless of discerning problems within his system—because he dedicated himself to serious thinking without any need for formal approval. Schopenhauer and Democritus' defiance towards their critics prompted Fritz to distinguish between philosophers who were free, independent, serious thinkers, and scholars of philosophy who adhere to the academic policy to pursue career advancement. Seriousness in thinking was not considered a vital attribute during the Democritus' or Schopenhauer's times, or even today, but "Democritus' claim that 'undisturbed wisdom is worth everything' struck a chord with Nietzsche," Swift claims.

"One becomes more cautious in speaking pronouncements of the priority of Leucippus and Democritus. It certainly is a great contribution to conceive of a totally new intuition, but there is a great spark to be hit upon from all the pages of Democritus. The wisdom of quiet thought, which remains undisclosed to the university student, has in the history of the sciences received a little claim for its worthiness,"[561] Fritz writes in notes for the essay.

"Democritus demonstrated a strict scientific view and method." Then he continues, seeing poesy in Democritean atomism. "An eternal shower of variant bodies appear in diversity. Movement occurs, and they are woven together, so a vortex originates.... In and for itself, there lies great poetry in atomism," Fritz presents his take on the a-metaphysical, materialistic reality. "Democritus was a beautiful Greek nature, like a statue appearing cold but fully concealing his warmth."[562] For Fritz, Democritus reinforced his rejection of the faith-based explanations of the world by excluding supernatural influence in creating the world. "With that, he became the first of the Greeks with scientific character, who endeavored to explain the unity behind the abundance of appearances without bringing in at difficult moments *deus ex machina*,"[563] Fritz explained, providing Democritus' determined rejection of this evasive plot devise.

Anyway, much of the notebook fragments Fritz dedicated to Democritus were concerned with the philosopher as a person.

Who then was this ancient thinker who agitated Fritz that he finally and decisively adjusted his career path? Although still only cryptically and internally—for formally, he was roaming the field of classical philology towards becoming, in a very near future, a professor of classics philology—Fritz was drastically changing his path of development. He came to conjecture that Democritus was motivated by "his will, which was the power (*Das macht sein Wille treibt*) that drove his senses of observation."[564]

He probably identified with Democritus, for he was also driven by an obsession to access the unknown. He did not speculate when and how it came to torment his unquenchable thirst for knowledge, but evidently, he exercised an attempt to recognize the power of his will (*Wille zur Macht)*.

Democritus utterly dedicated his life to science. He valued the scientific life [of] "having to work as a restless nomad full of self-denial," higher than any riches, Fritz wrote. "[Democritus] believed he found the scientific life to be the goal of all eudemonism. From this standpoint, he threw out the life of the masses and all earlier philosophers. He derived the pain and sadness of human beings from the unscientific life, all from the fear of gods."[565]

In Democritus, Fritz saw a person very close to himself, a person he could become, a beautiful Greek god, in total control of his emotions. An ascetic nomad who elevated philosophizing to the level of rejecting any idealistic (Platonic), metaphysical explanation. Through the life of hardship Fritz chose for himself, he rose above the masses suffering in fear of God; he found in his philosophizing more fulfillment than he could ever experience in the prevailing lifestyle of the masses he rejected.

Fritz never completed his Democritean project despite many notes accumulated throughout the years 1867–1870. Still, he continued to return to it while working on the other projects, considering it inspiration or validation of arguments or a script in pursuing his ideas. For Fritz at that time, I suppose, it would be unnecessary, or even against his budding principles, to produce a completed essay. The project in the form of rough notes, in its plasticity, was, in a sense, a reciprocal reflection of Fritz's attempts at becoming a revolutionary thinker. It was an intrinsic element of Fritz's thought and behavior formation. If it were finished, it would have been reduced to a lifeless ornament within the gallery of his achievements.

# RETROSPECT ON MY TWO
# YEARS AT LEIPZIG

The summer of 1867, the end of his two years at Leipzig University was the time of closure for Fritz. He threw himself into a celebratory mood of "nothing but the farewell parties, all rather happy than sad, Leipzig dies out slowly in our ears,"[566] he commented, already looking to the next chapter in his life. During that time, he saw Jacques Offenbach's *La belle Hélène*, whose melodies impressed him so much that he would hum it to cheer himself up, later during the military service.[567] Soon after, he left for Naumburg, where he began summarizing his life in Leipzig.

Unexpectedly, at the end of September—despite being rejected by the army on two separate occasions due to his poor vision—Fritz was declared fit for service and ordered to report for duty no later than October 9, 1867. Immediately he went to Berlin—where he stayed with Deussen but requested from Mushacke, to pick him up at the Berlin train station because of his "awkwardness (*Ungeschicktheit*) in a strange, big city"—trying in vain to join the service there. Instead, he was assigned a one-year military duty not in the major university city but to a cavalry artillery unit in Naumburg, his provincial hometown.[568]

However, the situation was not as bad as he thought initially. He could perform his service during a day, then, when he returned home, he could dedicate himself to his projects.

Following his own advice from a few months before as an imperative riposte to the critique of his own German style of writing, he commanded himself: "Thou shalt and must write."[569]

Thus, after this brief interruption, he continued with his summary, a new autobiographical essay, "Retrospect on My Two Years at Leipzig," prefacing it with a postulate of creating a "second nature" for himself, a concept of "a pivotal significance,"[570] writes Safranski. In a sense, he relieved the events of past two years by writing about them, reliving them as if they were completely new and not merely repeated events from the past.

Fritz, now a new gunner in the Prussian army, exemplifies the process of acquiring this alter ego by comparing the routine to a recruit's learning military discipline.

"Think of the foot soldier who initially fears to forget how to walk at all if he is taught the consciousness of lifting his own foot, and in the process keeps track of his mistakes. It only depends on his conforming to a second nature; then he walks just as freely as before."[571] In other words, Fritz claimed that the only solution to developing meaningful life would be the creation of a "second nature" in addition to the first one. "'First nature' reflects the manner in which people have been brought up and what inheres in them and their backgrounds, milieus, and characters. 'Second nature' is what people do with their potential. The young Nietzsche discovered that language and writing would enable him to make something of himself."[572] Writing is a method of self-configuration. And, it is not only the content of writing that is essential, he wrote in his first autobiographical sketch of 1858, but style acquired an overwhelming significance. And not just any but the style of his own—not Lessing, Stirner, or Schopenhauer's inspired form of writing but a style distinctively of his own making, which enabled his personal self-creation.

In his biography *Nietzsche*, Safranski describes Fritz's major pursuit throughout his life— the idea of "how one becomes what one is,"[573] which sprouted from the Pindar's adopted epigram, *Genoi' hoios essi, Become What You Are.*

"Self-configuration through language became a passion for Nietzsche," Safranski writes. "It contoured the unique style of his philosophy, which blurred the boundaries between detection and invention. Since he considered philosophy a linguistic work of art and literature, thoughts were inextricably bound to their linguistic form. The magic of his linguistic virtuosity would suffer considerable loss if his words were to be expressed any other way.... He considered himself, and what he had made of himself, inimitable. He felt at home on the boundary of communicability, which is where he chose to conduct his experiment with self-configuration. Nietzsche's remarkable language combined with his extraordinary ideas would initiate his self-configuration and the creation of a 'second nature.' ... Nietzsche would not restrict himself to developing ideas;

instead, he demonstrated how these thoughts originated from life and struck back into life and transformed him. He tried out their power to ascertain whether they could hold their ground against the physical pains from which he was suffering. Thoughts would have to be incorporated, he demanded—only then would they have value and significance for him. A person who is always asking himself, 'How do I form my thoughts, and how do my thoughts form me?' inevitably becomes the self-portrayer of his thinking." [574]

What is striking here is an acute awareness of the reciprocity of thought. Its impact-creation process does not stop when an idea arises and is formed into a consciously cognizable object. In response to its emergence, it immediately influences and reforms its creator, the subject. All the ideas are created by life to transform it to create a new one, endlessly, without the beginning and end. The only question that arises is whether a subject has a possibility of purposive influence on the content of an idea, and in consequence, himself? Or is the process by nature a-teleological, therefore wholly accidental, and random? If that is the case, we do not have any impact on our lives whatsoever. Hence, any attempt to purposely change is pointless?

Fritz, apparently, was asking these questions but did not consider them necessarily binding. He was interested in the observable changes in himself—in the effect of "strengthening of character"—as he put it. "My future is very unclear to me, but I am not concerned on account of it. I behave in a similar fashion regarding my past; on the whole, I forget it very quickly, and only changes in and strengthening of character show me, now and then, that I have experienced it. With such a way of life, one becomes surprised by one's own educational [developmental] progress (*Bildungsgang*), without apprehending it; and I do not deny that this has advantages, since the constant consideration [observation] and weighing [evaluation] (*Betrachten und Abwägen*) of simple manifestations of character is usually disruptive and seems to hinder its growth slightly," [575] he wrote his autobiography, now aware that a constant process of self-observation and assessment of its results would inhibit the development of his character. Nonetheless, he does not entirely reject it, Blue claims. [576] Therefore, Fritz postulated that the process of self-observation-evaluation must become instinctive, a "second nature," which he illustrated using the example of a foot soldier.

He attempted to capture this problem again, around the same time he was writing "Two Years in Leipzig," with the note "Introspection" *(Selbstbeobachtung),* a rough outline for perhaps another autobiography.

"Self-observation. It deceives. Know yourself. Through actions, not by watching. Those who measure themselves by an ideal learn to know themselves only in their weaknesses. But even the extent of these is unknown to them. Observation inhibits energy: it separates and breaks apart. Instinct is best. Self-observation, a weapon against outside influences. Self-observation as a developmental illness. Our acts must occur unconsciously."[577] He recognized that self-observation, or introspection, disturbs personal development. When confronted against ideals, which occur involuntarily, it is inaccurate, for it uncovers only the faults of a voyeur. Therefore, personal development must be achieved instinctively and unconsciously through action, not self-reflection. One could even say automatically, as one of the involuntary functions of the organism. But how to achieve it? Is Fritz's postulating self-development realized indirectly through observing, evaluating, and providing a written evaluation of other people's character?

Perhaps in that spirit, Fritz goes back to describe and relive the events he once experienced, but this time through written representation.

After the introduction, he continued not about himself but others. He began by retracing his stay in and departure from Bonn. Unlike the atmosphere at the university, he loved the city, "a beautiful place and such a prosperous land." Still, fellow students with their empty, pleasure indulging, day-to-day existence drove him away from it. "Everything was imposed on me, and I did not understand how to be master over that which surrounded me.... The crude philistine attitude amidst that excess of drink, rowdyism and indebtedness sprang forth, as something in me quietly began to protest,"[578] he confessed, adding that "constant rheumatic pain" made the situation even worse.

He left Bonn at midnight, "like a fugitive," sailing away on the steamer, not looking back with any regrets or "melancholy" as the lights marking the river's bank were slowly disappearing in the rainy darkness, Fritz remembers the event as if reliving it again.

His destination was Leipzig University, where he followed his teacher and adviser, Professor Friedrich Ritschl. Before the fall semester started, he stopped at the Mushacke family home in Berlin. He stayed there for a couple of weeks, regretting that he complained so much about everything while there. "Even our conversation fostered my bitter mood; for there was the sarcasm of the excellent Mushacke, his insights into secondary school administration, his anger about the Jewish Berlin, his memories from the time of the Young Hegelians, in short, the entire pessimistic atmosphere of a man who is much behind the scenes, to which my mood gave new supplies,"[579] Fritz reminisced, failing to remember that he was absolutely infatuated with older Mushacke and that they became close friends, although for a very brief time; failing to mention that Eduard Mushacke, during the times of Young Hegelians, had been an acquaintance of Max Stirner and most likely introduced Fritz to Stirner's magnum opus *The Ego and Its Own,* or perhaps even gifted him a copy of the work.

On the following day after their arrival in Leipzig, Fritz and Herman registered for the fall semester classes, learning, when congratulated by the rector, that a hundred years ago, on the same day Goethe began his education at the university, he reminiscences in his autobiography.

Another thing, which was "refreshing" and "pleasant" in this new place of education was an inaugural public lecture delivered by Friedrich Ritschl. Fritz was rapturous when the old professor, while looking around, "suddenly cried, 'Oh, there is Herr Nietzsche too,' and waved his hand at me in a lively fashion. Soon he had a whole circle of Bonn students gathered around him, with whom he chatted most pleasantly, while the hall became more and more crowded, and the academic dignitaries turned up. As he realized all this, he cheerfully and modestly ascended to the lectern and spoke his beautiful Latin address on the value and utility of philology. His candid view, the energetic youthfulness of his language, the flash of fire in his facial expression caused general astonishment. I heard a good-natured old Saxon remark afterward: 'Never had the old man displayed more fire.' The first lecture in Lecture Room No. 1 was also overwhelmingly crowded."[580]

Interestingly, he paid more attention to the ambiance, the *mise en scène* of lecture delivery, than its substance. The form of presentation, the literary form, or musical interpretation were becoming his focus. Renewing his memories from the years back, he became aware that, while attending lectures, he paid more attention to how they were delivered by the teachers than to their content. "What attracted me to most lectures was not the subject matter at all, but only the form in which the academic teacher conveyed his wisdom to everyone. It was the method in which I took a lively interest.... The exemplarity of the method, the way the text was dealt with, etc., was the point from which the transformative effect issue. I limited myself to paying attention to how they taught, how they conveyed the method of scholarship to young minds," – wrote a twenty-three-year-old student, foreseeing his own academic career. Then, immediately afterward, he precisely described his purpose in life. "The aim that lies before me is to become a really practical teacher and above all to awaken the necessary self-possession (*Selbstüberlegung*) [self-consideration] and reflection (*Besonnenheit*) [prudence] among young people that enables them to keep the Why? The What? and the How? of their scholarship in mind."[581] Next, he explained how he came to this conclusion of injecting a philosophical approach into scholarship. He postulated that young students should first of all fall into a state of astonishment, *philosophon pathos kat' exochēn* (philosophical pathos for excellence), then consciously concentrate on knowable things, referring to the discovery of his latest master, Arthur Schopenhauer, and the state of mind upon his arrival in Leipzig. "At the time, I was alone, just hovering in the air with some painful experiences and disappointments, without any help, without principles, without hopes, and without any pleasant memories. To construct a fitting life of my own was my endeavor from morning till night.... In the blessed apartness of my apartment, I was able to gather myself to myself (*mich selbst zu sammeln*) [to pull myself together]....— Now imagine how the reading of Schopenhauer's chief work must affect one in such a condition,"[582] Fritz addresses the reader directly, changing the narrative to the lovely story of his accidental discovery of Schopenhauer's main work, which, he claimed, was utterly unknown (*völlig fremd*) to him. A demon persuaded him to buy it. Back in his room, he threw himself on the divan and started to read. "Here every line screamed renunciation, denial, resignation, here I saw a mirror in which I caught sight of the world, life and my own heart and soul in terrible grandeur.

Here I saw the whole disinterested solar eye of art; here I saw sickness and health, exile and refuge, hell, and heaven. The need for self-knowledge (*Selbsterkenntniß*), indeed for self-gnawing (*Selbstzernagung*) seized me violently; for me, evidence of that revulsion is still the restless, melancholy pages of my diary from that time with their useless self-accusations and their desperate gazing upward for sanctification and transformation of the entire core of humanity,"[583] he remembered exposing himself to tortures of going to sleep at two in the morning, and getting up after only four hours of sleep, at six, in an attempt to refute the will to live.[584] He did that for two straight weeks until "the seductions of life, of vanity and the compulsion for regular studies" put an end to it.

Next, he recalled founding the Philological Society, which became a venue for the presentations of his work. At first, he started with the "Theognis" essay at the Lion restaurant on Nikolaistraße, where the first meeting took place. "There in the vaulted room, after I had overcome my initial shyness, I was able to speak forcefully and emphatically and even succeeded to the point that my friends expressed the greatest respect for what they had heard. Amazingly reinvigorated, I came home very late at night and sat at my desk, to write bitter words in my book of reflections and to cover up my indulgent vanity on the tablet of my consciousness," he wrote proudly of himself. The positive reception of the piece emboldened him to show it to Ritschl, who prized it and asked him to prepare it for publication. "My self-esteem and I were walking on air. In the afternoon, my friends and I took a walk to Gohlis [a district in Leipzig, where Friedrich Schiller worked and wrote his *Ode to Joy*]; it was beautiful, sunny weather, and my good fortune was on the tip of my tongue. Finally, as we had coffee and cake in the inn, I could hold back no longer and told my envyless, astonished friends what had happened to me. For some time, I wandered about in a whirlwind; it was the time when I was born into philology when I felt the sting of praise that made me pick this career,"[585] he swings back towards the realm of classical philology, yet again.

Then, he continued with the descriptions of the character of known philologists, including Ritschl, whom he prized but at the same time criticized, considering his writing about them as his gift of acknowledgement. Once again, he is not interested in their scholarship, but personalities and characters, and places he met or could have met with them, describing it in exhaustive detail. "At that time, I dined with my friends at Mahn in the Grant Blumenberg [Mahn was a restaurant in a hotel the Großen Blumenberg] in the immediate vicinity of the theater. From there, we regularly went to the Café Kintschy, which was a special privilege for me. Only a select circle of regular customers consorted there, including Prof. Wenzel, whom we called the 'tomcat,' a tiny man with lively doggedness and wavy white hair, at the time the editor of the Leipzig Signal, whom we had made the object of our waggish remarks in an innocent manner before we recognized the gentleman. We showed a lot of affection for Kintschy, the amiable Swiss, a kind, enlightened man who gladly remembered his previous customers, Stallbaum [philologist], Herloßsohn [novelist], and Stolle [poet], whose photos hung on the ancient brown walls. In these vaulted rooms, smoking was not allowed, something I found to be very pleasant. — At night, especially on Saturdays, we found ourselves in the newly established wine cellar of Simmer,"[586] remembers our unapologetic snob and elitist from a tiny village he had long forgotten.

Fritz was a keen observer and critic of peoples' interests, abilities, personality traits and characters, appearances and first impressions. By introducing those academics to the reader, therefore, giving them his "recognition," Fritz concentrated not on their work but their personae. He presents not the lifeless pages of their arguments but the multi-dimensional characters of blood and bones. His were like Leonardo Da Vinci's character studies reflected in the drawings of Florentines faces, not the Apollonian ideals of Greek statues.

Based on specific cases of acquaintances and colleagues, Fritz listed the multiplicity of attributes characterizing a person. When meeting someone new, he keenly sensed if one, for instance, was bound up in the illusionary magic or spellbound by the name of Schopenhauer. If one's qualities were hopelessly mixed, Fritz saw it as a perpetual inadequacy. Fritz always noticed if someone pursued the fine arts with zeal, especially music, or was a clever translator of French, or was very wealthy, swimming with ease against the stream of life. If one's musical judgments and feelings were more refined and better developed than his own. If one had seriously overestimated classical philology and therefore had an aversion to philologists closely involved with philosophy. If one was free from any scientific credo and was especially annoyed with an absolutely uncritical devotion to its findings.

Then he added an aspect of personality and character which would enrich his own self-portraiture. He listed the traits of other people that in many instances mirrored his own inadequacies. By paying attention to specific character traits, he ipso facto painted his own portrait as a strange, odd fellow with "English indifference and apathy," who looked at just about everything around him with a magnifying glass, especially his friends. Fritz flagellated himself with words as a person who lacked any inclination for philosophical profundity and the necessary educational background but had the restless, gnawing ambition that—because he could not find any satisfaction in anything—put his whole nature, especially his nervous system, into a state of excitement. He longed to eventually discover something through his scholarship and was sometimes happy about an allegedly significant find, but with enough inspection, they would turn out to be nothing but dross. He was a talented man, but easily offended people with his nonchalant disposition. A person with a personality that made an old-fashioned impression but who was, with his inquiring and seemingly fixed, intense gaze, possessed a trait that demanded that one should be on guard. With a repulsive mercantile egoism, he was inexhaustible in his outbursts of naive and imperturbable, offensive, and sometime nauseating vanity.

Then, with brisk touches, Fritz added several disparate traits: quick and clever, indeed diplomatically cunning, enthusiastic, frivolous, very perspicacious in his field, meticulous with his publications, naive, limitlessly vain, miserly, *defensor fidei* (defender of the faith), courtier, bookselling speculator, to finish the picture of variegated personality.

Also, he did not fail to describe his visual impressions of some of his acquaintances and had no qualms to ridicule them. On the contrary, he sounded like he was enjoying bringing out some frailties. It was almost like he was saying— look at this tiny, sickly little man with an old, beardless face, with a suppleness of movement, which reminds one in many respects of women with his embarrassing screaming voice. A small, somewhat hunchbacked man with a fresh rosy face and curly black hair threw his broad figure into a chair that cracked from his unusual weight and cried out: 'Uh-oh, this is not kosher,' offending Frau Ritschl.[587]

Some of these remarks somewhat puzzling, although I assume that the author was trying to camouflage some of the details that could be harmful or embarrassing. They were necessary in the undertaking of painting one's actual autoportrait.

Fritz accumulated a portrait of all these widely known philologists hoping that he would not become one of them. His casual tone of storytelling, almost gossiping, one could say, had become a derivative of philosophical reflection, a generator of Fritz's mysterious character.

In that sense, when I try to depict Fritz's *Bildungsgang*, do I indirectly write about myself too?

Nonetheless, while Fritz dismissed his career as a classical philologist, he was still more than enthusiastic about uncovering some of the "wonderful" secrets which the ancients tried to hide. Displaying his investigating vigor, he wrote enthusiastically of searching the libraries in an exploration of those enigmas.

"During the second winter I spent in Leipzig, I dedicated myself in earnest to paleographic studies. I had obtained through Ritschl almost unlimited access to the manuscript treasures of the Leipzig Municipal Library and situated myself there exceptionally well with the assistance of the librarian. In the dark rooms of the Gewandhaus, I sat cheerfully in the afternoon hours at the long green table, before me a Latin manuscript, one by Terence (190–158 BC) or Statius (AD 45–96) or Orosius (c. 375–418).... From the rich mass of older printings, I noticed a Walter Burley (1275–1345), something the bibliographic manuals do not mention: Walter Burley, *de vita philosophorum*, in the Leipzig Municipal Library [Catalog] HL q$^{aa}$ no name, no author and no date, 7-page index, two columns, 50 pages of text, next to the 50 on the right, 1 column explicit Gothic script."[588] Then Fritz even copied, although unskillfully, the drawing he found in the old manuscript, apparently zealous about this detective work.

Finally, as the last person in this portrait gallery of his acquaintances, Fritz introduced the reader to his friend Erwin Rohde, with whom he spent most of the summer of 1867, whose friendship he began to appreciate only from the distance of time of writing his "Two Years at Leipzig."

During that summer of 1867, while finishing "Diogenes Laertius" project, Fritz finally "surrendered" to Rohde's romantic advances. They moved into the same lodgings, although they decided to leave Ritschl and Leipzig University: Rohde for Kiel and Fritz for Berlin. Fritz could acquire a Prussian certificate allowing him to teach gymnasium there.

He also gave up his title of "student" because of his many interests and responsibilities outside routine classwork, and to lift the academic pressure. Not foreseeing a return to Leipzig, he obtained the *Sittenzeugnis*, a certificate of good conduct by the end of the semester.

When he completed the "Diogenes Laertius" paper, the first and only person he showed it was Rhode. "I spurred myself on with all my energy, and arriving there in time at 10 p.m., I was able to run over to Rohde's place with the finished manuscript in the dark, rainy night. My friend was ready, waiting for me there, and had already prepared a glass of wine for my refreshment," Fritz dramatizes the last minutes before meeting the deadline, then he reflects on their relationship.

"In a letter to me, Rohde once used the metaphor that both of us, in our last semester, sat, so to speak, upon a solitary stool. This is entirely true, but I was aware of it only when the semester was over. Without intending to, but guided by a sure instinct, we spent by far the greatest part of our time together. We did not do much work in the vulgar sense, and yet we reckoned each day we spent together was profitable. This was the first time in my life that I experienced the formation of a friendship with an ethical-philosophical background. Usually, it is the same way of studying that brings people together. However, we both have our own fields of scholarship quite distant from one another and only united in our irony toward and derision of philological manners and vanities. For we were usually at loggerheads, there were lots of things about which we were not in accord. But as soon as our conversation turned serious, the dissonance of our opinions died down, and they resounded with a more peaceful and richer harmony. Is it not, however, the opposite with most friendships and acquaintances? And is this not precisely where young people suffer some awful disappointment? That's why I now think of that entire time with great pleasure and often recall the image of those cheerful evenings in the clubhouse or those peaceful hours on a charming bend of the Pleiße River, which as artists we both enjoyed together, momentarily released from the impulses of the restless will to live and dedicated to pure contemplation."[589]

Since Fritz quoted their friendship as means to reject the Schopenhauerian will to live, their relationship must have been the not only way to artistic contemplation but also the most powerful instrument able to suspend the world in its implacable motion. Was it pure love?

As expected, Fritz received the first prize for his work, "*De fontibus Diogenis Laertii*", on October 31, 1867. Assuredly unhappily for him, for he loved all the celebrations, particularly about himself, he was unable to receive it in person, since he was already committed to military service in Naumburg.

The essay was eventually published in Ritschl's journal, *Rheinisches Museum*, in two installments, in 1868 and 1869. As James Porter and most scholars engaged in the topic claim, based on this work alone—which apparently was more than enough—Fritz could have obtained a professorship position, with Ritschl's backing, of course. The work alone established Fritz as a considerate classical scholar. "The studies were innovative indeed," writes Porter, "and full of novel insights. More vigorously systematic than their predecessors in this area, they contained vital implications for a new understanding of the entirety of Diogenes' *Lives*, a crucial source of information even today for the history of philosophy in antiquity. Clearly, the *Laertiana*, approaching two hundred printed pages and representing half Nietzsche's total published output, are a work to be reckoned with."[590]

Upon receiving the news from one of the members of the Philological Society, Wilhelm Roscher, on November 3, Fritz announced the event to Rohde. "I will not conceal from you that the Roscher's letter brought me the pleasant news that my Laertius work, on October 31 in the University Aula won a victory in the competition with *Herr Outi*s [Mr. Nobody]; I tell you that above all because I remember your friendly efforts which helped to launch the said *opusculum*."[591]

# 5

## A MOUNTED ARTILLERYMAN

In the same long letter, Fritz described his life in military barracks. However, rather than a description of himself, he cast himself in the role of narrator-spectator, a consciously self-consciousness observer, grasping the moment's activities as an exercise of his own philosophically inspired ideas. "Yes, my dear friend," he continued to Rohde, "if some *daimon* were ever to lead you early one morning between, let us say, five and six o'clock to Naumburg and were to have the kindness to intend guiding your steps into my vicinity, then do not stop in your tracks and stare at the spectacle which offers itself to your senses. Suddenly you breathe the atmosphere of the stable. In the lanterns' half-light, figures loom up. Around you, there are sounds of scraping, whinnying, brushing, knocking. And in the middle of it all, in a grab of a groom, making violent attempts to carry away in his bare hands something unspeakable, unsightly, or to belabor the horse with a comb—I shudder when I see his face—it is, by the Dog, none other than myself. A few hours later, you see two horses racing around the paddock, not without riders, of whom one is very like your friend. He is riding his fiery, zestful Balduin, and hopes to be able to ride well one day, although, or rather because, now he still rides on the blanket, with spurs and tights, but without a whip. Also, he had to forget in a hurry everything he had heard at the Leipzig paddock and, above all, to acquire, with great effort, a safe and statutory seat.

"At other times of the day, he stands, industrious and attentive, by the horse-drawn cannons and pulls shells out of the limber or cleans the bore with the cloth or takes aim according to inches and degrees, and so on. But most of all, he has a lot to learn.

I assure you, by the aforementioned Dog, my philosophy now has the chance to be of practical use to me."[592] Fritz turned the process of observing the performance of standardized military procedures into an experiment of developing one's self-conscious experience and learning from its application.

Around the same time, he relived the experience of repeating these observations in notebooks' entries, although from an added perspective, utilizing the Schopenhauerian postulate of performing self-observation through an artistic mode of originality. "It is a good ability to be able to observe one's condition with an artistic eye and even in pain and suffering, awkwardness, and matters of that sort to have the Gorgon gaze that instantaneously petrifies everything into a work of art: that gaze from a realm without pain. Another good ability is being able to recognize and assess everything that is personally relevant for us as a step toward refinement (*Bildungselement*)."[593]

Fritz was not an enthusiast of fossilizing one's life into a lifeless work of art, a discrete event, so one could, without agitation inspect it, Safranski construes, but he opted for a processual intervention, the "epic method" of incessantly forming one's personae. In other words, looking through one's life as a completed literary work, a book, was not a good option for Fritz. He chose his ever-developing writing work as a plastic modality through which he could gaze into his own tormented self within the unity of the world's suffering. Therefore, an output, a finished work of art, is irrelevant so as to be actually nonexistent. Instead, we should pay attention only to the plastic process of crafting a never-completed work.

The last part of Fritz's letter to Rohde was dedicated to their friendship, the subject which Fritz thought should have been addressed at the beginning of the letter. But he excused himself by not being in the right mood to do it, for "one does not write letters to friends whom one loves, as I love you, in any mood.... I am fairly lonely in Naumburg; I have neither a philologist nor a friend of Schopenhauer among my acquaintances.... When this morning I walked through the black, cold, wet darkness, and the wind blew restlessly round the dark masses of the houses, I sang to myself *Ein Biedermann muss lustig, guter dinge sein* (A man of honor must be merry and bright)[594] and thought of our crazy farewell party.... Today I am celebrating Sunday in my way, by remembering my distant friend and our common past in Leipzig and in Bohemian woods and in Nirvana, ... our memorial on the banks of that Leipzig River, which we christened Nirvana, and which bears the solemn words from me, which I have proved victorious: *Genoi' hoios essi* (*Become What You Are*). If, finally, I apply these words to you, dear friend, let them contain the best that my heart feels for you. Who knows when changeful fate will bring our paths together again: may it be very soon; but whenever it may happen, I shall look back with joy and pride to a time when I gained a friend *hoios essi* (*One that You Are*)."[595] For the first and probably the last time in his life, Fritz recognized himself for who he really was by openly and directly professing his love to Rohde. An event that has not happened with any other person in his life.

Towards the end of 1867, Rohde left Leipzig for Kiel, where, within a couple of years, he completed his doctorate and began his academic career. Fritz, all by himself again, turned his attention to pursue working on the essay concerning his latest philosophical idol, "On Schopenhauer" *(Zu Schopenhauer).*[596]

From the first moment in late October of 1865 when Fritz found a copy of *The World as Will and Representation* in Rohn's antiquarian bookshop, he was captivated by the thinker. He applauded the philosopher to heavens and tirelessly tried to make others follow him, but in moments of quiet, rational reflections, he was bluntly critical of the Schopenhauerian system. He specifically rejected Schopenhauer's claim that he knew the Kantian *thing-in-itself.* This epistemological analysis of Schopenhauer's claims was provoked by Fritz's concern with limitations of human intellect and the uniqueness of human consciousness within the animal kingdom and the world, Swift claims. "These issues also have direct implications for the classic philosophic quest for knowledge of self. The meaning of human life for the species and for the individual is not a nostalgic relic of pre-twenty-first century thinking but persists as a genuine philosophic concern."[597]

Swift further interprets Fritz's piece demonstrating that the theory of the will—that Schopenhauer replaced with Kantian, inaccessible to human intellect, *thing-in-itself*—is contradictory. In his piece, Fritz begins to explore the "limits of discursive representation," hence its consequences for the possibility of truth in philosophy. "An attempt to explain the world by an accepted factor. The *thing-in-itself* becomes one of its possible forms. The attempt fails. Schopenhauer did not consider it an attempt. His *thing-in-itself* was opened up by him.

That he did not see this failure can be explained that he did not want to feel the dark contradictoriness in the region where individuality ceases to be. He did not trust his judgment. The dark drive (*Trieb*), lying under the [realm] apparatus of representation breaks through, revealing itself as world,"[598] Fritz argued, postulating that the whole ontological schema of the world is encompassed already within the title of Schopenhauer's work: the world as will and representation. Thus, the world consists of the realm of the will (which is in Fritz's vocabulary the dark drive) and the reality of representation as the world (*Welt*), a phenomenal realm accessible by human senses.

Taking this argument into account, one question comes to mind: are there representatives of organic life including the human species, which have the ability, to some degree, to access the realm of the *thing-in-itself* or the dark drive? If it is true, and cannot be ruled out as false, then Schopenhauer may have possessed the ability to see across the screen of representation into the realm of the *thing-in-itself.*

However, Fritz saw in Schopenhauer's argument nothing but the Kantian formula, where the unknowable *thing-in-itself* was merely replaced with the will. And by which will, through the mechanism of representation, reveals itself as the world. Therefore, as Schopenhauer claims that he knows the *thing-in-itself* to be the will, Fritz showed it as an error:

"The so-called solution then: In order to comfortably get ahold of in what the redeeming and explanatory elements of this formula are to be found, it is recommended that they be transposed partly into images: the groundless, unknowing will reveals itself, through a representation mechanism, as world.

When we subtract from this sentence, what passed to Schopenhauer as the legacy of the great Kant, a legacy which he always, in his grand manner, regarded with the most proper respect: there remains the one word 'will' along with its predicates. It is a clumsily coined, very encompassing word, when with it such an important thought, going well beyond Kant, is to be labelled differently."[599]

He noticed that there is not a single piece of proof supporting Schopenhauer's claims. In Fritz's interpretation, Schopenhauer delivered his system in such a "triumphant tone" as if his claims should be accepted at face value, without the necessity of any proof. "How in the world a man can reach such a level of pretension with a system so full of holes," he asked with a hint of audacity in his voice. However, subscribing to his old maxim of profiting from even the worst situations, he affirmed that "the errors of great men (*großer Männer*) are worth honoring because they are more fruitful than the truths of small men."[600] Then, after these introductory remarks, Fritz arrived at his rational self, pointing out four concerns without scruples or hesitation.

The first objection was that Schopenhauer did not surpass Kantian *thing-in-itself* as an inaccessible category but, as the structure of the system, it remained in the same position. Then, he replaced it with "the will," relying on his "poetic intuition," without any justification or logical or rational proof for such an act. Schopenhauer claims that the predicates of the will are in opposition (contradiction) (*Gegensätze*) to the world of representation. Still, Fritz noticed that "between the thing-in-itself and its appearance not even the concept of this opposition has any meaning." In other words, Schopenhauer has invented a relationship of opposition between the will and its predicates, discarding the Kantian absence of meaning in the relationship between the *thing-in-itself* and the world of representation. And lastly, Fritz continues, "an opposition is unprovable between *thing-in-itself* and appearance but can still be thought. Against such a knot of possibilities every ethical thought could explain itself: but even against this ethical pretext one could still object that the thinker who stands before the riddle of the world, has no other means than to guess in the hope that a moment of heightened awareness (*ein genialer Moment*) will place the word upon his lips. A word which offers the key to that text lying before all eyes still unread, which we call world. Whether this world is will? Here is the point at which we must make our fourth attack. The Schopenhauerian warp and weft gets tangled in his hands: in the smallest part as a result of a certain tactical clumsiness of its author, but mostly because the world does not let itself be so easily fastened into the system as Schopenhauer had hoped in the first inspiration of discovery. In his old age he complained that the most difficult problem of philosophy had not been solved in his own [philosophy]. He meant the question concerning the borders of individuation."[601] Fritz further elaborated that Schopenhauer simply took the concept of will not from the realm of *thing-in-itself*, which he could not know regardless of his claims otherwise, but rather, from the world of appearance.

Fritz presented sophisticated philosophical proof of Schopenhauer's mistakes; however, one may feel that the academic argument was not within Fritz's concerns, for he never clearly rejected Schopenhauer. On the contrary, he continued his on-and-off reverence towards the philosopher. Because "the errors of great men are worth honoring,"[602] Fritz showed yet again that he was more interested in the man than his philosophical system. He valued Schopenhauer's vulnerable courageousness submitting his error to criticism instead of providing the bulletproof way out from a pitfall he dug up for himself, utilizing a transcendental copout.

It is puzzling that in his piece, Fritz concentrated solely on the errors in the philosopher's system but not on the functions of arts, specifically music, through which—Schopenhauer claimed, we are "attuned to the authentic condition of life, without any interference from language"[603]—Fritz could have incorporated music into his reasoning since he was exalted about the similarities between himself and the philosopher in the thought processes. It would be fully justified since Schopenhauer wrote:

"Music expresses in an exceedingly universal language, in a homogeneous material, that is, in mere tones, and with the greatest distinctiveness and truth, the inner being, the in-itself, of the world, which we think of under the concept of will, according to its most distinct manifestation. Further, according to my view and contention, philosophy is nothing but a complete repetition and expression of the inner nature of the world in very general concepts, for only in these is it possible to obtain a view of the entire inner nature which is everywhere adequate and applicable. Thus, whoever has followed me and has entered into my way of thinking will not find it so very paradoxical when I say that, supposing we succeeded in giving a perfectly accurate and complete explanation of music which goes into detail, and thus a detailed repetition in concepts of what it expresses, this would also be at once a sufficient repetition and explanation of the world in concepts, or one wholly corresponding thereto, and hence the true philosophy. Consequently, we can parody in the following way the above-mentioned saying of Leibnitz, in the sense of our higher view of music, for it is quite correct from a lower point of view: 'Music is an unconscious exercise in metaphysics in which the mind does not know it is philosophizing' *(Musica est exercitium metaphysices occultum nescientis se philosophari animi)*."[604]

Nevertheless, despite the exclusion of music in his piece on Schopenhauer, Fritz devoted his first book to the ontological considerations flowing from the spirit of music just a few years later. Apparently, his way of thinking about *The World as Will and Representation* have not been forgotten. He purposely dismissed useless academic arguments, whether correct or incorrect, in favor of accessing a particular way of thinking, the method which he could appropriate for his own subjective purposes, and of which he refused to notify his readers. But he still proved that he could efficiently deliver an academic argument to be reckoned with.


At last, by the end of 1867, Fritz disclosed his involvement with Rohde to his friend Carl von Gersdorff. Why had he waited so long? Was it an apprehension of losing a friend or needing to unfurl the veil of mystery around himself?

He did not write Gersdorff for more than eight months, but in any case, if we consider theirs a close friendship, Fritz was indeed embarrassed that he "owed" Gersdorff a letter for such a long time. When eventually he got to writing it, he described the events of last summer, starting with winning the first prize for the "Diogenes Laertius" paper. He cited Ritschl's congratulatory remarks while emphasizing Pindar's motto of *becoming what you are.* Then, he connected it with Schopenhauerian demand for putting ἄσκησις, askesis (ascesis, exercise) into a praxis of life he later adhered to his entire productive life. However, he did not write about the blatant nepotism he was obviously aware of. Still, paradoxically, he was "very glad because Ritschl's *iudicium (judgment)* encouraged him and drove him forward on a path of which he was tempted, out of skepticism, to leave."[605]

He complained again that he could not attend the award ceremony in a fully packed Aula due to his military obligations, but anyway, he rewarded himself for the work. After its completion "in early August," he writes, "as soon I was free of it, I fled with a friend Rohde to the Bohemian woods to bathe my tired soul in nature, mountain, and forest. Here I must say something of Rohde, whom you have also known from an earlier time. We were together most of this summer and felt a strange intimacy between us. It was without saying that over this friendship hovered the genius of the man whose picture Rhode sent me a few weeks ago from Hamburg—Schopenhauer. I think you will be very glad to hear that precisely such robust and good natures as Rohde has, in the best sense, are gripped by that philosophy,"[606] Fritz continues his story. By the end of the excursion, they attended a music festival held by the *Zukünftler* (*Zukunftsmusiker*), a group of music practitioners associated around Liszt and Wagner, "who were celebrating their strange musical orgies here. Abbé Liszt was presiding. This school has thrown itself passionately into the arms of Schopenhauer. A Symphonic poem by Hans von Bülow, *Nirvana*, was based on a collection of Schopenhauer sentences; but the music was frightful. On the other hand, Liszt himself, in a few of his sacred pieces, has hit off the character of that Indian [Buddhist] Nirvana excellently, above all, in his *Seligkeiten* (Bliss), '*beati sunt qui'* (Blessed Are Those) and so on."[607] Then, fate intervened. Fritz was drafted for one-year volunteer military service as an artilleryman at the 4th Field Artillery Regiment stationed in Naumburg. He did not complain about the turn of events; after all, he was trying to enlist for quite some time. Contrary, he was even glad to find himself under the "military shackles," for "only now am I really thankful for our Schopenhauer," he wrote to his friend, "now that I have a chance to practice a little ἄσκησις (ascesis). During the first five weeks, I also had to perform stable duties: every morning at five-thirty I was in the stables to clean out the manure and to groom my horse with comb and brush.... I like the riding lessons best. I have a very good-looking horse, and people say that I have a talent for riding. When I whirl around the exercise area on my Balduin, I am very satisfied with my lot. On the whole, I am treated excellently well. Above all, we have a pleasant captain."[608] In the end, he recommended two books to Gersdorff. One was a novel by Friedrich Spielhagen (1829–1911), *In Rank and File (In Reih und Glied)* and the other, a philosophical treatise by Julius Bahnsen (1830–1881) *Contributions to Characterology (Beiträge zur Charakterologie, 1867)*.

Spielhagen's novel was published in 1866, the third work in a cycle of three books proceeded by *Problematische Naturen* (1861–2) and *Die von Hohenstein* (1864). The three novels' theme was a call for unified Germany, a project which, as the author fictionally portrayed, was impossible to realize. Spielhagen's "insistent calls for Germans to unite in common purpose thus were countered by his portrayals of starkly conflicting purposes.... An all-out collision between aristocratic privilege and middle-class values," writes Katherine Roper.[609] Spielhagen experimented with the possibilities of successful unification, providing the most accurate critique of the socio-political reality of Germany. "The novels serve as vivid evidence of the making of a German democrat during the 1860s," Roper continues, "years in which the authoritarian course of the Bismarckian Reich had not yet been set. Critics inclined to dismiss the *Ratlosigkeit* (helplessness) of Spielhagen's liberalism miss the historical importance of his struggles against formidable countercurrents and of his commitment to educating German readers then and throughout the rest of his life in taking political responsibility to bring the promise of 1848 to fulfillment."[610] Reading perhaps all three novels, Fritz would benefit not just with a documentarian description of political, social, and economic realities of Germany but also could learn from the way it was delivered. As he was more and more sensitive to the process of artistic creation, he could have realized that the form of Spielhagen's works was as important as their content.

"Writing for Spielhagen was not only a political act; it was an aesthetic creation. As he wrestled with the problems of literary representation in a long succession of essays, he repeatedly emphasized that the first task of the novelist was to create an artistic totality of a complex world of individuals living in a distinctive society. He realized that a significant problem with conveying that social reality was dependent upon language and that, in turn, was molded by the perspectives of the observer. A genuine literary realism, then, had to convey not simply the perspectives of the author, but those of the whole range of characters he was creating... Rather than depicting one 'reality,' his novels are replete with characters who perceive widely differing 'realities' according to their social station, their material condition, or their psychological stance. His detailed and usually respectful portrayal of such perspectives gave rise to multifaceted episodes that revealed deep social conflicts, but it also undermined his effort to enunciate an overarching diagnosis for German society's ills and prescription for a cure. His insistent calls for Germans to unite in common purpose thus were countered by his portrayals of starkly conflicting purposes,"[611] writes Roper.

Thus, the works by Spielhagen must have had an effect on Fritz, for the author was very popular during his prime as a writer. The books were not only mines of information about sociopolitics but also a blueprint on how to deliver complex and unpopular truths about the readers themselves. The Spielhagen's prose was not only relevant as a historical narrative but also as a work of art, which perhaps interested Fritz the most, for he was still searching for the style of his own.

The other feature of Spielhagen's fiction, which could arouse Fritz's curiosity, was a theme of the origin of nobility: "The secret class origin seems to have deterministic psychological effects; some form of superiority or delicacy is detectable before the circumstances of birth are revealed. Oswald Stein in *Problematische Naturen* developed, despite the influence of his fiercely class-conscious alleged father, initially incomprehensible aristocratic instincts, a love of fine clothes and comfort, an attraction to refinement and poesy.... In *Sonntagskind*, when Justus finds himself in the garden of the manor, he feels a longing for beauty and elegance."[612] In many of the author's novels, this narrative device reoccurs, sometimes straying into the areas suggesting biological inheritance. But, as Jeffrey Sammons claims, "it is always difficult to tell in the late nineteenth century whether the implication of blood inheritance are merely of metaphorical usage or are the precursors of genetic ideas.... But notions of genetic inheritance are grounded in ancient folk perceptions, and I do not think Spielhagen [is] entirely free of them in his understanding of class determinations.

[Katherine Roper] has remarked that his [Spielhagen's] 'critique is seriously weakened by countervailing hints that the notion of inborn superiority might have merit.'[613]"[614] Nevertheless, this type of lecture, if they would not have strengthened Fritz's reveries of his inherent nobility, they would undoubtedly allow him to introduce an element of mystery into his writing.

# JULIUS BAHNSEN'S
# CHARACTEROLOGY

The other recommendation to Gersdorff was the newly published *Contributions to Characterology* by Julius Bahnsen. At first, Fritz enthusiastically recommended Bahnsen's work, but later, while reading and appropriating his ideas, he never mentioned him by name. Eventually he dismissed him as the "old claptrap Bahnsen,"[615] a naïve but fairly frequently used trick, to quash any opinion which would suggest he was borrowing from others' works.

Julius Bahnsen was one of the three leading pessimists in German philosophy with Philipp Mainländer and Eduard von Hartmann, who grown out of Schopenhauerian teachings, and whom Fritz read frequently. Bahnsen was obsessed with Schopenhauer, even visited him personally on two occasions, recognizing later, that "from then on I regarded him and honored as my master,"[616] nonetheless, in his writings, refuting his teachings.

Bahnsen's philosophy was quite unusual, far from the accepted academic practice, so it contributed to many unsuccessful attempts at securing an academic position for him. Harry Slochower writes interestingly about Bahnsen's attitude towards philosophy, perhaps not accidentally describing what Fritz was striving for his entire philosophical life. "Philosophy was to [Bahnsen] rather an attitude of faith, practical ethics, bound up with man's basic emotions and having direct life-significance. His own philosophic orientation was determined throughout by the deepest and most intimate sources of his being. The high moral pathos of his argument, the rhythmic intensity, and the individual character of his idiom are striking indications of the significant extent to which his entire personality entered into his work. Ideas possessed personal values for him. However, the passion with which he fought for his persuasions involved him in constant controversies, carried on in a brilliant yet extremely polemical manner. Everywhere he takes the position of a fighter, now assailing with fast rapier-thrusts, now defending with passionate counterattacks, always disputatious. Indeed, the entire form of his presentation received its stamp from the controversies carried on against von Hartmann, Volkelt, and others. His heated and militant tone has irritated many critics and has doubtless been a strong factor contributing toward the inadequate consideration that his system has received."[617]

Bahnsen's philosophical debut was a work titled *Contributions to Characterology,* which Fritz read immediately after its publication. It is a work concerning the personality and individuality of a human being. And, from a different point of view, *the book*, as Frederick Beiser writes, is a documentation of a process of becoming an independent philosopher (in this case, independent but indebted to Schopenhauer[618]), themes which were of decisive interest to Fritz. The science of personality—in Bahnsen's terms, characterology—was based on the Schopenhauerian concept of the will. "Bahnsen not only states that the philosophical foundations of characterology lies in Schopenhauer's philosophy but he also defines his discipline in Schopenhauerian terms. The whole discipline revolves around Schopenhauer's central concept: the will. Characterology, Bahnsen writes, is 'a phenomenology of the will' whose task is to describe how the will appears in different individuals. The debt to Schopenhauer is especially apparent when Bahnsen makes the will and its various motives the basis for his classification of personality,"[619] writes Beiser.

Making a distinction between philosophy and empirical sciences, Bahnsen claimed that characterology has a metaphysical foundation like any other field of scientific inquiry. It was necessary to explore it to obtain the complete picture of that discipline. Hence, he discerned two "fundamental metaphysical questions" to address this concern: "First, what is the relationship of the will as such and its manifestations in individuals? Second, what is the relationship between the will and its representation?"[620]

While declaring his debt to Schopenhauer, Bahnsen was severing himself from the "master's" idealism by developing his own path of thought. He approached the problem of the will confronting it as one universal, indiscrete force *versus* individual phenomena of observable differences between people. He saw an error in Schopenhauer's limiting the *principium individuationis* of the will to the empirical world of human differences exclusively. That Schopenhauer could not explain why the universal will, due to its universality and sameness in all people, produces inexhaustible phenomenal differences. Therefore,

Bahnsen concluded, it cannot be the basis for the *principium individuationis.* Bahnsen discovered that the will must be different in each person, thus arriving at the concept of individualism. He argued that if the world consists of a multiplicity of individual substances, then there is not just one but a variety of wills, different in each person and—not expanded further by Beiser—in every substance. Thus, if an object is a conglomeration of various substances, it would be a conglomeration of different wills. Or perhaps, this conglomeration of wills would homogenize into one, but a different will, which would always be in a state of continuous transformation to accommodate the change of an object or *vice versa,* reciprocally. The concept of individuality is intertwined with the idea of individual responsibility, which consequently provides the power of autonomy, the source or a cause of an individual's own actions. And this would have been the point which Fritz would totally embraced. Fritz was seeking confirmation of his intrinsic desires to truly own his person.

Further, considering the second question concerning the relationship between will and representation, Bahnsen focuses on Schopenhauer's aesthetic experience. He thought Schopenhauer was wrong separating the will from the aesthetic sensation and declaring it a will-less, "disinterested contemplation" of the works of art. Baffling, because for Schopenhauer, art was the only possibility of slipping out of the clutches of the will—in an effort to alleviate suffering, music could suspend the will's unrestrained forces.

"Aesthetic interest has its basis in the will, and that it is an exaggeration to write of its 'disinterestedness.' Although esthetic experience abstains from the lower ends or interests like self-preservation and procreation, that does not mean that the will is absent; on the contrary, it appears in feelings of 'self-promotion, self-confirmation, self-satisfaction.' The pleasure we take in art, and in intellectual activity in general, Bahnsen claims, is a species of 'self-affirmation.' The experience of beauty consists not in the elimination but the expansion of our willing self,"[621] Beiser paraphrases Bahnsen. Bahnsen came to the conclusion that the intellect and the will should join one another: "Just as the will should know, so the intellect should will.… Volition and cognition should never be separated, because the will is always the force and power behind cognition: 'intellect functions are only a special case of functions of will,'"[622] Beiser reads Bahnsen.

Bahnsen's *Weltschmerz* philosophy (willing what one does not will and not willing what one will) arose from the grounds of Schopenhauerian pessimism and his misfortunes in family and professional life, providing him with ideas concerning pessimism and the possibility of redemption.

He dismissed Schopenhauer's preponderance of suffering, insisting that "the pessimist knows all too well that most of his hopes and ideals will be frustrated by the world, and that he can realize a few of them only through enormous struggle and then by paying the price." But the pessimist never gives up, "he stands and fights for them even when he knows that it requires sacrifice and sorrow"[623]—Bahnsen personifies Fritz's favorite heroic character, the tragic hero. Through not willing what one will, therefore through self-denial, Bahnsen believed in the possibility of release from the urges of the will and, though with a dash of doubt, the possibility of redemption.

Fritz seemed elated in recommending Bahnsen's work to Gersdorff, but despite undoubtedly being influenced by his philosophy while adopting Bahnsen's will theory, he never discussed him as a source or an inspiration in his works.[624]

He repeatedly reached into anything creative, famous, or significant to shamelessly appropriate it into his self-created myth about himself as a great thinker. It did not matter to him if he was plagiarizing, borrowing, or simply influenced by others. For him, it was just a fertilizer to nurture his own person. He was beyond common morality from the beginning, following only his own prerogatives of making an image of himself by himself. Bahnsen's philosophy was just an additional element in the whole schema, for Fritz understood that the art of inventing conspicuous impressions is more potent than any argument or mechanistic scientific discovery.

However, all his lofty tone when writing philosophy disappeared when confronted with the reality of his military service. During the first days of February 1868, he complained to Rohde about the lack of friends, books, and time to contemplate in order to think and write. "My dear friend, this life of mine is now really very lonely and friendless. There is no stimulation except that I give myself, nothing of that harmonious accord of souls that many good hours in Leipzig brought together. Rather, alienation of the soul from itself, the pre-ponderance of a dominant influence which pulls the mind into a knot of fear and teaches it to look at things with a seriousness of which they are not worthy. This is the downside of my present existence, as you can certainly feel it from me," Fritz complains at the very beginning of a long letter, but then, finding, as always, a right within a wrong, a beneficial meaning in the whole ordeal, he changes the tone: "let's turn the coin over. This life is uncomfortable, but useful when enjoyed as an entremets between courses. It is a constant appeal to the energy of a person, and it tastes particularly good as ἀντίδοτον, *(antidoton)* (antidote) against the paralyzing skepticism which effects we have experienced together. In this way, one gets to know one's nature, as it manages to reveal it-self among strangers, mostly rough people, without the aid of *Wissenschaft* and without that traditional *fama* (reputation) which determines our worth for our friends and society."[625]

Then, Fritz referred again to the "Diogenes Laertius" essay with em-phasis on its inscription γένοι᾿ οἷος ἐσσί (*Genoi' hoios essi), Become What You Are.* By connecting "knowing one's own nature" with "becoming what you are," Fritz undeniably formulates a metaphysical path of continuous recreating anew of his own person in terms of somatic materialism.[626] In other words, the realization of the process of ongoing development through one's action.

A couple of weeks later, he repeated and strengthened his concerns of self-knowing and self-becoming through complaining, although finding benefit in his military service, in letters to Mushacke and Gersdorff on Feb-ruary 13 and 16, respectively. He once again recommended works by Lange, Schopenhauerians Spielhagen and Bahnsen, and Darwin, whom he discov-ered in *The History of Materialism,* probably his initial encounter, as indicat-ed in Fritz's notes and letters.[627]

At first, he acknowledged to Mushacke a problem of the one-sidedness of one's perspective in perceiving development of a person: "I thought of myself in a state of affairs which, although contained various discomforts, was at the same time surrounded by a sphere that breathed courage, determination, and manliness. After all, the savory dish had been offered to me at the table of my life, which I was no longer able to refuse. I tasted enough, and I didn't even find it that bad tasting. It tasted particularly of the effeminacy that ensues in a student's way of life and study." Then, realizing that his soldering was not merely a waste of time but a necessary feature in self-cultivation. "Hence, I got used to looking at the military year as one of those benefits through which we avoid one-sided formation (*einer einseitigen Ausbildung*). To primarily find in it a specific antidote to a stiff, pedantic, narrow-chested erudition against which I always struggle (*Kämpfe*), wherever I could uncover it."[628]

This concentration on the body must have been corroborated by Darwin's theory of evolution—a theory which in later years he went on to criticize, mainly because he did not read Darwin firsthand, but knew him through secondary literature, not realizing that he was through-and-through Darwinian,[629] John Richardson claims.

Excited about Darwinian theory, he wrote Gersdorff three days later: "If you feel like truly informing yourself about the materialistic movement of our times, in the natural sciences with their Darwinian theories, their cosmic systems, their animated camera obscura, etc., at the same time ethical materialism, about the Manchester theory, etc., then l can recommend nothing better than *The History of Materialism* by Friedrich Lange (Iserlohn 1866), a book which gives infinitely more than its title promises, and which one can go back and read through again and again as a true treasure. In your subject of study, I cannot name anything more worthy."[630]

With the adoption of materialism, Fritz crossed boundaries of metaphysics and philology into the realm of scientific speculations, where he stayed interested in its philosophical implications. In Lange, he discovered that "Darwin has effectively refuted the various teleological views of nature, from those associated with ancient philosophy, such as Plato and Aristotle, to Christian theology and natural philosophy in debt to religious ideas. Like many of his contemporaries, Lange's judgment about the scientific merits of Darwin's views is somewhat equivocal: while he has undoubtedly made a great advance on previous worldviews in natural philosophy, Lange asserts, his contentions are based on hypotheses that have yet to be demonstrated. Lange, therefore, calls for experiments to confirm what Darwin has conjectured. He also intimates that Darwin's solution to the mechanism of evolution, which was the central issue troubling members of the scientific community who objected to Darwin's work, is only partially valid. Citing other prominent biologists critical of Darwin, Lange obviously believes that natural selection, which he views as an outgrowth of Darwin's preoccupation with artificial breeding, must be supplemented by internal mechanisms in order to account for the fecundity of species development. In general, Lange emphasizes the struggle for existence as the centerpiece of the Darwinian hypothesis, and we can imagine that Nietzsche was fascinated by an extended citation from *Origin of Species* in which Darwin writes about how one species of birds lives from insects and seeds, and how birds of prey and other animals, in turn, devour these birds,"[631] Holub paraphrases parts of Lange's work which might interest Fritz.

There is no question that Fritz was critical of Darwin's ideas almost from the beginning, but that does not mean that he did not use them in his philosophical inquiries. As with Schopenhauer and many others, Fritz always saw value in works he later dismissed, usually, as I claimed before, immediately after the initial moments of euphoric prizes.

## AN ACCIDENT AND TELEOLOGY SINCE KANT

On March 5 or 6, 1868, Fritz, one of the best, if not the best horse riders in the barracks, had an accident. While mounting a horse, due to his myopia, he missed the saddle, hitting a pommel with his chest, tearing two muscles, and fracturing his breastbone. He continued riding the horse, but after an hour or so, he fainted. Because of excruciating pain, he found himself confined to bed, taking morphine daily so he could sleep. Ice packs and chamomile tea compresses did not help much. His wound, instead of healing, was getting progressively worse: he developed internal hemorrhage, infection, and swelling spreading throughout his chest. The doctor had to cut the wound open and install drainage so the pus could discharge externally, about which he wrote to Rohde on April 3.

Two months later, on June 6, 1868, he wrote him again, mostly about his work and work-related affairs but then, at the end of the letter about the illness: "First of all, from my state of health, it became sadly clear to me how badly one can live in self-deception for a long time. Not only can I not tell you that my illness is over, but that the worst is likely to be expected. The suppuration continues, the sternum is affected, and today the doctor even predicted that an operation is hardly doubtful very soon for me. It is a question of the rejection of a whole piece of bone; they will have to cut the soft parts of it and then 'reduce' the affected bone, namely the sternum, as the doctor put it, 'sawing it off.' But if one is under the knife and the saw of the surgeon, then you know on how a thin thread hangs the thing, what is called life. Then comes a pus fever—and the little light goes out. It was strange when the first bone of my skeleton suddenly swam out of a pus drain. It gradually became clear to me that the plans for our Paris trip and the habilitation are probably impossible things. The fragility of existence is never demonstrated to one so *ad oculos* as when one sees a piece of one's skeleton,"[632] Fritz explicitly realized how vulnerable his existence was. Sticking to his beliefs, disregarding the fear of death, and accepting suffering as an intrinsic part of his life, he not only did not succumb to the illness but utilized it as a source to produce more work than ever when actively in service.

Released from duty, being cared for by his mother and sister, and having plenty of time on his hands, Fritz threw himself into a frenzy of work, sometimes collapsing out of exhaustion after he finished. "Incidentally, I work eagerly 'while it is day' on philological issues… I have generally devoted my involuntary idleness to a greater focus on and tidying up of my studies. Specific intentions are poured into a more specific form. Half-sensed insights germinate on all sides. No, dear friend, one does not extinguish me quite so quickly,"[633] he resolutely announced. With his "Democritus" essay and a new major project, called "On Teleology" or "Teleology since Kant," or "The Concept of the Organic since Kant" *(Der Begriff des Organischen seit Kant)*,[634] intended as his doctoral dissertation still to come, he was putting a massive weight of responsibilities on his shoulders.

Once again, unquestionably suffering but not giving up, he revisited his relationship with Christianity and philosophy. "Anyone who keeps an eye on the course of the relevant investigations—especially the physiological ones since Kant—can have no doubt that limitations [of our cognitive faculties] (*Erkenntnisvermögens*) have been determined so reliably and infallibly that apart from theologians, a few philosophy professors and the *vulgus* (commoners), nobody here has any illusions about it anymore. The realm of metaphysics, thus the province of 'absolute' truth, has inevitably been brought into line with poetry and religion. Anyone who wants to know something is now content with conscious relativity of knowledge - such as all well-known naturalists. Metaphysics, which belongs, for most people in the sphere of emotions, is essentially edification. On the other hand, it is art, namely that of conceptual poetry. It should be noted, however, that metaphysics, neither as a religion nor as art, has anything to do with what is known as 'truth or, that what is in itself,'"[635] he wrote Deussen by the end of April and beginning of May 1869, elaborating on his materialistic considerations.

"[Fritz] equates religion with metaphysics and claims that it is relevant for art and for the building personality and culture but has nothing to do with truth,"[636] writes Brobjer. Fritz counters religion and metaphysics with bio-materialism pushing back *thing-in-itself* squarely into its original domain, preferring a scientific approach towards reality over emotional and faith-based considerations. Interestingly, he again diminished the importance of the Schopenhauerian solution of realizing the *thing-in-itself* through art, placing the artistic activities in the domain of personal edification. At that time, art for Fritz ceased being a method of inquiry, becoming, together with metaphysics and religion, a way of cultivating one's persona. Thus, Fritz was not wholly faithless, but indifferent or emotionally withdrawn from it. He merely treated faith as one of the possible interpretations of reality. At that point in his life, he divided its cognizance into emotional and rational perspectives, with preference for the latter. But, of course, this was happening in a time of crisis, looking into death's eyes, when most ordinary people would have turned themselves towards God praying for relief from suffering. But Fritz was not a commoner anymore—if he ever was—but an exceptional young man.

The views he expressed in the letter to Deussen reflected a subject of his research: he was gathering materials and making notes for his doctoral dissertation. But he was not interested or focused on merely philological matters. The ideas for "Teleology Since Kant," practically a philosophical thesis, came mainly from his work on Democritus, and reading Empedocles, to whom he was introduced back in Pforta through Hölderlin's *The Death of Empedocles*, and later in Leipzig, Laertius' *Lives of Philosophers*; readings of Schopenhauer's *The World as Will and Representation*, Lange's *History of Materialism*, Kuno Fischer's study of Kant, *Kants Leben und die Grundlagen seiner Lehre* (1860), and Kant's *Critique of Judgment*, which he probably read firsthand in its entirety, and Goethe, whom he read from the early age.[637]

"By the way," he announces this new project to Rohde, "when at the end of this year, you receive my doctoral dissertation, you will notice a few things which will explain this point of limits of knowledge. My theme is 'the concept of the organic since Kant,' half philosophical, half natural science. My drafts are almost ready.... For a long time, I have had a philosophical project in mind, ... (namely to write 'Concerning the concept of the organic since Kant') and have collected enough material for it; on the whole, however, this theme cannot be realized as the conscious goal just mentioned unless one goes about it no less carefully than a fly."[638] Fritz, though in the middle of the project, was already skeptical about the whole endeavor.

As is typical with his other early writings, there are very few academic attempts at the interpretation[639] of the "Teleology Since Kant" material, possibly because he abounded the work shortly after the compilation of notes. However, regardless of its noncompletion, they are his most extensive writings on Kant, showing his growing concern with ontology and epistemological limitations.

Fritz began with Kant's postulate that the organic (organic or natural bodies) came to existence by a premeditated purpose, in accordance with teleology, introducing right at the beginning the concepts of purpose, premeditation, teleology, and intelligent design in order to refute them later.

He hypothesized that the organic came to existence only by chance, although we humans are stuck with an assumption of teleology in the natural world. Wherefore, it is necessary "to offer a proof of unpurposiveness"[640]—a problem to be resolved in his dissertation.

He started with an assumption that there is "no unified teleological world but creative intelligence" or an "unconscious creative power" [641] in nature, and this "creative intelligence," or "knowing" is not lying outside the world but, refuting metaphysics and the *thing-in-itself*, within it. What sporadically appears purposive only accidentally arises from the unpurposive and "reveals itself as being completely without reason."[642]

It seems that organisms (the organic) as built from interdependent parts exist only through an intrinsic purposiveness, except, that it is a mere illusion. What appears within the organic as a purposiveness is only a "capacity for life."

Fritz cited Empedocles as an originator of collaboration between the whole and its parts as an organism. Emphasizing the significance of life in a schema of cosmic purposelessness, he concluded that life arose by chance without any intervention from an intelligent designer.

To illustrate the parts-whole collaboration as a mechanism of survival, he cited Empedocles' monsterland: "Many foreheads without necks sprang forth, and arms wandered unattached, bereft of shoulders, and eyes strayed about alone, needing brows... Limbs wandered alone... Many creatures were created with a face and breast on both sides; offspring of cattle with fronts of men, and again there arouse offspring of men with heads of cattle and creatures made of elements mixed in parts from men, in parts of the female sex, furnished with hairy limbs."[643] Those freaks did not last but perished, Empedocles explains, what Fritz rationally interpreted: "Functionality determines survival, and the 'design' is really contingent, spawned by luck."[644]

He transferred the lack of purposiveness within the organic into the world as an organism (*Weltorganismus*), merging the organic with the inorganic, and "the origin of evils,"[645] as the products of intellect, other words, of human invention.

Fritz came up with the ontological concerns that existence (*Existenz*) and its means are purposive in the sense of common consideration of being. We assume that the astonishing complexity of interrelated parts of the organic necessitate purposiveness, but we do not see purposiveness in the inorganic (*Unorgan*), supposing nothing but its pure unity (*lauter Einheiten*).

Purposiveness, thus teleology, is "like optimism, an aesthetic product" of human imagination. Therefore "existence is perforated with miracles," Fritz wrote, entering yet another mode of existence.

We assume that if things exist, they must have the ability to exist; they must have the condition for existence (*Bedingungen zur Existenz*). If someone constructs a thing, he names the conditions for its existence as purposive. However, things and events are neither purposive nor unpurposive, but are brought about by pure chance. Chance is a necessary condition for continuing existence.

If we could eliminate purposiveness, thus teleology, we would remove the "concept of higher reason" [646] (*Erscheinung*) which is an intention of the existence of things. Only human representation (*Vorstellung*) of things, which seems different from appearance, could be cognized as a purposive and mechanistic organization (*mechanische Entstehung)* of things.

We only recognize the organic at the level of a cognizable existence of organic things within their bodies, where the parts are bonded together purposively. Still, the origin of the organic is beyond our cognitive reach. And so, the concept of the organic is merely a human creation.

The ability to life (*Lebensfähige)* grew out of an enormous number of failed attempts in the inorganic at nascency of the organic. But is this a nascency of a process or a substance, or a particular consolidation? At organizing? Reciprocally interrelating the parts into a whole? We still should ask.

The concept of the whole, of the unity, is a product of human invention. The organisms we call unities are still multiplicities and are an invention of human ingenuity. Fritz locked himself up in the inability to ask about the origin of life.

Additional concepts which are inventions of our creativity include force, matter, individuals, law, organism, atom, purposive cause, together with the idea of unity. So, "we are not allowed to go beyond them,"[647] for we are prisoners of our cognition.

The same refers to the concept of purposiveness. As it is "only the capacity for existence,"[648] we cannot speak about its reason.

In his notes, Fritz gathered material referring primarily to the concept of organic, although he deviated into the territory of the inorganic on occasions.

However, his ideas could have been applied similarly to both—separately or in the unity of organic-inorganic—for the organic and inorganic are maintained by the same principle (*Princip*) of force (*Kraft*).

"The method of nature in her treatment of things is the same. She is impartial mother, equally harsh to her inorganic and organic children,"[649] Fritz noted, poetically as always.

However, we can only grasp the changing forms, not the change in itself. "The eternal becoming (*ewig Werdende*) is life... We grasp only forms.... Our intellect is too blunt to perceive the perpetual change"[650] (*fortwährende Verwandlung*). Again, only the appearance unveils itself to us.

Only the everchanging forms and the forms as individuals are accessible to us, but through our intellect, we consolidate these infinite multiplicities of differences onto abstract unities. "The unity is only a coarse intuition, perhaps first inferred from the bodies of humans."[651]

The organic and inorganic are generated out of an accident, therefore not according to the purposing cause. "Thus [it] means that the form is added after,"[652] revealing an inexhaustible potentiality of always anew organic-inorganic forms.

Because of our assumption that an appearance is not by itself but of something, or in Kantian terms of the *thing-in-itself*, frustrated by the inability to access it, we invented a whole spectrum of representations of that assumed world, declaring illusion as reality.

It sounds like a copout, and according to Fritz, it was. He suggested a different perspective on the illusions we have constructed. He looked beyond the pejorative connotations that the concept of illusion generates into a process of inexhaustible human ingenuity creating this edifice.

The world thus, as we experience it, is an illusion, a substitute spawned by the impotence of our cognition, appropriating a role of the real thing, nonetheless mediating the airs of limitless ingenuity of humankind.

Fritz, being mired in the process of continuous creation of his own interpretation of the world, allowed himself to produce some thoughts about the *thing-in-itself*, perhaps forgetting that not that long ago, he criticized

Schopenhauer for precisely the same attempt. Enabled by an insatiable will to create, he employed a different method than the knowing mode of cognition, proposing instead an emotional approach of sensing and feeling to access the unknowable.

In just the same way as Schopenhauer, he postulated that the *thing-in-itself* is the will. Perhaps not recognizing, for he had closed the door to his artistic career, that he himself was becoming an artist-philosopher or a practitioner of philosophy as a form of art, who could sense the real through his genius but could not explain it discursively. Fritz examined the human perspective of perceiving the world as faulty. Nonetheless, in human consciousness and intellect, he saw an inexhaustible source of creativity, the power to create the intelligible in places where human cognition is powerless.

Instead of Kantian concepts of order, purpose, unity, design, commonly accepted notions of reality, "a distinctively human product,"[653] as properties recognizable through a passive polarity of cognition, Fritz postulated plastic creativity enabled by human imagination.

Our understanding is determined by the ability or inability to see the world as it is. The visual perception of the world is negotiated by the cognitive capability of a human subject, delivering the world as it appears, not as it is, therefore offering not a scientific but a distinctively aesthetic view of the world. Fritz "interprets the world of phenomenal appearance to be a type of illusion in the sense of [appearance as an illusion], a problem that still lingers in the final analysis for both Schopenhauer and Kant."[654]

Fritz was touching on all the ideas he appropriated from Kant, Lange, Fischer, Schopenhauer, and others, transforming them into his own thoughts around the materialistic concept of the organic and life.

"The concept of the whole is our work. This is where the source of representation of the purpose lies. The purpose of the whole does not lie in the thing but in us. But once again, these unities which we call organisms are still multiplicities. There are in reality no individuals. Moreover, individuals and organisms are nothing but abstractions. They are unities manufactured by us into which we transfer the idea of purpose.

"We assume that there would be a unitary force which brings about organisms. Then the method is to observe this force of the organisms which allows them to create and preserve themselves. Here it is demonstrated what we call purposive is only that which proves itself to be capable of living. The secret is only 'life.'

"The capacity for life is constructed from an unending chain of failing and half-successful attempts. The existence of the organism points only to the blindly acting force.

"Do we need purposive causes to explain the life of a thing? No, to us 'life' is something wholly dark, through which no light can shine by purposive causes,"[655] Fritz postulated.

In the end, he did not follow with any of the books he listed to develop the topic further. Instead, he gave up on the project altogether, concluding that it is not suitable for a doctorate in classical philology.

He was trying to avoid the Schopenhauerian approach of inquiry into the world through an artistic endeavor, limiting himself to the scientific materialistic method, which, if successful, would provide absolute knowledge of the world, the *thing-in-itself*, therefore making him God.

If an unknowable thing is truly unknowable, there is no way of knowing it. Therefore, knowing as such is out of the picture. Why then waste time trying to speculate with a helpless reason?

Can life emerge spontaneously from inorganic matter now, without any intervention or contamination by the existing life? Or was this a done deal when life came into existence 3.7 billion years ago. Concerning the organic-inorganic dichotomy, what is the difference between a mustard seed, a conglomerate of inorganic elements and a grain of sand, purely inorganic stuff?

Fritz, I am sure, was aware of these problems before he started on the road of this materialistic but futile approach. He attempted it probably to exercise his ability to think through an otherwise unsolvable problem. Or he was curious about the language necessary to think of it or prove that the mystery could ever be resolved. Or, as in the past, Fritz concentrated not on the content but the form of delivering information, expecting, in its plasticity in itself, to recognize that the process of creation dominates everything.

We "clever animals" invent a purpose, meaning, sense, or final goal in our lives to veil the unimaginable suffering of our helplessness in comprehending the world, suffering from the futility to harness the chance, the ruler of the world's existence.

Only our creativity gives us solace. The creative, plastic process that, like a tranquilizer, shields us from the world of suffering.

The world creates itself without any purpose or a goal. The creation process is the world, an artist or an "aesthetic phenomenon" consistent with an a-teleological aesthetic. Suppose the world, as the relentless process of infinite possibilities, is represented by us, or "is" an appearance. In that case, there must be, should be, or is the different spectral form of representation and appearances.

Like Rembrandt, Picasso, or Beethoven, we "argonauts" are at the most creative, daring, and impudent stages at the beginning and the end of our natural lives. Those, like Rimbaud, who died too early did not have a chance to realize the second phase. In the beginning, we are the poets, by the end, the philosophers. But what happens in between? We succumb to conventions, sacrificing our dreams. Even if it appears that we stay within the realm of creativity, we still conform to the requirements of the masses. At the dawn of our lives, we do not know if we are "right," so we suffer in some instances, to the point of suicide, not realizing that that is the point of the whole enterprise. Except, if we do not succumb to Camus' alternative, in the end, we do not care anymore about "right" or "wrong"–we simply start over our projects of youth–while ironically still suffering the pointlessness of creation. Although, "one must imagine Sisyphus happy."[656] Is that what makes us human?


And Fritz indubitably suffered. The doctors who look after him were gradually giving up proposing surgery as the last and only resort. But Franziska found yet another doctor in a neighboring Halle, Richard von Volkmann, to whom, on June 25, 1868, Fritz traveled for consultation. Volkmann dissuaded surgery proposing treatment at his spa of salt-water baths in Bad Wittekind (*Solbad Wittekind*). On the same day, Fritz went back to Naumburg, packed his bags, and left for Wittekind, stopping in Leipzig to visit Sophie Ritschl and friends.

On July 1, 1868, the first day at the spa, he wrote to his mother and sister that his most pleasant call was with the Ritschls, especially with Sophie, whom he called in a letter to Rohde *"meine intime 'Freundin.'"*[657]

"The highest point of his trip, he wrote, was conversation and playing the piano with Frau Ritschl. He notified his family and Rohde that she was now his intimate *Freundin*, a term that almost connotates 'girlfriend' here. What they played together was Wagner, about whose music Nietzsche still had serious reservations. But now he began to speak of Schopenhauer and Wagner in the same breath,"[658] writes Pletsch. Fritz must have made some kind of blunder because he apologized to her. "Wagner's and Schopenhauer's drawbacks (*Pferdefüße*) are hard to hide. But I will get better,"[659] he writes her on the second day in Wittekind. In the spirit of his ever-changing resolves, he confides to her that he would like to merge music with philology as one presentation (*Darstellung*). "Maybe I will find a philological subject that can be treated musically, and then I will babble like an infant and heap up images like a barbarian who has fallen asleep in front of an antique head of Venus, and still be in the right despite the 'flourishing haste' of the exposition."[660]

Perhaps submitting to the vigilance of his own body, he turned his gaze towards himself in self-observation (*Selbstbeobachtung),* yet again, as he continued to do from the early age, but this time, critically: "'It is deceiving / Know yourself. / By action, not by observation. / Those who measure themselves against an ideal do not get to know themselves but their own weaknesses, of which the degrees are also unknown to them. Observation saps your energy: it corrodes and crumbles. / Instinct is best.' He paused and thought over what he had written. Did self-observation really just impede and subvert? After observing his own self-observation, he realized that it had worked to his benefit 'Self-observation a weapon against influences from without,' he appended,"[661] Fritz sways back and forth, always finding a positive in the negative. Introspection wears you down in an unending assault of external influences, but in consequence, we need a weapon to have at least a chance to defend ourselves. Fritz realized, years before it was scientifically shown, that human instinct—in contemporary terms what would be called "autopilot," relying on habitual and mindless processes—is the primary mode of human behavior.

Whereas self-conscious decision-making provides some kind of assurance of an error-avoidance but consumes significantly more time and effort. But, it's only partial certitude, for we have a tendency for habitual, automatic behavior even as we try to reason. Our instincts or gut feelings win out, redirecting us, sometimes to the most disadvantageous situations. Conversely, introspection is not enough either, for it never allows a self-observer to reach the depths of selfhood; therefore, the self-investigator turns to the material concretes out of frustration. Consequently, we have a continuous swaying between or attempts at the consilience of two or more inquiry sources into one's own I.

A month-long stay at Dr. Volkmann's spa proved to be good for Fritz. The salt baths and iodine dressings saved his life. On August 2, 1868, he left Wittekind for Naumburg, almost completely healed. There was a permanent scar over the recess in the middle of his chest, so he continued his coalescence at home, working and relaxing on the first-floor veranda of his mother's house. Rohde, finally at ease that Fritz survived such an ordeal, wrote, asking him for a photograph, a request which Fritz, without hesitation, fulfilled within a couple of days from his arrival, posing at the studio of Ferdinand Henning in Naumburg. "Here is a photograph that shows me in a somewhat defiant pose. Basically, it is rude to appear before one's friends with a drawn sword and, on top of that, with such a peevish, furious expression on one's face. There is something brutish about such a warrior. But why do we let a bad photographer annoy us, why do we let all the rubbish of life annoy us so that we no longer look like freshly washed girls? Why do we always have to stand with the sword at the ready? And if we now want to attack the photographer with gusto, what does he do? He crouches behind his [camera's] cowl and shouts, 'Now!'"[662] – Fritz wrote to Rohde on August 6, 1868.

Then again, as in often repeated instances during his life, Fritz was standing at the crossroads, indecisive of what to do next. He was still working on the *Rheinische Museum* index for Ritschl, a dull and mechanistic occupation which probably gave him as much solace as any other chore of one's dull existence would. He looked at all the tasks unrelated to his philosophically driven explorations into himself as a foolish waste of time; nevertheless, he continued to perform them. Any automatic and mindless task, being easy and with a distinctive beginning and end to provide closure, always gives us a feeling of satisfaction by delivering an illusion of accomplishment. So, it can perhaps be a remedy for our restlessness and constant anxiety, the sensation of the impossibility of comprehending our and the world's existence—the complete and utter hopelessness. However, Fritz was never entirely dedicated to philosophy only. He never bet everything on one card, always keeping up his sleeve the alternative that he could take the well-beaten path of prestige and recognition if the original dream did not work out. It took him many years before he could give himself entirely to the endeavor of self-cultivation on his own terms. Or perhaps, these deviations into the well-beaten paths of prestige and recognition were merely the periods of relaxation, convalescence, and regaining strength before the next battle.

Why not, since most of us are doing nothing but living on-automatic, avoiding the struggle and suffering of an encounter with one's life that is like taking a drug to feel better all the time. But Fritz, on the contrary, suffered continuously throughout his life and felt better only sporadically.

On September 19, he wrote to Ritschl a detailed letter about the structure of the index asking for corroboration, for—speaking between words—did not want to work in vain, not mentioning that he was way overdue with it. Next, he reluctantly turned to his abounded task, his dissertation: "So much for the index. In October, I will move back to Leipzig for six months; maybe then there will also be an opportunity to do a doctorate, for which I have a *commentatio altera de Laertii Diogenis fontibus* (the other commentary concerning sources of Diogenes Laertius) in mind. – Or, if you like, *de Aristotelis librorum indice Laertiano* or *Analecta Democritea* or *quaestiones Cynicae* or *de fontibus Latinorum artis veterinariae scriptorum*!! etc., easily *in infinitum*,"[663] Fritz almost nonchalantly produces several prospective themes for his thesis. Evidently, it was not essential or necessary work for him. It was merely a way "to avoid being counted among the *pecus* of '*Literaten*' (crowd [cattle] of scribes),"[664] he opened up to Rohde, adding that he decided to become a "society man" (*Gesellschaftsmensch*), using connections to a sister of Richard Wagner, arranged by his friend Ernst Windisch, a fellow philologist, who previously arranged for Fritz's position as a contributor for *Literarisches Centralblatt* journal, and who was one of only two friends who visited him, while he recovered from the accident in Naumburg.[665]

At that point in his life, Fritz was still critical of Wagner but, it seems, attracted to the composer's notoriety, his music, and probably his writings, and indeed to the reports about the composer.

"Recently I also read (for the first time, what is more) Jahn's essays on music, including the ones on Wagner. One needs to have some enthusiasm to do such a person justice, whereas Jahn has an instinctive antipathy to him and hears with his ears half shut." Fritz already recognized Wagner's significance, but not without reserve. "Yet I grant him many points, particularly his maintaining that Wagner is representative of modern dilettantism which consumes and digests all varieties of artistic interest; but precisely from this standpoint one cannot be astonished enough at the significance that one single artistic disposition has in this man, a disposition that allies indestructible energy with many-sided artistic gifts, whereas 'culture' [*Bildung*], where more various and embracing it is, usually appears with dulled eyes, weak knees, and enfeebled loins. Moreover, Wagner has a sphere of feeling which is totally hidden from O. Jahn: Jahn remains a frontier hero, a healthy man, to whom the *Tannhäuser* saga and the *Lohengrin* atmosphere are a closed world. In Wagner as in Schopenhauer, I like the ethical air, the Faustian odor, Cross, Death, Grave, and so on."[666]

Intoxicated by the lecture of Schopenhauer and his recent near-death experience, embracing suffering, disease, and death, Fritz asked: "how much of it he could bear without losing his lust for life."[667] But then he turns back to his philological publication, denouncing them: "O how repulsive I find this whole work! ... There is nothing more to it! So much is actually wrong. ... My only excuse is the fact that I shall be of age only on October 15 of this year, on which day I also take off my military coat,"[668] he announced his discharge.

On October 15, 1868, on his twenty-fourth birthday, Fritz was officially dismissed from military duty as temporarily unfit for service, although, to be declared a commissioned artillery officer, he arranged to serve yet another month the following spring.[669]

# 6

## A PERPETUAL FELLING
## OF RAPTURE

The next day, he left Naumburg for Leipzig, mysteriously stopping for two days in Dresden. On October 18, he arrived at his new lodgings of Professor Karl Biedermann, the editor of the *Deutsche Allgemeine Zeitung,* at Lessingstraße 22, on the 2nd floor, where Windisch arranged a room for Fritz.

The same day he wrote to his mother and sister describing the apartment, its surroundings, food and prices, and of course did not fail to complain about his missed package of books, and the last day of Leipzig Trade Faire that "fortunately rescued us from the stink of fat and the many Jews."[670] Then, considering his student years over, and despite not having a doctorate, he requested from them to be addressed in writing as *Herr Doctor Nietzsche*—he was certainly rearranging his demeanor, the wrappings of his own person.

In addition to his contributions to *Literarisches Zentralblatt,* "as a book reviewer, covering the whole field of Greek philosophy except Aristotle,"[671] Biedermann offered him a position of a music and opera critic at his newspaper. Although he had been mocking his host for a couple of years already, Fritz was nevertheless impressed, or perhaps even idealized Biedermann in his own way, so, in the end he accepted the offer.

Within a few days, he described these new living arrangements in Leipzig in a letter to Deussen: "I live here. Well, it is not as a student. It is more than a year that I have quit that intolerable condition. Rather, I am here, the future *Privatdozent* of Leipzig, and am systematically arranging my existence in accordance with this object in view. The family where I have made my nice home is that of Professor Biedermann, a former member of Parliament and now editor of the *Deutsche Allgemeine*. Through him I able to make several interesting appointments, such as smart women, pretty actresses, important authors and politicians, etc. A number of larger essays are awaiting the blessed event about which I shall write you later. Ritschl, the teacher whom I esteem, and his wife who is very close to me, show me many favors. Also, I flourish in the circle of ambitious friends and associates and only regret that I do not have around me the excellent Paul Deussen."[672] Fritz indeed settled himself in the most advantageous position to realize his latest dream of becoming "a society man," an academician and a person of significance through the conventional means of the rat race.

Was that what he wanted? I think not, for, in the same letter, he defended philosophy and Schopenhauer, sarcastically mocking philology. "Your mythological conception of philology as a daughter (daughter no less! *heu! heu!*) of philosophy which as such is supposed to be beyond all control and jurisdiction. Should I speak mythologically, I would say philology is the miscarriage (*Mißgeburt*) of the Goddess Philosophy, conceived by an idiot or cretin."[673] Sneering at Deussen that he did not visit when he was sick as if he had considered him dead, Fritz, capitalizing on his recent bout with illness, suggested dependency between one's health and philosophy. He proclaimed that profound philosophy (*tieferer Philosophie*) requires certain unhealthiness. He taught Deussen "to realize that φιλοσοφεῖν and being sick are not really identical concepts, but that, on the contrary, there is a certain 'health,' the eternal foe of profound philosophy."[674] Then he moved to criticize Schopenhauer, while defending his genius, regardless—as he formulated it—of some "faulty passages, unsuccessful proofs, or tactic ineptitudes," explicitly declaring his fascination with the philosopher: "You cannot adequately conceive of the respect I have of 'this genius of the first order of magnitude' if you think *I* (*i.e., homini pusillullullo!*) have the ability to make mincemeat of said giant. … Someone who does not smell the fragrance of a rose surely should not be permitted to criticize it; and if he smells it, *à la bonheur*! he will not have the inclination to criticize it,"[675] Fritz clearly approaches Schopenhauer's thought not from an analytical perspective, but from emotional-aesthetic absorbency. It seems that he dismissed the mechanistic analysis of a philosophical text as an inadequate method of reception. His recent accumulation of extensive notes for the strictly scientific treaty did not estrange him from leaning towards the sensual as a mode of experiencing the world.

# RICHARD WAGNER

On October 27, 1868, Fritz, under the auspices of his new position as a music and opera critic, attended for the first time a concert of the preludes to *Tristan und Isolde* and *Die Meistersinger von Nürnberg*, at the Euterpe Music Society of Leipzig (*Euterpe Musikgesellschaft*). Although he knew and played both pieces before, he never heard them performed in a concert hall. Not only had he changed his attitude towards Wagner, but the music made an enduring impact on his thought and, in fact, life. It was again one of the pivotal moments which opened yet another phase in Fritz's development. Like with discovering Schopenhauer, Fritz was smitten with Wagner through his music.

On the same day, right after the concert, he wrote to Rohde about the experience. "Tonight, I have been to the Euterpe, which started its winter concerts and revitalized me with the prelude to *Tristan and Isolde* as well as with the overture to the *Meistersinger*. I cannot find it in my heart to keep a cool critical detachment from this music: every fiber and nerve of my being is tingling, and it has been a long time since I experienced such a perpetual feeling of rapture."[676]

Though right in the next paragraph, always sober-minded, he did not fail to trivialize the profundity and sublimity of that experience by bragging about who-is-who sitting next to and around him, in the "sharp corner" (*scharfe Ecke*) of music critics: Eduard Bernsdorf (1825–1901), chief music critic for the *Signale für die Musicalische Welt*; Oskar Paul (1836–1898), music critic of the *Leipziger Tagblatt*; Friedrich Stade (1844–1928), music critic of the *Neue Zeitschrift für Musik*; and Fritz. Our twenty-four-year-old newly minted socialite, undoubtedly rising in the social circles and enjoying it, joined the Wagnerian crowd with a new objective on his mind: meeting the maestro in person.

Being in a specific milieu with adequate performance on Fritz's part was becoming more important to him than the value of the contents. On Monday, November 9, 1868, he wrote Rohde a long letter, with two points worth mentioning.

First, he wrote about his inaugural lecture to the Philological Society, which he delivered at Café Zaspel at Klostergasse 12, on November 7, merely mentioning its theme and focusing entirely on the ambiance and form of his presentation. "The first lecture of the semester for our philological club was scheduled for that evening: and they had asked me very courteously if I would take this on. I, who need opportunities to arm myself in academic weapons, was also prepared, and I had the pleasure to see the black mass of 40 people on my entering the Zaspel's. Raymond was instructed by me to be personally very attentive so that he could tell me how the theatrical side (*die theatralische Seite*) had been, and how effective—the delivery, voice, style, organization of the material. I was completely extemporizing (*frei gesprochen*), helped only by notes on a slip of paper, my topic being Varro's satires and the cynic Menippus: and lo and behold, everything was καλὰ λίαν (kala lian – very good, the Greek saying in Genesis, as cited with derision by Schopenhauer). It will be all right in this academic career!"[677]

The other subject was Fritz's wish to meet Richard Wagner. On arriving home on that Saturday, he found a note from Windisch that if he wants to meet Wagner, he should come to Café Theater at 3:45 pm. The meeting was initiated by Wagner himself, who heard of Fritz from Sophie Ritschl through her friend Wagner's sister Ottilie Brockhaus, wife of Professor Hermann Brockhaus, an orientalist at the Leipzig University. Wagner, who was traveling incognito visiting his sister in Leipzig, finding out from Frau Ritschl that Fritz often played his music with her, expressed his wish to meet the young man at Brockhaus' house. Fritz was flabbergasted by this unexpected acquaintance "verging on the realm of a fairy tale," though as always, down-to-earth and "something of a dandy,"[678] ordered a new evening suit. However, unable to afford it, he settled on a black jacket to call on the Brockhauses on Sunday evening.

"We enter the very comfortable drawing room of the Brockhauses," he scrupulously describes the first meeting with Wagner, "nobody is there apart from the family circle, Richard"—Fritz did not fail to make a point of being on first name terms with Wagner—"and the two of us. I am introduced to Richard, and address to him a few words of respect; he wants to know exactly the details of how I became familiar with his music, curses all performances of his operas except the famous Munich ones, and makes fun of the conductors who call to their orchestras in a bland voice: 'Gentlemen, make it passionate here! My good fellows, a little bit passionate!' W. likes to imitate the Leipzig dialect.... Before and after dinner Wagner played all the important parts of *Die Meistersinger*, imitating each voice and with great exuberance. He is, indeed, a fabulously lively and fiery man who speaks very rapidly, is very witty, and makes a very private party like this one an extremely gay affair. In between, I had a longish conversation with him about Schopenhauer; you will understand how much hearing him speak about Schopenhauer with indescribable warmth, what he owed to him, how he is the only philosopher who has understood the essence of music, then he asked how the academics nowadays regarded him, laughed heartily about Philosophic Congress in Prague, and spoke of 'vassals of philosophy.' Afterword he read an extract from his biography, which he is now writing, an utterly delightful scene from his Leipzig student days, of which he still cannot think without laughing; he writes too with extraordinary skill and intelligence. Finally, when we were both getting ready to leave, he warmly shook my hand invited me with great friendliness to visit him, in order to make music and talk philosophy; also, he entrusted to me the task of familiarizing his sister and his kinsmen with his music, which I have now solemnly undertaken to do. You will hear more when I can see this evening somewhat more objectively and from a distance."[679] Undeniably, from the first moment of meeting Wagner face to face, Fritz was bewitched by the composer's personality and music. Although, as in other instances of encountering new ideas of art or philosophy, the question arises. Was he overwhelmed more by Wagner's music, or his personage?

These emotionally charged events must have evoked in Fritz a creative potentiality built upon reciprocally founded relations between Schopenhauer as a thinker and his philosophy and Wagner as an artist and his music, consolidated into an unnamed, yet to arrive, emerging concept of artist-philosopher.

Just as he had with *The World as Will and Representation*, Fritz threw himself at *Opera and Drama* (1851), Wagner's artistic manifesto, and Wagner's poetry, where the composer argues that "the real drama needs heightened, poetic language to express the larger-than-life emotions of its characters."[680] This idea of the musicality of language was not new to Fritz, but the reading reinforced his convictions of being on the right track. Within a month, Fritz returns to these events in his correspondence with Rohde, trying, this time more coolly, to describe his perspective towards Wagner and Schopenhauer as a consolidated concept. "Wagner whom I now know from his music, his poetry, his writings on aesthetics and, not least, from happy personal acquaintance with him, is the most vivid illustration of what Schopenhauer calls a 'genius'; the similarity in all particulars springs immediately to the eye. I wish I could tell you all the details of his life which I mostly know through his sister. How I wish we could read his poems together (which Romundt values so highly that he considers R.W. to be by far the greatest poet of the generation, and about whom, as Wagner told me, Schopenhauer thought very well); to allow ourselves to go through its bold, subversive and uplifting aesthetics; we could finally let ourselves to be swept away in this Schopenhauerian sea of sound, in the most secret breaking of the waves, so that when listening to Wagnerian music joyful intuition one experiences an astonishing discovery of oneself (*Sichselbstfinden*),"[681] Fritz intuitively employs an aesthetic experience in describing the process of self-cultivation.

During the same period, in halls of academia, Fritz had a different supporter. Prof. Ritschl also was singling out and favoring his pupil. He was immersed in the behind-the-scenes machinations, which, yet again, would change Fritz's life. The professor has received a request to recommend one of his students for a recently vacated position of a philology professor from the chair of the department of classical philology, Adolf Kiessling, at the University of Basel, Ritschl's former student. The request explicitly mentioned Fritz, for his work published in *Rheinisches Museum* was known and prized by Kiessling. Ritschl responded in an astonishingly enthusiastic spirit: "As many young scholars as I have seen developing under my supervision in the last 39 years, I have never known a young man, never tried to advance a career of anyone in my discipline, who so early and so young was as mature as this Nietzsche.... If he lives long— and may God grant it— I prophesy that he will stand in the front rank of German philologists. He is now twenty-four years old, strong, vigorous, healthy, valiant in body and spirit, well built, and made to impress similar natures. In addition, he has an enviable ability to speak clearly and persuasively in public. He is the object of admiration and the leader (without wanting to be) of the whole philological world of Leipzig, who can hardly await the time when they will hear him as their docent. You will say that I am describing a kind of 'phenomenon;' well he is that, and modest and approachable besides.... I would stake my entire academic reputation [on my opinion that appointing Nietzsche to the post in Basel] would turn up happily."[682]

Although it was an impeccable letter of recommendation, yet there was a problem: Fritz lacked a doctorate (*Promotion*), not to mention habilitation (*Habilitation*), necessary requirements for an academic position in German academia. But Fritz was still taking his time with deciding on a subject of his dissertation. Instead, he was frequenting theaters and concerts and was often invited by the Ritschls or the Brockhauses. Occasionally, he hosted parties himself, and took up horse-riding again. He was less frequently writing to his mother and sister, planning to spend barely three days at home in Naumburg during the Christmas of 1868. He was once again abandoning some of his followers, but this time, they were also his loved ones. "He excused himself from writing the songs they had requested for Christmas, 'for some of them I had no music and for none have I any words,' announcing that there would be no presents from him this year. Wagner was already so important as a father-figure that the need for mother and sister was dwindling, while Nietzsche was conscious that the bonds of family life had come to mean less to him than the bonds of friendship."[683]

"Whoever is lonely," Fritz writes to Rohde, "because of a caprice of nature, because of a curious brewed mixture of wishes, gifts, and endeavors of the will, he knows what an 'incomprehensibly lofty marvel' a *friend* is; and if he is an idolater, he must first and foremost erect an altar to the 'unknown god who created the friend.' Here I have an opportunity to observe from close at hand the ingredients of a happy family life; here there is no comparison with the loftiness, the singularity of friendship. Fillings clad in a dressing gown, the most quotidian and trivial things shimmering with this comfortably expensive feeling—that is the joy of family life, which is much too common to be of any great value. But Friendship! Yes, it is a choice delicacy, allotted only to few people, to those exhausted travelers whose way through life leads through the desert; a friendly spirit consoles them when they lie in the sand, and he moistens their parched lips with the divine nectar of friendship. But in the crevices and caves where, far from the world's noise, they bring sacrifices to their gods, these few sing beautiful hymns to friendship, and there too the old high priest Schopenhauer swings the censer of his philosophy,"[684] he confided his deepest anxieties to his one and only friend.

## PROFESSOR RITSCHL'S SURPRISE

While writing to Rohde, Fritz was summoned to the Ritschls. The time has come that his secret endeavor appeared to be successful, Professor Ritschl decided to inform Fritz about his efforts to secure for him an appointment as a professor *extraordinarius* of classical philology at the University of Basel. On hearing the news, Fritz was both pleased, for he was offered a position of high prestige that was only available to a very few, and dispirited, for he had to abandon traveling to Paris with Rohde in pursuance of his philosophical projects. Overall, he was deeply dissatisfied that he was faced with a *fait accompli*, he had no choice but to concede to it.[685] But one detail about the new position was unambiguously exhilarating: Basel was about eighty kilometers from where Wagner lived in Tribschen, outside Lucerne, so Fritz could conveniently and often visit his newfound idol.

After leaving the Ritschls, he walked around Leipzig singing melodies from *Tannhäuser*.[686] Back home, he returned to finish the letter to Rohde: "Now returned, I am trembling all over and cannot free myself of it even by pouring out my heart to you. *Absit diabolus! Adsit amicissimus Earwinus*"[687] – notwithstanding, Fritz did not mention Ritschl's efforts to arrange a faculty position for him.

He was undoubtedly gratified and excited about being offered an academic appointment at such a young age and, what's more, without a doctorate. But he had entirely different plans for the immediate future. First, he counted on the trip to Paris with Rohde, where he could study subjects of interest and be with him while postponing his entry into the adult world of bureaucratic drills, routines, and the insignificance of academic life.

Fritz was looking forward to a few more years of luxuriant freedom, beauty, art, and philosophy but instead was coerced by the institutional mandates to become a cog in the antiquated apparatus of classical philology. Although it was not his decision, nevertheless, to be faithful to his own convictions, he had to welcome this quirk of fate with opened arms and make the best of it.

After six days, on January 16, 1869, he wrote Rohde again, dared to tell him about the possibility of an appointment in Basel. "A great circumstance has fallen on my head, and the joint Paris plans have vanished into thin air. And with them flew away my wonderful hopes.

I really wanted one more time, before they put on chains of the profession, to savor the deep seriousness and the magical charm of a wandering life, once again the indescribable happiness of being a spectator and not a player, to sip life with the most faithful and understanding friend. I imagined the two of us walking with a serious gaze and smiling in the middle of the Parisian crowd. A couple of philosophical *flâneurs*, to whom one would get used to seeing together everywhere, in museums and libraries, in the La Closeries des Lilas and the Notre Dame – everywhere carrying the seriousness of thinking and tender understanding of togetherness. What would I exchange for such a wandering, such closeness to a friend! Oh, dearest friend, I believe that the bridegroom feels the same way as I do: our graceful informality, our ideal summer stroll, never seemed so desirable as it does now."[688]

Rohde was so devastated by Fritz's cancellation of their trip that, when writing back about his disappointment, he forgot to congratulate Fritz on his appointment. Only within a few days, he corrected himself, however still grieving that their relationship was practically over. "This means the end of any long-lasting relationship between us.... Never before have I felt so deeply how the best parts of my life are inseparably linked with my love for you.... What our life together has meant to me, and would continue to mean to me, is something more easily felt than expressed,"[689] he wrote, painfully aware that Fritz replaced his utter devotion with a mere career opportunity. Fritz did not respond to his friend's plea for over a month. Instead, he could not resist, but confidentially inform Gersdorff and Elisabeth about his prospects of appointment, then ordered new calling cards with his new professional title:

*FRIEDRICH NIETZSCHE.*
*Professor extraord. der klass.*
*Philologie in Basel.*[690]

By the end of January 1869, Fritz traveled to Dresden to attend his first complete performance of Wagner's *Die Meistersinger von Nürnberg.* It was a powerful experience which he described to Rohde, a few weeks later in a letter on February 22 (Schopenhauer's birthday), as the "greatest artistic feast that this winter brought me. God knows I must be a musician in large part of my body, for a while listening, I suddenly had the strongest feeling of homecoming and being at home (*heimisch),* and my other activities seemed like a distant fog from which I was released"[691] – in adequately Schopenhauerian manner, the Wagnerian music allowed him to steal a glimpse of a true view of himself.

"Since the opera's first act starts with the music of his homeland, a Lutheran chorale, Nietzsche had a special reason to feel *heimisch.* But his reaction was, I think, quite typical, even among those skeptical of Wagner's other works. What is immensely reassuring about the opera is that the startlingly new music of Walther von Stolzing's prize song, after many trials and tribulations, is ultimately accepted by the mastersingers' guild, thus demonstrating the power of tradition to bend without breaking, to absorb the novel energy of (in Nietzsche's later terminology) the 'free spirit' while yet preserving the integrity of tradition. And presiding over the entire work is the wisdom of Hans Sachs, who, though given to melancholy, is, nonetheless, surely the most reassuring father figure in the whole of opera,"[692] Young pointedly captures the essence of sentient formative experience that Wagner's music must have had on Fritz.

This sublime artistic experience coincided with a request from the accepting committee of Basel University for Fritz's Curriculum Vitae. During this time of change, he started sketching drafts for yet another autobiography, the *"Aus den Jahren 1868/69",* the notes as a source for an official CV.

Fritz began with a vision or a dream reoccurring throughout his life as a reminder of his hopeless inability to comprehend the things that existed outside the reach of the senses. "What I am afraid of is not a frightful shape behind my chair, but its voice; also, not the words, but the terrifyingly unarticulated and inhuman tone of that shape. Yes, if only it would speak as human beings do,"[693] he lamented, knowing that any communication was impossible. Therefore, he turned his gaze into himself, towards not what was merely possible but the only option. "A chain of events and endeavors, in which one looks for the contingencies of external fate (*äußern Schicksals*) or baroque moodiness, later reveals itself as a path traced out by the sure hand of instinct,"[694] he focuses not on an external causality of events but an instinctual internal drive, the *modus operandi* of one's life.

Then, after very briefly and matter-of-factly mentioning his date and place of birth, his father's death, and, in consequence, move to Naumburg and the schooling at Domgymnasium and acceptance to Schulpforta, he turned to describe his childhood. "My upbringing was left up to me in its principal aspects. My father, a Protestant country minister in Thuringia, died all too soon; I lacked the strict and superior guidance of a masculine intellect. When as a boy, I came to Schulpforta, I got to know only a surrogate for fatherly upbringing, the uniform discipline of a regulated school. But just this almost military coercion which, because it is supposed to work on the mass, treats the individual coolly and superficially, led me back to myself again" – he did not mention his mother or the other family members but an institution, the Schulpforta as a father surrogate. So, it seems he saw himself as a product of institutional upbringing, along with the influence of his own efforts of self-cultivation.

He reminisced about his childhood years of wonder and innocence and his love of music and poetry. "I saved my private inclinations and attempts from the monotony of laws, I lived a hidden cult of particular arts, in an overexcited addiction to universal knowledge and enjoyment, I tried to break the rigidity of a legally determined order and use of time. If not for a few external coincidences, I would have dared to become a musician back then. Since I was nine years old, I felt the strongest pull towards music; In that happy state in which one does not yet know the limits of one's talent and considers everything one loves to be attainable, I had written down countless compositions and acquired a more than amateurish knowledge of musical theory. It was only in the last part of my Pforta life that, in true self-awareness (*richtiger Selbsterkenntnis*), I gave up all my artistic plans for the rest of my life. From then on, philology stepped into the newly formed void."[695] Then, he continued explaining further the intervening "true self-awareness" as "a certain philosophical seriousness (*philosophischer Ernst*) [that] saved me from vague wonderings of my talents in too many directions. The [philosophical seriousness] was never satisfied but only in the face of naked truth and fearlessness, even affection for severe and evil consequences. The feeling of not getting to the bottom of universality drove me into the arms of rigorous science. Then simply, there is the desire to save oneself from the artistically prone rapid changes of emotions in the harbor of objectivity."[696]

Next, Fritz asked how one becomes a philologist, responding that people go to the field of classics because they are "driven by an innate teaching talent, but for them, science is only an effective tool, not the serious goal of their wandering life, viewed with longing eyes." The other smaller group "amuse themselves with aesthetic pleasure of Greek world of forms," and even fewer people are interested in problems which "thinkers of antiquity did not think through to the end,"[697] He recounted all the roads leading to philology, but did not rank himself into any of these groups, "for the road on which I came to philology is as far from the practical wisdom and low egoism as from the enthusiastic love of antiquity....This last is not easy to say, but it is honest."[698] Then, he is precise and to the point: "I sought a counterweight to the changeable and restless earlier propensities, a field, which could be promoted with cool sobriety, with logical coldness, with steady work, without the results immediately touching the heart. I then thought to find all of this in philology.... [And] I found splendid teachers on whose personalities I based my judgment of their discipline."[699]

Following it, he described briefly his one year stay in Bonn, where he claimed he researched a philological side of the New Testament and its sources; then, following Professor Ritschl, transfer to Leipzig where, with "a number of like-minded comrades," he founded a philological society in which he delivered "five major lectures."[700]

In these notes to Curriculum Vitae, Fritz attempted to evoke cold-mindedly of whom he was by remembering the paths he traveled in his life. Admitting that all the unexplained and even irrational turns of events had determined his formation, but without a doubt, considering himself a philologist. "Perhaps I am not at all one of those specific philologists"—he acknowledged with honesty

(*Ehrlichkeit*)—"that nature draws on their foreheads with an iron stylus: that is a philologist who travels the path laid out for him with the greatest steadfastness and naiveté of a child. When one comes across such philological demigods here and there, he realizes how everything that instinct and the violence of nature creates is fundamentally different from that which is produced through education, reflection, and perhaps even through resignation. I do not mean to say that I belong wholly and completely to these submissive philologists (*Resignationsphilologen*). But when I look back how I got from art to philosophy, from philosophy to science and here again into an even narrower field, it almost seems like a conscious renunciation (*bewußte Entsagung*),"[701] he was trying to rationalize his decision-making, claiming, that *summa summarum*—at least, at that moment in his life—all was over for him, predetermined and beyond his will. "I should think that a man of twenty-four already has behind him the most important things in his life, even if it is not until later that he produces what makes his life worthwhile. Until about this age the young soul still extricates what is typical from all its experiences of living and thinking, and it will never be prized away from the world of these types. Later on, when this idealizing gaze is extinguished, we remain under the sway of that world we receive as a legacy from our youth."[702] With an attitude of philosophical fatalism (*Resignationsphilosophie),* he convinced himself that he would capitalize on his development for the rest of his life, hoping that *resignation* would connote its other side: relentless attempting. On February 1, 1869, Fritz wrote a letter to Professor Wilhelm Vischer-Bilfinger accepting employment, attaching his succinct Curriculum Vitae.

From then on, things concerning his appointment moved rapidly. On February 10, the accepting committee at Basel decided to hire Fritz, of which Vischer-Bilfinger notified him in advance, three days before the official decision date of February 13, 1869.

The day before that, Fritz wrote several letters to his family and friends announcing his new position, citing a salary of 3,000 Swiss Francs, and sent them with his already-printed calling cards.[703] In return, he expected admiration, especially from his colleagues.

But, when Deussen, instead of dedicating his letter to Fritz's achievements, drew "a parallel between [Fritz's] brilliant success and [his] depressing situation, and a little envy may have shone through between the lines," Fritz responded abruptly, terminating their many years of friendship: "Dear Friend, unless perhaps accidental mental disturbance was to blame for your last letter, then please consider our relations to be over. F. N."[704]

In this milieu of such exhilarating events, instead of rejoicing his good fortune, Fritz found himself again in deep bouts of depression. In his letter to Rohde from February 22 and 28, he saw himself as a philistine pursuing opportunity for a career, a loner in the crowd. "In fact, I live here in the ash-gray cloud of loneliness, which is all the worst for having so many sociable arms held open to me on many sides, and almost every evening, the dismal flow of invitations keeps up its pressure. In these gatherings, I hear so many voices. I never come to myself at all.... At the moment, dissipated and pleasure-seeking, I am living through a desperate carnival before the Ash Wednesday of the profession, philistinism. It grieves me to the heart, but none of my present acquaintances notice anything of this. Dazzled by the title 'professor,' they think me the luckiest man on earth."[705] But even if he was not "the luckiest man on earth," he nevertheless was utterly focused on locking himself up in this new facility of fierce rivalry in intellectual achievements, where the prestige and power of a high social position are of the highest value.

Much to Fritz's surprise, on March 23, 1869, again thanks to Ritschl, Fritz was awarded a doctorate degree *in absentia* from Leipzig University in recognition of his essays published in the *Rheinisches Museum*[706] instead of a formal dissertation. Finally, completing all the necessary bureaucratic requirements, Vischer-Bilfinger asked Fritz to give up his Prussian citizenship "so he would not be drafted in the event of war."[707] Fritz followed up on the request and was relieved from Prussian citizenship in April 1869, becoming a stateless person, as he would remain for the rest of his life.

On April 11, 1869, the last evening in Naumburg before departure, he wrote to Gersdorff, closing a chapter in his life. "The golden time of free, unrestricted activity, the independent existence, the enjoyment of art and the world as a spectator—this time is irretrievably over. Now the strict goddess, the duty of the day, reigns," he summed it up nostalgically.

"I must now be a Philistine myself! ... One is not unpunished in position and dignity; it is only a matter of whether the fetters are made of iron or of thread. After all, I still have the courage to tear up the fetters and try the dubious life elsewhere and in a different way. I still feel nothing of the professors' obligatory hump. To be a Philistine, ἄνθρωπος ἄμουσος (*antropos amousos*), a herd man—Zeus and all the Muses protect me from that!" – he still hoped that one day, through philosophical seriousness (*philosophische Ernst),* he would be able to experience a true life of ideas.

"The real and essential problems of life and thought were shown to me clearly by the great mystagogue Schopenhauer, to ever have to fear a shameful fall from the 'idea.' To infuse my science with this new blood, to transfer to my listeners that Schopenhauerian seriousness that is pronounced on the forehead of the nobleman (*erhabnen Mannes*), this is my wish, my bold hope; I would like to be a little more than a disciplinarian of competent philologists.... Since we have to bear our lives, we should try to use it in such a way that others will bless it as valuable when we are happily redeemed from it,"[708] he declared himself a disciple of Schopenhauer. Nevertheless, he was ready to pursue the life of a philistine in exchange for prestige, dignity, and perhaps money, although he did not mention it this time.

On April 12, 1869, "wearing clothes chosen to make him look older, he was taken to the station at Naumburg, in an old-fashioned fly-coach, driven by the coachman who in 1843 took his parents to their wedding,"[709] Fritz began his journey visiting and saying goodbye to his old hangouts in Cologne, Bonn, and Heidelberg. He took a steamer ride on the Rhine to Biebrich near Wiesbaden and attended *Die Meistersinger* in Karlsruhe.[710]

Leaving Germany behind, Fritz arrived in Basel on April 19, 1869, into his new life as Herr Professor Dr. Friedrich Nietzsche.

# NOTES

## CHAPTER ONE

1   FS vol. 1 (hereafter abbreviated as FS 1), pp. 16-18, in NWS, pp. 14-15.

2   FS vol. 2 (hereafter abbreviated as FS 2), p 71, in NWS, "Euphorion,"
    Chap. I, p. 77.

3   Safranski 2006, (hereafter abbreviated as Safranski), p. 353.

4   FS 1, p. 27, in NWS, p. 22.

5   Ibid., p. 11, in NWS, p.10.

6   Ibid.

7   FS 1, p. 14, in NWS, p. 13.

8   Safranski, p. 352; Brobjer 2008, p. 43.

9   Brobjer 2008, p. 186.

10   FS 1, p. 28, in NWS, p. 23.

11   Brobjer meticulously lists authors. Brobjer 1999, p. 309-310.

12   Ibid.

13   FS 1, p. 28, in NWS, p. 22.

14   Ibid.

15   Brobjer 1999, p. 309, n. 24.

16   FS 1, p. 31, trans. with minor modifications in Grundlehner, p. 5;
    Luchte and Leadon, p. 9.

17   Ibid., p. 32, in NWS, p. 26.

18   On plastic discourse see Jachimczyk, p. 143-5.

19   Ibid., p. 28.

20   FS 1, p. 1, in NWS p. 3.

21   Köhler, p. 1; NWS, p. 105; Schlechta vol. 3 (hereafter abbreviated as
    Schlechta 3), p. 107-8.

22   FS 1, p. 1, in NWS, p. 3.

23   Ibid., p. 6, in NWS, p. 7.

24 Alternatively, Parkes puts the onset of Fritz's losing faith in God at precisely this period in his life. Parkes 2013, p. 35.

25 eKGWB, BVN-1858, #18.

26 FS 1, p. 1, in NWS, p. 3.

27 Hayman, p. 24.

28 Köhler, p. 14.

29 Oehler, p. 55.

30 KSW, vol. 12, p. 15, in Köhler, pp. 14-15.

31 FS 1, p. 31, in NWS, p. 25.

32 Nietzsche Reader, p. XXII.

33 "According to Nietzsche himself, his first philosophical speculations, at the age of twelve, concerned the problem of evil and the nature of God.", Brobjer 2008, p. 43; "[In 1856] N. writes his first philosophical essay 'On the Origin of Evil.'", Safranski, p. 353.

34 GM, Preface, § 3.

35 Ibid.

36 FS1 p. 12, in NWS, p. 11.

37 Hayman, p. 23; There is conflicting information about when Franziska bought the piano for Fritz to learn music: by the end of 1850, when he was 6 (Safranski, p. 353) or, in 1855, when he was 11 (NWS, p. 29, n. 42; and in Hayman, p. 23). It was most likely in 1850 after they left Röcken and arrived in Naumburg to begin a new life after Ludwig's death, for the ideal age to start piano lessons is about six years of age.

38 FS 1, p. 26, in NWS, p. 21.

39 Ibid., p. 18, in NWS, p. 15.

40 NSW, p. 29, n. 42.

41 FS 1, p. 27, in NSW, p. 22.

42 Ibid., p. 8, in NWS, p. 29, n. 8.

43 Ibid., p. 24, in NWS, p. 19.

44 Parkes 2013, p. 23

45 Hayman, p. 32

46 FS 1, p. 147-8, in Brobjer 2008, p. 43.

47 Ibid., p. 24, in NWS, p. 20.

48 Safranski, p. 32

49 Hayman, p. 20.

50 Ibid.

## CHAPTER TWO

51    Brobjer 2001, p. 322, n. 1.

52    Ibid., p.323.

53    Brobjer 1999, p.302.

54    Hayman, p. 27.

55    Pletsch, p.48

56    eKGWB BVN-1859, #55.

57    Hayman, p. 28.

58    eKGWB, BVN-1858, #30, in Pletsch, p. 50

59    Pletsch, p. 49.

60    eKGWB, BVN-1858, #26.

61    Schlechta 3, p. 48, in Kohler, p. 29.

62    Ibid., p. 46, in Parkes 1994, p. 32.

63    Parkes 1994, p. 32.

64    FS 1, p. 24, in NWS, p. 20.

65    Hayman, pp. 29-30.

66    KSW, vol. 6, p. 107, in Pletsch, p. 29.

67    Pletsch, p. 30.

68    eKGWB BVN–1859, #69, in Lecznar, p.38.

69    FS 1, p. 69, in Safranski, p. 33.

70    Lecznar, p. 38.

71    This term I own to Friedrich Ulfers, my mentor and friend.

72    Holub, p. 81.

73    Köhler, p. 31

74    Hayman, p. 32; Köhler, p. 31.

75    Köhler, p. 27.

76    HH, vol. 1, sec. 5, pp. 12, 13.

77    Hayman, pp. 33-4.

78    eKGWB BVN-1958, #30, in Pletsch, p. 50.

79    FS 1, p. 120, in Hayman, p. 33.

80    eKGWB BVN-1860, #126, in Hayman, p. 35.

81    Ibid., #129, in Hayman, p. 35.

82    eKGWB BVN-1860, #129.

83    FS 1, pp. 152, 154, in Blue, p. 109.

84   Gilman, p. 10.
85   Diethe, pp. 25, 27.
86   Safranski, p. 246.
87   Hayman, p. 36.
88   Anti-Education, p.5.
89   Hayman, pp. 36-7; Pletsch, pp. 51-2.
90   eKGWB, BVN-1861, #203, in Liebért, p. 19; Brobjer 2001a, p. 139.
91   Ibid., #202.
92   Ibid., #215, in Hayman, p.38.
93   Blue 2016 (hereafter abbreviated as Blue), p. 118.
94   Hayman speculates what Blue questions. Blue claims that "Steinhart in the Hebrew class at sixth-year level explained the Forty-Fifth Psalm completely as a secular wedding song. Such an account should be treated with caution. The Steinhart lecture occurred during Nietzsche's final year at Schulpforta, and his Confirmation took place during his third." Blue, pp. 120-121.
95   Hayman, p. 39; Brobjer 2001a, p. 139.
96   Brobjer 2001a, p. 138.
97   FS 1, pp. 232-235.
98   Blue, p. 123.
99   FS 1, pp. 235-243.
100  Ibid., p. 237, in Safranski, p. 33.
101  FS 1, 235-243.
102  Blue, p. 124.
103  FS 1, pp. 276-284.
104  Parkes 1994, p. 35.
105  Safranski, p. 34.
106  FS 1, p.277, in Parkes 1994, p. 36.
107  Ibid., p. 278.
108  Ibid.
109  Ibid.
110  Safranski, pp. 33-34; Nietzsche does not, however, use the term *der Gott*, contrary to what Safranski writes. Not even once, but uses phrases like original soul, primeval spirit, eternal essence, primordial spirit, or higher being. All these terms, he will use quite often, later after he sundered from Christianity.

111   FS 1, p. 278.

112   KGW, I-3, p. 291, in Blue, p. 73.

113   "On October 6, 1858, the day after Nietzsche's arrival at Pforta, the king was officially removed from his throne, and his brother Wilhelm was installed as regent. All birthday celebrations for the king were canceled at the school. This had to have come as a blow to Nietzsche, if only as a dash of cold water thrown on his own birthday two weeks later (October 15). As a boy, he had liked the holiday festivities which accompanied the day he shared with the king, and at least one biographer believes that he had viewed Friedrich Wilhelm as a symbolic parent." Blue, p. 98.

114   FS 1, p. 281.

115   Ibid.

116   Ibid, p. 284.

117   Beiner, p. 22.

118   FS 1, pp. 290-299, in NWS, p. 40

119   Safranski, p.31.

120   FS 1, pp. 290-299, in NWS, p. 40

121   Ibid., in NWS, p. 42

122   Forster-Nietzsche, p. 110.

123   Brobjer 2001a, p. 139.

124   eKGWB, BVN-1861, #257, in Hayman, p. 41.

125   Hayman, p. 40.

126   Gilman, p. 10-11.

127   Brobjer 2001a, p. 139-140.

128   Ibid., p. 140.

129   Safranski, p.246-247.

130   Ibid., p. 247; Walther.

131   Walther, p. 4.

132   FS 2, pp.187-189, in Safranski, p. 247.

133   Safranski, p. 247; Schmidt, Hermann Josef (1991), *Nietzsche Absconditus, oder Spurenlese bei Nietzsche*, Parts 1-3, Berlin Aschaffenburg: IBDK.

134   Blue, p. 146.

135   FS 2, pp. 1-5, in Middleton, pp. 4-6.

136   eKGWB, BVN-1861, #281.

137    Parkes 1994, p. 33.

138    FS 2, pp. 1-5, in Middleton, pp. 4-6.

139    Brobjer 2001b, p. 402.

140    Ibid.

141    Brobjer, in *Nietzsche's Philosophical Context*, claims that "Nietzsche's borrowing, without citing sources, sometimes verged on plagiarism. The young Nietzsche, at Schulpforta, began this bad habit and directly plagiarized several times. The essays written between 1861 and 1864 were, to a large extend, plagiarized: 'Brief an meinen Freund,' where Nietzsche strongly prizes Hölderlin, (FS 2, pp. 1-5); 'Napoleon III als Praesident,' (FS 2, pp. 23-28); and 'Primum Oedipodis Regis Carmen Choricum,' (FS 2, pp. 364-394). Two of these essays were handed in as school assignments without the teachers noticing the plagiarism. Such copying from other sources is not easy to discover, and other early essays may well also be plagiarized.... The cases mentioned here are early and extreme cases, but it was not uncommon for the mature Nietzsche, to borrow significantly without mentioning his sources; see, for example, his use of Gustav Gerber in "About Truth and Lies in an Extra-Moral Sense" and Julius Wellhausen in *The Antichrist*." Brobjer 2008, n.1, p. 111.

142    eKGWB, BVN-1862, #338, in Blue, p. 158.

143    Hayman, p. 42.

144    Blue, pp. 110, n. 88, 89.

145    eKGWB, BVN-1861, #288.

146    Blue, pp. 161, 177.

147    "He had once roused my mother and Aunt Rosalie (who was an authority on dogma) to a positive storm of indignation when he recommended *The Life of Jesus* (Strauss) and *The History of the Church*, by Professor von Haase, as Christmas present for myself." Föster-Nietzsche, pp. 89-90.

148    KGB I-1, p. 374, in Blue, pp. 161-162.

149    eKGWB, BVN-1860, #197.

150    Large, p. 45; Hayman, p. 43.

151    Blue, p. 145.

152    Blue, pp. 152-153.

153    Parkes 1994, p. 27.

154    He writes in his second to last work; "I must be profoundly related to Byron's *Manfred*: all these abysses I found in myself; at the age of thirteen I was ripe for this work." EH, Why I Am so Clever, §4, in Parkes 1994, p. 28.

155    Köhler, p. 40

156    Ibid.

157    FS 2, p. 10, in NWS p. 49.

158    Ibid., p. 13, in NWS, p. 51.

159    Kaufmann, pp. 307-308.

160    Emerson, pp. 157–175.

161    Cybulska, pp. 1–2.

162    Parkes 1994, p. 31.

163    Blue, p. 154.

164    Byron, *Manfred*, Act II, Scene 2; lines 50-69; in Parkes 1994, p. 31, modified from the original text.

165    A person who sees himself. A term coined in Siebenkäs by Jean Paul Richter (1763-1825) with who's writings, according to Safranski, Fritz was familiar already in 1959: "The fragments of his works that I have read appeal to me uncommonly with their blooming, effusive descriptions, their subtle ideas, and their satirical wit." Safranski, p. 354.

166    eKGWB, BVN-1862, #339.

167    Gilman, p. 11.

168    Pletsch, p. 58.

169    eKGWB, BVN-1883, #471; in Hayman, pp. 43-44.

170    KGB I-1, p. 335, in Blue, p. 147.

171    Gilman, p. 9.

172    Blue, pp. 147-148.

173    eKGWB, BVN-1861, #288.

174    FS 2, p. 23.

175    Safranski, p. 35.

176    Hayman, p. 44.

177    "The term 'Caesarism' was coined by Johann Friedrich Böhmer in 1846, though the term's first systematic treatment may be found in Francois Auguste Romieu's *L'ere des Cesars* (1850). Peter Baehr writes that according to Romieu, with the dawn of Caesarism 'will come a violent new order, the regime of military commanders, and a

quasi-permanent state of civil war as the normal form of future society.' Romieu employed the terms' Bonapartism' and 'Caesarism' in an affirmative sense. He 'predicted that since liberalism was impotent and monarchial legitimism dead, the rule of force by the military would succeed indecisive parliaments.' Romieu was also the author of *Le spectre rouge de 1852*. His' books…helped lay he ground for the coup [of Napoleon III] by calling for a new Caesar to save society from an impending jacquerie'; that is to say,  from an impending popular revolution. Proudhon much less favorably utilized the term 'Caesarism' in his criticism of Napoleon III. Proudhon viewed 'Napoleon-Caesar as a despot who maintained his hegemony through corruption, cunning, and terror. The multitude of people was reduced to an ignorant and miserable mass.'" Dombowsky, p. 81. The term was further employed by Oswald Spengler in his monumental *The Decline of the West*, as an inevitable evolutionary step of the Western Culture.

178    Brobjer 2008, p. 2, n. 1.
179    Dombowsky, p. 11a.
180    FS 2, p. 23.
181    Ibid.
182    KSAB II, p. 138, in Blue, p. 236.
183    Krell, p. 46
184    Brobjer, p. 23.
185    Ratner-Rosenhagen, p. 10-11.
186    FS 2, p. 54-59, in Nietzsche Reader, p. 13.
187    Ibid., p. 12.
188    Ibid., p. 14.
189    Ibid., pp. 12-15
190    Ibid., p. 12.
191    Richardson, p. 3
192    Fritz took it from "Circles," in *Versuche* by R. W. Emerson, a copy he owned; in NWS, p. 65.
193    FS 2 p. 57, in Nietzsche Reader, p. 13
194    Safranski, p. 36.
195    Nietzsche Reader, p. 14.
196    Ibid.
197    Ibid.

198    Ulfers and Cohen 2007, p. 3.

199    FS 2, pp. 60-62, in Nietzsche Reader, pp. 16-17.

200    Nietzsche Reader, p. 17.

201    eKGWB, BVN-1862, #30, in Safranski, p. 39.

202    Brobjer 2004, pp. 25-26.

203    Brobjer 2008, p. 44.

204    Blue, pp.140-141.

205    Ibid., pp. 154-155.

206    FS 2, p. 68.

207    Ibid., in Pletsch, p. 58.

208    Förster-Nietzsche, p. 100.

209    eKGWB, BVN-1862, #312; in Krell, pp. 25, 27.

210    Gilman, p.10.

211    eKGWB, NF 1882 21[2], in Förster-Nietzsche, pp. 5-6.

212    Oehler, Max.

213    "[Byron] was not only a poetic genius but also a freedom fighter, who, heedless of danger, had made his way to the native land of Homer to liberate it from the Ottoman yoke. His role was soon over. In 1824 he died [age 36] of a mixture of fever and boredom. The perversions that punctuated his life, from incest to pedophilia to sadomasochism and the pleasures of the transvestite, did nothing to shake his great reputation. Rather, already during his lifetime, they helped to create that demonic aura about whose origin people were reluctant to enquire." Köhler, p. 41.

214    Goethe, Johan Wolfgang von, letter to Eckermann, 5 July 1829, in Hayman, p. 46.

215    FS 2, pp. 70-71.

216    Ibid., p.71, in Krell and Bates, p. 26.

217    Ibid.

218    At Louisiana's Hilliard University Art Museum, Jun 08, 2018 — Jan 18, 2019.

219    KGB, I/3, p. 53; in Köhler, p. 44.

220    Hayman, p. 48.

221    eKGWB, BVN-1862, #336, in Blue, p. 157.

222    FS 2, p. 10, in Blue, p. 157.

223    Ibid., p. 100

224    Ibid., pp. 89, 114, 171-172.

225    Schlechta, vol. 3 "Meine musikalische Tätigkeit im Jahre 1863," p. 110-113, in NWS, p. 83, n.1.

226    FS 2, p. 114, in NWS, p. 82.

227    "This idea that the first form of human communication was more like wordless song than what we would recognize as language. The idea originates with Rousseau, Condillac, and Herder and plays an important role in Wagner's *Opera and Drama* (1852), which is possibly the more or less direct route by which it came to Nietzsche. It has recently been revived in the archaeologist Stephen Mithen's *The Singing Neanderthals* (Mithen, 2005). These leads, in Nietzsche's mature philosophy, to a suspicion of words, paradoxical in one of the supreme wordsmiths of the German language. The wordier we become – he suggests in *Wagner at Bayreuth* – the more distant we become from true feeling and insight." Young, p. 39.

228    The usual ancient Greek sense, supernatural agent or intelligence lower than a god, ministering spirit is attested in English from 1560s and is sometimes written daemon or daimon for purposes of distinction. Meaning destructive or hideous person is from 1610s; as an evil agency personified (rum, etc.) from 1712. OED.

229    Young, p. 39.

230    Förster-Nietzsche, p. 110.

231    Hayman, p. 49.

232    Förster-Nietzsche, pp. 97-98.

233    Developed later in Nietzsche's *Untimely Meditations*; in Jachimczyk.

234    The idea of music as a means for self-introspection is developed further by Nietzsche in Birth of Tragedy and Gay Science, §354, as referenced in Higgins' article. Higgins, p. 663.

235    FS 2, pp. 101-105, in NWS pp. 85-90.

236    Ibid., p. 102, in NWS, pp. 87-90.

237    Ibid., p.120, in Safranski, p. 30.

238    Safranski, p. 30.

239    FS 2, p. 129, in Hayman, pp. 49-50.

240    Hayman, p. 49.

241    eKGWB BVN-1862, #337, in Hayman, p. 49.

242    Blue, p. 157.

243    Ibid., p. 158.

244    The only preserved letter concerning the incident was written as a gentle rebuke. KGB I: i, p. 388, in Blue, p. 158, n. 91.

245    eKGWB BVN-1862, #338, in Blue, pp. 158-158, n. 92.

246    There are many inconsistencies between the drinking incident and the timing of Meyer's expulsion from the school. Deussen writes that Meyer left in 1862 (Gilman, p 12), whereas Blue puts the expulsion in late February 1863.

247    eKGWB, BVN-1863, #343, in Köhler, p. 44.

248    Pletsch, p. 58.

249    Blue, p. 159.

250    eKGWB, BVN-1863, #350, in Blue, p. 160.

251    Ibid., #352, #353, #355.

252    Ibid., #353.

253    Köhler, p. 44.

254    FS 2, pp. 193-200.

255    Large, pp. 45, 61 n. 5.

256    Nehamas, p. 227.

257    FS 2, p. 193.

258    "It has gradually become clear to me what every great philosophy up till now has consisted of – namely, the confession of its originator, and a species of involuntary and unconscious autobiography; and moreover, that the moral (or immoral) purpose in every philosophy has constituted the true vital germ out of which the entire plant has always grown." BGE, Ch. 1, 6.

259    eKGWB, BVN-1863, #343, in Köhler, p. 44.

260    KGB I-I, p. 401, in Blue, p. 164.

261    FS 2, pp. 214-219.

262    Ibid., pp.214-215.

263    Ibid., pp. 215-219.

264    KGW I-4, p. 63, in Blue, p. 188.

265    KGB I-I, p. 401, in Blue, p. 164.

266    Safranski, p. 355.

267    FS 2, pp. 287-289.

268    Ibid., p. 287.

269    Ibid., p. 190-191, in Grundlehner, pp. 21-22; Reich, August 18, 1863.

270    Ibid., pp. 249-254

271    KGW I-3, p. 144-145.

272    FS 2, pp. 262-266.

273    Luchte, pp. 11-12.

274    Reich, p. 100; Hayman, p. 52.

275    eKGWB, BVN-1863, #376.

276    Hayman, p. 52.

277    eKGWB, BVN-1863, #377, in Diethe, p. 28.

278    Ibid., #376, in Safranski, p. 355.

279    FS 2, pp. 269-272, in NWS, p. 97-101.

280    Nietzsche Reader, pp. 18-20.

281    Ibid., p. 18.

282    Ibid., p. 19.

283    Ibid., p. 20.

284    Ibid., p. 19.

285    FS 2 p. 364.

286    "At least until the 1880s, he was an unexpectedly conventional think-
       er, borrowing more from other thinkers including his contemporaries,
       than has been recognized before now." Brobjer 2008, pp. 2, 111 n.1.

287    Blue, p. 160, n.15.

288    FS 2, pp. 406-48, 415-416, in Nietzsche Reader, pp. 21-23.

289    Hayman, pp. 54, 364 n. 52.

290    Nietzsche Reader, p. 21.

291    Ibid., p. 22.

292    Ibid.

293    Ulfers and Cohen 2018.

294    Strawson.

295    FS 2, p. 406.

296    Nietzsche Reader, p. 22.

297    The term is commonly attributed to William James who used it in 1890
       in his *The Principles of Psychology.*

298    Nietzsche Reader, p. 22.

299    Porter, pp. 32-33.

300    Schlechta 3, p. 151, in Young, p. 31.

301    FS 2, p. 374-378.

302    Ibid., *Primum Oedipodis regis carmen choricum, commentario il-*

*lustravit dissertationibus adornavit*, pp. 364-399.

303   Ibid, p. 374, in Walther.

304   Ibid., p. 378, in Walther.

305   Ibid., p. 376, in Walther.

306   Ibid., pp. 376-377, in Walther.

307   Sloterdijk, p. 41.

308   eKGWB, BVN-1864, #426.

309   Lanham.

310   Gilman, p. 14.

311   Gast's letter to Carl Fuchs, Jan. 1890, in which he wrote: "It seemed, horrible though this is, as if Nietzsche were merely feigning madness, as if he were glad for it to have ended this way." Overbeck's letter to his wife, February 24, 1890: "I cannot escape the ghastly suspicion ... that his madness is simulated." Breazeale, pp. 20, 29 n. 9.

312   Sloterdijk, p. 35.

313   Ibid., p. 34.

314   "Nietzsche learned this evasiveness at least in part from Shakespeare. In Henry IV, Part 1, Hotspur's rival, Prince Hal, plays the role of a wayward, drunken youth in order to lull his enemies into complacency. He cavorts in an Eastcheap tavern with fat Jack Falstaff, a Greek satyr or Silenus if ever there was one. When Hal's father, King Henry IV, takes him to task for his time slumming it in the tavern, though, Hal promises to "be more myself," a fierce warrior and a Machiavellian politician. But Hal is so convincing as a bawdy brawler in the tavern–indeed, it took Shakespeare an entire sequel, Henry IV, Part 2, to complete Hal's journey of redemption from drunkard to the magisterial King Henry V–that neither role seems truer than the other. So too with Nietzsche's many roles in his writing." Lanham.

315   "Duncan Large has assembled a provocative archive of Nietzsche's meditations on the Bard, arguing that Nietzsche consistently uses Shakespeare as a mask for himself." Lanham.

316   Large, p. 49.

317   Ibid., pp. 48-49.

318   Ibid., pp. 60-66 n. 4, 5.

319   FS 2, pp. 412-414.

320   eKGWB, BVN-1864, #432.

321   Nietzsche Reader, pp. 22-23.

322   This term I owe to Graham Parkes 1994.

323   Nehamas, p. 40-41.

324   Jachimczyk, pp. 182-183.

325   eKGWB, BVN-1864, #434.

326   Ibid.

327   Ibid., #435.

328   "The lyric poet, a Dionysian artist, has become entirely at one with the primordial unity, with its pain and contradiction, and he produces a copy of this primordial unity as music, which has been described elsewhere, quite rightly, as a repetition of the world and a second copy of it." BoT, p. 30, in Jachimczyk, p. 182.

329   eKGWB, BVN-1864, #435.

330   Schlechta 3, p. 117, in NWS, p. 115-118.

331   NWS, p. 118.

332   Hayman, p. 57.

333   Ibid., p. 56.

334   eKGWB, BVN-1864, #426, in Hayman, p. 55.

335   "At the time though, the work helped to establish the reputation of the then twenty-year-old Nietzsche and considerably facilitated his later academic career. By all accounts, it was a considerable achievement, especially considering when it was written: it entailed an expert knowledge, not just of classical-philological literature, but also of codicology." Kerr, Preface.

336   Kerr, Preface.

337   Ibid., p. 81.

338   Ibid., p. 73.

339   Ibid.

340   Ibid., pp. 73, 75.

341   Ibid., p. 77.

342   Ibid., p. 75.

343   Ibid., p. 81.

344   Ibid.

345   Ibid., p. 89.

346   Ibid., p. 83.

347    Young, pp. 31-32.

348    "Fortunately, and for unknown reasons, although there are legends, the Schulpforte synod elected to override this lapse, and Nietzsche was cleared to take his degree. Förster-Nietzsche attributes her brother's graduation to a dramatic confrontation in the Schulpforte synod. She further claims that she received this highly confidential information from Diederich Volkmann. However, she tells this story only in her second biography, which was published after Volkmann was dead and unable to respond." Förster-Nietzsche, pp. 116–117, in Blue, p. 177.

349    Grundlehner, p. 25.

350    FS 2, p. 428, in Grundlehner, pp. 25-26.

351    Grundlehner, p. 27.

352    Ibid., p. 28.

353    Blue, pp.176-177.

354    "Cause is effect, the cause is in the effect, and the effect is in the cause, within a process of becoming. ... Cause and effect are essentially the same concepts, or in Hegel's words: 'there is nothing else in the cause but what is in the effect.' Causality is a manifestation of substantial otherness, or substantial differences, that is the 'absolute contingency of the original unity of substantial difference, and therefore absolute contradiction.' Causality is then the potentiality, the origin-heterogeneous, the plasticity that as an effect necessarily sublates itself to freedom." Jachimczyk, pp. 22, 52.

355    Sloterdijk, pp. 33-34.

356    eKGWB, BVN-1864, #441a.


## CHAPTER THREE


357    Ibid., #445.

358    "Intoxicated with wine and camaraderie, we allowed ourselves, in spite of having very little money, to be persuaded into hiring horses to ride up the. It is the only time I have ever seen Nietzsche on horseback. He was in a mood to interest himself less in the beauty of the scenery than in the ears of his horse. He kept trying to measure them and make up his mind whether he was riding a donkey or a horse. In the

evening, we acted still more insanely. The three of us were wandering through the streets of the little town, making overtures to the girls we assumed to be concealed behind the windows. Nietzsche whistled and cooed, 'Pretty darling, pretty darling.' Schnabel was talking all kinds of nonsense, making out that he was a poor Rhineland boy, begging for a night's shelter." Gilman, p. 20.

359    eKGWB, BVN-1864, #446.

360    Ibid., #447.

361    Ibid.

362    Ibid., #448, in Young, p. 52

363    Ibid., in Young, p. 53.

364    KGB I-4: 338, in Walther; in Blue 2016a.

365    Blue, p. 178.

366    eKGWB, BVN-1864, #448.

367    Brobjer 2008, p. 47

368    Blue, pp. 182, 191.

369    Ibid., pp. 182-183.

370    Brobjer 2008, p. 46.

371    A comedic play written by Titus Maccius Plautus (c. 254–184 B.C.); eKGWB, BVN-1864, #449a

372    Young, p. 53.

373    Ibid.

374    Hayman, p. 61

375    eKGWB, BVN-1864, #453.

376    Gilman, p. 22.

377    Ibid.

378    Liébert, p. 2.

379    eKGWB, BVN-1864, #452.

380    Hayman, p. 63.

381    eKGWB, BVN-1864, #456.

382    A piece for piano and violin written in 1864. eKGWB, BVN-1865, #455, in Young, p. 60.

383    eKGWB, BVN-1864, #458.

384    Blue, p. 194.

385    FS vol. 3 (hereafter abbreviated as FS 3), p. 79-80.

386    Ibid.

387    eKGWB, BVN-1865, #459.

388    Ibid., #460.

389    Blue, pp. 187-188.

390    eKGWB, BVN-1865, #476.

391    Liébert, p. 31

392    Ibid.

393    Pletsch, p.66.

394    Ibid., p.67.

395    Gilman, p. 24.

396    FS 3, "Bücher für die Ferien mitzunehmen," p. 99.

397    eKGWB, BVN-1865, #462, in Hayman p. 66.

398    The notebook under catalogue number GSA 71-41, Goethe-Schiller-Archiv, Weimar. Brobjer 2008, p. 47.

399    eKGWB, BVN-1865, #468.

400    Ibid., #467

401    KGB I.3, p. 97, in Young, p. 59

402    eKGWB, BVN-1865, #469, in Young, pp. 59-60.

403    Ibid., in Blue, p. 196.

404    Pletsch, pp. 69-70

405    Ibid., #476, in NWS p. 120.

406    eKGWB, BVN-1865, #469.

407    Hayman, p. 70

408    Gilman, p. 25.

409    KGW I-4, pp. 508, 507, in Blue, p. 207.

410    eKGWB, BVN-1865, #478, in Young, p. 62.

411    Ibid., in Blue, p. 204.

412    Blue, p. 212.

413    eKGWB, BVN-1865, #479, in Laska.

414    Ibid., #483, in Laska.

415    Laska.

416    Safranski, pp. 125-131.

417    Stirner 2017, p. 169.

418    Safranski, p. 129.

419    Stirner 2017, p. 56.

420    KGW I-4, p. 509, in Blue, pp. 211, 212.

421    Safranski, p. 126.

# CHAPTER FOUR

422 KGW, I.2, p. 60 [I], in Young, p. 63.

423 FS 1, p. 24, in NWS p. 20.

424 eKGWB, BVN-1865, #483, in Hayman, p. 71.

425 Ibid., #482, in Young, p. 62.

426 Young, p. 64.

427 Blue, p. 213.

428 eKGWB, BVN-1865, #481.

429 KGW I-4, pp. 510–511, in Blue, p. 225.

430 KGW I.2, p. 60 [I], in Young, p. 64.

431 FS 3, p. 298, in Hayman p. 72.

432 eKGWB, BVN-1865, #486

433 Berman, p. xviii.

434 Schopenhauer 1969 vol. 1 (hereafter abbreviated as Schopenhauer 1969 1), p. 3

435 Young, p. 82; Schopenhauer 1992, p. 216.

436 Schirmacher, in Schopenhauer 2010, p. xiv

437 Hegel, p. 82.

438 Stirner 2017, p.25

439 Ibid., p.27

440 Ibid., p.179.

441 "Ownness" is best understood as a variety of self-mastery, a form of substantive individual autonomy which insists that any actions or desires which involve waiving or suspending individual judgment violates the self-mastery and independence of a person concerned. David Leopold, Introduction, in Stirner 1995, p. xxii.

442 Stirner 2017, p.183.

443 Schopenhauer 1969 1, p. 312.

444 Stirner 2017, p. 333.

445 Ibid., p. 169.

446 Ibid., p. 208.

447 Ibid., p. 238.

448 Ibid., p. 208.

449 Ibid., p. 75.

450    Schopenhauer 2010, pp. 36, 13.

451    Schopenhauer 1969 1, p. 326.

452    "The double declaration of the illusion of illusion, or double negation, is offered in *The Birth of Tragedy* where Nietzsche discusses the value of dreams. In the first stage of negation, we are motivated by the need for the 'the rapturous visions, the pleasurable illusions' to redeem, 'through illusion, the eternal suffering and contradictory' caused by viewing the Apollonian illusion as the real, despite the fact that it is a mere construct of reality.
       The second stage of the process is a self-contradiction that reality is an illusion of primal unity (first original negation) and, as Nietzsche points out, may be looked upon through the prism of our dreams as representations of mere appearances, or as a double negation of reality through the prism of naïve works of art: 'If we conceive of our empirical existence, and of that of the world in general, as a continuously manifested representation of the primal unity, we shall then have to look upon the dream as mere appearance of mere appearance, hence as a still higher appeasement of the primordial desire for mere appearance. And that is why the innermost heart of nature feels that ineffable joy in the naïve artist and the naïve work of art, which is likewise only 'mere appearance of mere appearance.'" Jachimczyk, pp. 88-89.

453    Schopenhauer 1969 1, p. 399.

454    Ibid., p. 398.

455    Safranski 1991, p.112.

456    Kant 1929, p. 7.

457    Safranski 1991, p.113.

458    Schopenhauer 1969 1, p. 178.

459    Ibid., p. 196.

460    Ibid., p. 262.

461    Ibid., p. 264.

462    Ibid., p. 332.

463    Ibid., p. 380.

464    Ibid., p. 383.

465    Ibid., p. 401.

466    Schopenhauer 1969 vol. 2, p. 463.

467    Tolstoy.

468    "Eigenheit can also be translated as property, peculiarity or individuality, in the sense of something that distinguishes a particular individual," in Stirner 2017, p. 170.

469    Stirner 2017, p. 185.

470    Ibid., 175.

471    Ibid., 179.

472    Ibid., 178.

473    Ibid., pp. 179, 178.

474    Stirner 1995, p. 70.

475    Stirner 2017, p. 195.

476    KGW I-4, pp. 512-513, in Blue, p. 222.

477    Young, pp. 66-67

478    Safranski, p. 45.

479    Blue, p. 225.

480    Diethe, p. 30.

481    Holub, 2016, p. 41.

482    Hayman, p. 75.

483    Pletsch, p. 72

484    HKGW 3, p. 299, in Pletsch, p. 72.

485    Ibid. 3:299-300, in Pletsch, p. 73.

486    FS 3, pp. 212-226, in Barnes.

487    KGW I.4, p. 60 [I], in Young, pp. 65-66.

488    Hollinrake, p. 164.

489    eKGWB, BVN-1866, #497.

490    Ibid., #500, in Middleton, pp. 10-11.

491    One of Schumann's late works, labeled as the composer's magnum opus, completed before attempted suicide and eventual death in an asylum for the insane in 1856.

492    eKGWB, BVN-1866, #500, in Middleton, p. 12.

493    Ibid., pp. 11-12.

494    Hayman, p. 78.

495    eKGWB, BVN-1866, #502

496    Ibid., in Holub 2016, p. 43.

497    Ibid., #504, in Holub 2016, p. 43.

498    Holub 2016, p. 41.

499    eKGWB, BVN-1866, #504, in Hayman, p. 78

500    Ibid., #511.

501    Ibid., #515, in Hayman, pp. 82-83.

502    Köhler, p. 61

503    "Prussia's conversion to German reunification took place in the 1860s, largely as a means for breaking out of the German Confederation and the hopeless entanglement with Austria. In the early years of William I (r. 1861-88), Prussia's affairs had reached very ambiguous conditions. The authoritarian establishment had been strengthened by the military reforms of von Roon, whilst the Landtag elections had produced a liberal majority headed by the Fortschrittspartei of Waldeck.... In 1862 Otto von Bismarck (1815-1898)—the 'Iron Chancellor,' more than anyone else, was the architect of the European order which emerged from the turmoil after 1848, the year when he entered politics, and whose revolution he detested—was appointed premier to sort out the resultant crisis, if necessary, by the unconstitutional measures. ... His aim was to put Prussia' in the saddle' in Germany and Germany in the saddle in Europe. Immense friction is being caused by the joint Prusso-Austrian administration of Schleswig-Holstein. William I could not decide whether to lead the Confederation or to leave it to Francis-Joseph, as he did for the Frankfurt Fürstentag in 1863. All these issues were settled by Bismarck's determination to create a new North German Confederation without Austria, and by the masterly use of limited war. In 1864 Prussia attacked and defeated Denmark for annexing Schleswig. In 1866, when Austria referred the Schleswig Question to the Confederation Diet,Prussia promptly walked out, attacking and defeating Austria and Austria's German allies. The lighting victory at Sadová, near Hradec Králové (Königgrätz), ensured Prussia's supremacy, and the formation of the North German Federation." Davis, pp. 824-826, 841.

504    eKGWB, BVN-1866, #511.

505    Ibid., #509, in Middleton, p. 14.

506    Hayman, p. 83.

507    eKGWB, BVN-1866, #517.

508    Ibid., in Brobjer 2008, p. 33.

509    Yet another example that Fritz must have known about Stirner. Lange, p. 256.

510    It is worth noting that Lange makes only two references to Schopenhauer in the book and, thus, for Nietzsche, who was a dedicated

Schopenhauerian the first times he read the book, this is likely to be a central sentence in the book. Brobjer 2003, p. 113, n.6.

511    Lange, p. 3.

512    Brobjer 2004a, p. 26.

513    Ibid. p. 26.

514    Brobjer 2008, p. 36.

515    eKGWB, BVN-1866, #519.

516    KGW I-5, p. 47, in Blue, p. 253.

517    eKGWB, BVN-1866, #523, in Young, p. 64.

518    Ibid., #526.

519    Ibid.

520    Ibid, #535.

521    Ibid., #536, in Middleton, p. 20.

522    KGB I-3, pp. 183-185, in Blue, p. 247.

523    eKGWB, BVN-1867, #538,

524    KGB I-3, pp. 321-322; in Blue, pp. 249-250.

525    Ibid.

526    Köhler, p. 62.

527    Ibid., p. 61.

528    eKGWB, BVN-1867, #540, in Middleton, p. 22.

529    Strong, p.8,

530    eKGWB, BVN-1867, #540, in Middleton, p. 22.

531    Ibid., p. 23.

532    Janz vol. 1, p. 210, in Köhler, p. 61.

533    KSW 15, p. 32, in Köhler, p. 61.

534    KGB I/3, p. 321, in Köhler, p. 62.

535    FS vol. 4 (hereafter abbreviated as FS 4), pp. 269-358.

536    Ibid., pp. 217-268.

537    Barnes.

538    Diogenes Laertius vol. 2, pp. 134-143, in Blue, pp. 264-265.

539    Swift 2013, pp. 3-4.

540    Swift 2008, pp. 18-19.

541    In *Pythian II* by Pindar, an ancient Greek lyric poet from Thebes (c. 518–438 BC), in Bowra.

542    Babich.

543    Porter 2000, p. 34.

544    Ibid.

545    eKGWB, BVN-1867, #588.

546    Ibid., #548.

547    Porter 2000, p. 32.

548    FS 3, pp. 345-347, in Swift 2005, p. 30.

549    Berry, p. 98.

550    Ibid., p. 104.

551    Power, pp. 121-122.

552    Ibid., p. 130.

553    Swift 2008, p. 13.

554    Ibid., pp. 12, 13.

555    Ibid., p.14.

556    Ibid., p.15.

557    Ibid.

558    Ibid., p.14.

559    Swift 2008, pp.19, 38 n. 38; Neiman, 2015, p. 212.

560    FS 4, p. 213, in Swift 2008, p. 19.

561    FS 3, p. 328, in Swift 2008, pp. 20-21.

562    Ibid., p. 349, in Swift 2008, p. 25.

563    Ibid., p. 346, 345, in Swift 2008, pp. 25, 29.

564    Ibid., p. 348, in Swift 2008, p. 25.

565    Ibid., pp. 348-349, in Swift 2008, p. 25.

566    KSAB II, 223, in Blue, p. 268.

567    KSAB II, 235, in Blue, p. 268.

568    eKGWB, BVN-1867, #549.

569    Ibid., #540, in Middleton, p. 22.

570    Safranski, p. 54.

571    NWS, "Retrospect on My Two Years at Leipzig," p. 121.

572    Safranski, p. 55.

573    It is a subtitle of Nietzsche's last book, *Ecce Homo. How One Becomes What One Is*, written in 1888 and published in 1908.

574    Safranski, pp. 55-56.

575    NWS, "Retrospect on My Two Years at Leipzig," p. 121.

576    Blue, p. 316.

577    FS 4, p.126, in Blue, p. 315.

578    NWS, "Retrospect on My Two Years at Leipzig." pp. 121-122.

579    Ibid., p. 123.

580    Ibid., p. 125.

581    Ibid.

582    Ibid., p. 125.

583    Ibid.

584    Schopenhauer 1969, §68.

585    NWS, "Retrospect on My Two Years at Leipzig," p. 127.

586    Ibid., p. 128.

587    Ibid., pp. 127-133.

588    FS 3, pp. 309-310, in NWS, "Retrospect on My Two Years at Leipzig," pp. 133-134.

589    Ibid., pp. 312-313, in NWS, "Retrospect on My Two Years at Leipzig," p. 135.

590    Porter, p. 117.

591    eKGWB, BVN-1867, #552, in Middleton, p. 25.


## CHAPTER FIVE


592    Ibid., pp. 26-27.

593    FS 3, p. 344, in Safranski p. 27.

594    Jacques Offenbach's opéra bouffe, *Die Schöne Helena*.

595    eKGWB, BVN-1867, #552, in Middleton, pp. 27-28.

596    FS 3, pp. 352-361, in Nietzsche Reader, pp. 24-29.

597    Swift 2008, pp. 43-44.

598    Nietzsche Reader, p. 24.

599    Ibid., pp. 24-25.

600    Ibid., p. 25.

601    Ibid., p. 26.

602    Ibid., p. 25.

603    Schirmacher, in *The Essential Schopenhauer*, p. viii.

604    Schopenhauer 1969 1, p. 264.

605    eKGWB, BVN-1867, #554, in Middleton, p. 29.

606    Ibid., pp. 29-30.

607    Ibid., p. 31.

608    Ibid., pp. 31, 32.

609     Roper, pp. 427, 430.

610     Ibid., p. 445.

611     Ibid., p. 429.

612     Sammons, p. 80.

613     Roper, p. 431.

614     Sammons, p. 81.

615     GS, §357.

616     Bahnsen, p.45, in Jensen 2016, p. 104.

617     Slochower, p. 368.

618     Beiser, pp. 238-239.

619     Ibid., p. 239.

620     Ibid., p. 240.

621     Ibid., p. 242.

622     Ibid., pp. 242, 243.

623     Ibid., p. 243.

624     Jensen 2016, p. 109-110.

625     eKGWB, BVN-1868, #559.

626     Eagleton 2016, p. 103.

627     Around the same time, Fritz made an entry in his notes about Lange's reference to Darwin. "–Diese Ansicht entspricht der darwinschen Theorie Gesch des Mat. p. 404." FS 4, p. 54.

628     eKGWB, BVN-1868, #561.

629     Richardson. This source I owe to Alexander Nehamas who mentioned it during our conversation at Princeton, in 2017.

630     eKGWB, BVN-1868, #562.

631     Holub 2018, p. 323.

632     eKGWB, BVN-1868, #574, in Blue, pp. 287-288.

633     Ibid.

634     FS 3, pp. 371-395.

635     eKGWB, BVN-1868, #568.

636     Brobjer 2001a, p. 142.

637     Gardner; Brobjer 2008, p. 43.

638     BVN-1868, #568; #569, in Crawford, p. 105.

639     Crawford; Swift 2008; Gardner.

640     Swift 2008, "Teleology Since Kant," p. 95.

641     Ibid.

642     Ibid. p. 96.

643     Ibid., p. 106 n. 5.

644     Ibid.

645     Swift 2008, p. 97.

646     Ibid.

647     Ibid., p. 101.

648     Ibid., p. 102.

649     Ibid.

650     Ibid., p. 103

651     Ibid.

652     Ibid., p. 104.

653     Swift 2008, p. 74.

654     Ibid., p. 76.

655     Swift 2008, pp. 99, 100, 104.

656     Camus 1955, p. 91.

657     eKGWB, BVN-1868, #583.

658     Pletsch 1991, p. 94.

659     eKGWB, BVN-1868, #578

660     Ibid., in Safranski 2002, p. 59.

661     FS 4, p. 126, in Safranski 2002, p. 42

662     eKGWB, BVN-1868, #583, in NWS p.156.

663     Ibid., #589.

664     Ibid., #591, in Middleton p. 33.

665     Blue, p. 289.

666     eKGWB, BVN-1868, #591, in Middleton p. 33.

667     Safranski, p. 46.

668     eKGWB, BVN-1868, #591, in Middleton p. 34.

669     Young, p. 74.

## CHAPTER SIX

670     eKGWB, BVN-1868, #593.

671     Hayman, p. 96.

672     eKGWB, BVN-1868, #595, in Leidecker, p. 49.

673     Ibid., p. 48.

674    Ibid., p. 46.

675    Ibid., p. 47.

676    Ibid., #596, in Safranski, p. 56.

677    eKGWB, BVN-1868, #599, in Middleton p. 36.

678    Young, p. 77.

679    eKGWB, BVN-1868, #599, in Middleton p. 39.

680    Eichner.

681    eKGWB, BVN-1868, #604, in Young, p. 78.

682    Pletsch, p. 99.

683    Hayman p. 101.

684    eKGWB, BVN-1868, #607, in Middleton p. 43.

685    Blue, p. 305.

686    Hayman, p.102.

687    eKGWB, BVN-1868, #607, in Middleton p. 43.

688    Ibid., #608.

689    KGB I 3, 340, in Köhler, p. 63.

690    Blue, p. 306.

691    eKGWB, BVN-1869, #625.

692    Young, pp. 75-6.

693    Schlechta 3, "*Aus den Jahren 1868/69*", p. 148-154, in Hayman p. 103.

694    FS vol. 5, p. 250.

695    Ibid., pp. 252-3.

696    Ibid., p. 250.

697    Ibid., p. 251.

698    Ibid., p. 251.

699    Ibid., p. 253, in Blue, p. 309.

700    Ibid., p. 255.

701    Ibid., p. 251.

702    Ibid., p. 252, in Hayman, p. 104.

703    Hayman, p. 102.

704    Gilman, pp. 30, 31.

705    eKGWB, BVN-1869, #625, in Hayman p. 103.

706    Hayman, p. 102; Blue, p. 305.

707     Blue, p. 307.

708     eKGWB, BVN-1869, #632, in Middleton, pp. 43-44.

709     Hayman p. 105.

710     Blue, p. 311; Hayman, p. 10

# BIBLIOGRAPHY

All cited works are provided with translation sources. Any unattributed translations are by the author.

## WORKS BY FRIEDRICH NIETZSCHE

### Abbreviation of collected works of Nietzsche

**eKGWB**     *Digitale Kritische Gesamtausgabe Werke und Briefe. http://
              www.nietzschesource.org/#eKGWB*

**FS**        *Frühe Schriften 1854–1869, 5 vols., Verlag C. H. Beck,
              München 1994.*

**HKGB**      *Historisch-kritische Gesamtausgabe: Briefe, editors Wilhelm
              Hoppe, Karl Schlechta, 4 vols., Munich Beck, 1938-1942.*

**HKGW**      *Historisch-kritische Gesamtausgabe: Werke, editors Hans-
              Joachim Mette, Karl Schlechta, and Carl Koch, 5 vols., Mu-
              nich Beck, 1933–1940.*

**KGB**       *Kritische Gesamtausgabe: Briefwechsel, Giorgio Colli and
              Mazzino Montinari eds. Berlin, Walter de Gruyter, 1975–.*

**KGW**       *Kritische Gesamtausgabe: Werke, Begründet von Giorgio
              Colli und Mazzino Montinari et al. Berlin, Walter de Gruyter,
              1967–.*

**KSB**       *Sämtliche Briefe. Kritische Studienausgabe, 8 vols., Giorgio
              Colli and Mazzino Montinari eds. Berlin: Walter de Gruyter,
              1986.*

**KSW**       *Sämtliche Werke: Kritische Studienausgabe, 15 vols., Gi-
              orgio Colli and Mazzino Montinari eds, Berlin: Walter de
              Gruyter, 1988.*

**Middleton** *Selected Letters of Friedrich Nietzsche edited and translated
              by Christopher Middleton, Hackett, 1996.*

**NWS**       *Nietzsche's Writings as a Student, The Nietzsche Chanel 2012.,
              http://www.thenietzschechannel.com/*

**Schlechta**    *Werke in 3 Bänden, edited by Karl Schlechta, Munich 1956.*

## Abbreviations of works by Nietzsche

**Anti-Education**    *Anti-Education. On the Future of Our Educational Instittions edited by Paul Reitter and Chad Wellmon, trans. by Damion Searls, New York Review Books, 2016.*

**BGE**    *Beyond God and Evil, trans. by Walter Kaufmann, Vintage Books, 1989.*

**BoT**    *The Birth of Tragedy, trans. Ronald Speirs, Cambridge University Press, 1999.*

**EH**    *Ecce Homo. How To Become What You Are, trans. Duncan Large, Oxford University, 2007.*

**GM**    *Genealogy of Morals, trans. by Walter Kaufmann, Vintage Books 1989.*

**GS**    *The Gay Science, trans. by Walter Kaufmann, Vintage Books 1974.*

**HH**    *Human, All Too Human, trans. by R. J. Hollingdale, Cambridge University Press, 1996.*

**Nietzsche Reader**    *The Nietzsche Reader, edited by Keith Ansell Pearson and Duncan Large, Blackwell Publishing, 2006.*

**Theognis**    *Friedrich Nietzsche De Theognide Megarensi (Theognis from Megara) trans. by Robert M. Kerr, The Nietzsche Chanel, 2015, http://www.thenietzschechannel.com/*

## WORKS BY OTHER AUTHORS

**Babich, Babette E. (2003),** *Nietzsche Imperative as a Friend's Encomium: On Becoming the One You Are, Ethics, and Blessing, Nietzsche-Studien, academia.edu.*

**Bahnsen, Julius (1931),** *Wie ich wurde, was ich ward, ed. Rudolf Louis, Leipzig: J.A. Barth. Bahnsen, Julius (1967), Beiträge zur Charakterologie, 2 vols., Leipzig: Brockhaus.*

**Barnes, Jonathan (2014),** *Nietzsche and Diogenes Laertius, in Jensen, Anthony and Heit, Helmut Nietzsche as a Scholar of Antiquity, Bloomsbury Academic, pp. 115-139.*

**Beiser, Frederick C. (2016),** *Weltschmerz, Pessimism in German Philosophy 1860-1900, Oxford University Press.*

**Beiner, Ronald (2018),** *Dangerous Minds: Nietzsche, Heidegger, and the Return of the Far Right, University of Pennsylvania Press.*

**Berman, David (1995),** *Introduction, in Schopenhauer A., The World as Will and Idea, Everyman.*

**Berry, Jessica N. (2004),** *Nietzsche and Democritus: The Origins of Ethical Eudaimonism, in Nietzsche and Antiquity: His Reaction and Response to the Classical Tradition, edited by Paul Bishop, Boydell and Brewer.*

**Blue, Daniel (2016),** *The Making of Friedrich Nietzsche. The Quest for Identity, 1844-1869 (abbreviated as Blue), Cambridge University Press.*

**Blue, Daniel (2016a),** *Nietzsche's Views on Plato Pre-Basel, S. Ph. Essays and Explorations, Volume 1, Issue 1, Spring-Summer 2016.*

**Bowra, C. M. (1937),** *Pindar, Pythian II, Harvard Studies in Classical Philology, Vol. 48, 1937, pp. 1-28.*

**Breazeale, Daniel (1991),** *Ecce Psycho. Remarks on the Case of Nietzsche, International Studies in Philosophy, Vol. 23, Issue2, pp. 19-33*

**Brobjer, Thomas H. (1999),** *Nietzsche's Education at the Naumburg Domgymnasium 1855-1858, Nietzsche-Studien, 28, pp. 302-322.*

**Brobjer, Thomas H. (2001),** *Why did Nietzsche Receive a Scholarship to Study at Schulpforta? Nietzsche-Studien, 30 (1),2001, pp. 322-328.*

**Brobjer, Thomas H. (2001a),** *Nietzsche Changing Relation with Christianity, in Nietzsche and the Gods, Edited by Weaver Santaniello, SUNY.*

**Brobjer, Thomas H. (2001b),** *A Discussion and Source of Hölderlin's Influence on Nietzsche Nietzsche-Studien 30, 2001, pp. 397-412.*

**Brobjer, Thomas, H. (2003),** *A Possible Solution to the Stirner-Nietzsche Question, Journal of Nietzsche Studies, Issue 25, 2003.*

**Brobjer, Thomas H. (2004),** *Nietzsche's Reading and Knowledge of Natural Science: An Overview, in Nietzsche and Science, edited by Gregory Moore, Thomas H. Brobjer, Ashgate.*

**Brobjer, Thomas H. (2004a),** *Nietzsche's Reading and Knowledge of Natural Science: An Overview, in Nietzsche and Science, edited by Gregory Moore and Thomas H. Brobjer, Routledge (2017).*

**Brobjer, Thomas H. (2008),** *Nietzsche's Philosophical Context: An Intellectual Biography, University of Illinois Press.*

**Camus, Albert (1955),** *The Myth of Sisyphus, Vintage Books.*

**Crawford, Claudia (1988),** *The Beginnings of Nietzsche's Theory of Language, Walter de Gruyter.*

**Cybulska, Eva,** *Nietzsche's Übermensch, Indo-Pacific Journal of Phenomenology, vol. 15, 1, May 2015, pp. 2-13.*

**Davis, Norman (1996),** *Europe. A History, Oxford University Press.*

**Diogenes Laertius (1925),** *Lives of Eminent Philosophers, 2 vols., translated by R. D. Hicks, Harvard University Press.*

**Dombowsky, Don (2014),** *Nietzsche, and Napoleon: The Dionysian Conspiracy, University of Wales Press.*

**Eagleton, Terry (2016),** *Materialism, Yale University Press.*

**Eichner, Barbara (2018),** *Wagner the Poet, paper presented at 'Insights: Discover the Ring' event at the Royal Opera House, London, on 14 October 2018.*

**Emerson, Ralph Waldo (1979),** *The Over-soul, in The Collected Works of Ralph Waldo Emerson, J. Slater, A. R. Ferguson and J. Ferguson Carr, eds., The Belknap Press of Harvard University Press.*

**Forster-Nietzsche, Elisabeth (1912),** *The Life of Nietzsche. Volume I, The Young Nietzsche, Sturgis and Walton, New York.*

**Gardner, Sebastian (2019),** *Nietzsche on Kant and Teleology in 1868: "'life' is something entirely dark...", An Interdisciplinary Journal of Philosophy, Volume 62, Issue 1, pp. 23–48.*

**Gilman, Sander L. editor (1987),** *Conversations with Nietzsche. A Life in the Words of His Contemporaries, Oxford University Press.*

**Grundlehner, Philip (1986),** *The Poetry of Friedrich Nietzsche, Oxford University Press.*

**Hegel, G. W. (1969),** *Hegel's Science of Logic, trans. by A. V. Miller, Humanity Books.*

**Higgins, Kathleen (1986),** *Nietzsche on Music, Journal of the History of Ideas, vol 47, No. 4, Oct-Dec.*

**Hollinrake, Roger (2010),** *Nietzsche, Wagner, and Philosophy of Pessimism, Routledge.*

**Holub, Robert C. (2016),** *Nietzsche's Jewish Problem, Princeton University Press.*

**Holub, Robert C. (2018),** *Nietzsche in the Nineteen Century. Social Questions and Philosophical Interventions, University of Pennsylvania Press.*

**Hayman, Ronald (1982),** *Nietzsche. A Critical Life, Penguin Books.*

**Jachimczyk, Andrzej (2013),** *Reading Hegel After Nietzsche, Atropos Press, New York Dresden.*

**Janz, Curt Paul (1978),** *Friedrich Nietzsche: Biographie, 3 volumes, Hanser.*

**Jensen, Anthony and Heit, Helmut (2014)** *Nietzsche as a Scholar of Antiquity, Bloomsbury Academic.*

**Jensen, Anthony K. (2016),** *Julius Bahnsen's Influence on Nietzsche's Will-Theory, Journal of Nietzsche Studies, Spring 2016, Vol. 47, No. 1, Penn State University Press.*

**Kant, Immanuel (1929),** *Immanuel Kant's Critique of Pure Reason, Macmillan.*

**Kant, Immanuel (1991),** *Idea for a Universal History with a Cosmopolitan Purpose (Idee zu einer allgemeinen Geschichte in weltbürgerlicher Absicht (1784), in Reiss, H. S. editor, Kant Cambridge Texts in the History of Political Thought (2nd ed.), Cambridge University Press.*

**Kaufmann, Walter (1974),** *Nietzsche: Philosopher, Psychologist, Antichrist (4th ed.), Princeton University Press.*

**Kerr, Robert M. (2015),** *Friedrich Nietzsche De Theognide Megarensi (Theognis from Megara), The Nietzsche Chanel.*

**Köhler, Joachim (2002),** *Zarathustra's Secret. The Interior Life of Friedrich Nietzsche, trans. Ronald Taylor, Yale University Press.*

**Krell, David F., Bates, Donald L. (1997),** *The Good European. Nietzsche's Work Sites in Word and Image, The University of Chicago Press.*

**Lange, Frederick Albert (1925),** *The History of Materialism and Criticism of Its Present Importance, with an Introduction by Bertrand Russell, Harcourt, New York.*

**Lanham, Andrew (2016),** *Shakespeare Contra Nietzsche, Marginalia – LARB, May 9, 2016.*

**Large, Duncan (2000),** *Nietzsche's Shakespearean Figures, in Why Nietzsche Still? Reflections on Drama, Culture, and Politics, edited by Allan D. Schrift, University of California Press.*

**Laska, Bernd, (2001)** *Nietzsche's Initial Crisis, New Light on the Stirner/ Nietzsche Question, Germanic Notes and Reviews 33, Fall 2001, pp. 109-133.*

**Lecznar, Adam (2013),** *Aryan, German, or Greek? Nietzsche's Prometheus between antiquity and modernity, Classical Receptions Journal Vol 5. Issue 1, pp. 38–62.*

**Leidecker, Kurt F (1959),** *Friedrich Nietzsche. Unpublished Letters, Philosophical Library New York.*

**Liébert, Georges (2004),** *Nietzsche and Music, The University of Chicago Press.*

**Luchte, James and Eva Leadon translators (2003),** *The Peacock and the Buffalo: The Poetry of Nietzsche, Lampeter Wales: Fire and Ice.*

**Nehamas, Alexander (1985),** *Nietzsche: Life as Literature, Harvard University Press.*

**Neiman, Susan (2015),** *Evil in Modern Thought, Princeton Classics.*

**Oehler, Adalbert (1940),** *Nietzsches Mutter, Verlag C. H. Beck, München.*

**Oehler, Max (1938)** *Nietzsches angebliche polnische Herkunft, in Ostdeutsche Monatshefte. Jahrgang (Jg.) 18. Danzig. H. 11, S. 679-682.*

**Online Etymology Dictionary (OED),** *etymonline.com*

**Parkes, Graham (1994),** *Composing the Soul, Reaches of Nietzsche's Psychology, The University of Chicago Press.*

**Parkes, Graham (2013),** *Nietzsche and the Family, in The Oxford Handbook of Nietzsche, ed. Ken Gemes and John Richardson, Oxford University Press.*

**Pletsch, Carl (1991),** *Young Nietzsche. Becoming a Genius, The Free Press.*

**Porter, James I. (2000),** *Nietzsche and the Philology of the Future, Stanford University Press.*

**Power, Nina (2001),** *On the Nature of Things: Nietzsche and Democritus, Pli: The Warwick Journal of Philosophy, 12 (2001), pp. 118-130.*

**Ratner-Rosenhagen, Jennifer (2012),** *American Nietzsche. A History of an Icon and His Ideas, The University of Chicago Press.*

**Reich, Hauke (2000),** *Friedrich Nietzsche. Chronik in Bildern und Texten, Carl Hanser.*

**Richardson, John (2004),** *Nietzsche's New Darwinism, Oxford University.*

**Roper, Katherine (2000),** *1848 in the Early Novels of Friedrich Spielhagen: The Making of a German Democrat, German Studies Review, Oct. 2000, Vol. 23, No. 3.*

**Safranski, Rüdiger (1991),** *Schopenhauer and the Wild Years of Philosophy, Harvard University Press.*

**Safranski, Rüdiger (2001),** *Nietzsche. A Philosophical Biography (abbreviated as Safranski), translated by Shelly Frisch, W. W. Norton & Company, New York*

**Sammons, Jeffrey L. (2004),** *Friedrich Spielhagen, Novelist of Germany's False Dawn, Max Niemeyer Verlag, Tübingen.*

**Schopenhauer, Arthur (1969),** *The World as Will and Representation, vol.1 and 2, translated by E. F. J. Payne, Dover Publications.*

**Schopenhauer, Arthur (1992),** *On the Will in Nature, trans. E. F. J. Payne, New York: Berg.*

**Schopenhauer, Arthur (2010),** *The Essential Schopenhauer, Schirmacher, Wolfgang, editor, Harperperennial.*

**Slochower, Harry (1932),** *Julius Bahnsen, Philosopher of Heroic Despair, 1830-1881, The Philosophical Review, July 1932, Vol 41, No. 4, Duke University Press.*

**Sloterdijk, Peter (1989),** *Thinker on Stage: Nietzsche's Materialism, University of Minnesota Press.*

**Stirner, Max (1995),** *The Ego and Its Own, edited by David Leopold, Cambridge University Press.*

**Stirner, Max (2017)** *The Unique and Its Property, translated by Wolfi Landstreicher, Underworld Amusements.*

**Strawson, Galen (2021),** *What does "physical" mean? A prolegomenon to physicalist panpsychism, forthcoming in Mind and Being, Academia.edu.*

**Strong, Tracy B. (2013),** *In Defense of Rhetoric: Or How Hard is to Take Writer Seriously: The Case of Nietzsche, Political Theory, XX(X), SAGE.*

**Swift, Paul A. (2008),** *Becoming Nietzsche. Early Reflections on Democritus, Schopenhauer and Kant, Lexington Books.*

**Swift, Paul A. (2013),** *Wieland and Nietzsche's Use of Democritus as Role Model for Character Development, Axiology and Ethics: Special Volume for 23rd WCP, edited by John Abbarno, International Society for Value Inquiry, Hubei University; Academia.edu.*

**Tolstoy, Leo (2004),** *The Death of Ivan Ilyich and Master and Man, translated by Ann Pasternak Slater, The Modern Library.*

**Ulfers, Friedrich, Cohen, Mark (2007),** *Nietzsche and the Future of Art, Hyperion, vol. II, issue 4, 2007.*

**Ulfers, Fred and Cohen, Mark (2018),** *Nietzsche's Panpsychism as the Equation of Mind and Matter, in Nietzsche on Consciousness and the Embodied Mind, Manuel Dries editor, DeGruyter.*

**Walther, Helmut,** *Nietzsche Hauptseite, http://f-nietzsche.de/*

**Walther, Helmut (2003),** *A 'Romantic' or an Educational Experience? Nietzsche and Ortlepp, Lecture before the Gesellschaft für kritische Philosophie (Society for Critical Philosophy) Nuremberg, April 30, 2003, http://www.f-nietzsche.de/ortlepp_vortrag_e.htm*

**Young, Julian (2010),** *Friedrich Nietzsche. A Philosophical Biography, Cambridge University Press.*

www.ingramcontent.com/pod-product-compliance
Lightning Source LLC
Chambersburg PA
CBHW070022100426
42740CB00013B/2575